# essential
# herbs

Enhancing your life with aromatic herbs and essential oils

## lesley bremness

Photography by Clay Perry and Pia Tryde

Recipes by Marie-Pierre Moine
Photography by Jean Cazals

QUADRILLE

Both metric and imperial quantities are given in the recipes in this book. Use either all metric or all imperial, as the two are not necessarily interchangeable. All recipes for food serve 4, unless otherwise indicated.

First published in 2000 by
Quadrille Publishing Limited
Alhambra House
27-31 Charing Cross Road
London WC2H OLS

This title previously appeared in hardback as Crabtree & Evelyn Fragrant Herbal

British Library Cataloguing in Publication Data
A catalogue record for this book is available from the British Library

ISBN 1 902757 24 6

Printed in Hong Kong

**Important Notice**
This book contains a range of information on herbs and essential oils including cosmetic and culinary recipes. Before trying any herbal preparations, the reader is recommended to sample a small quantity to establish whether there is any adverse or allergic reaction. Neither Crabtree & Evelyn, the authors nor the publisher can be held responsible for any adverse reactions to the recipes, recommendations and instructions contained herein, and the use of any herb or essential oil is entirely at the reader's own risk. If in doubt, consult professional advice.

# Contents

# Creating an Aromatic Mood

Herbs are a glorious group of plants with a rainbow of illuminating gifts for humankind. A herbal is a book 'with descriptions and accounts of the properties of herbs', and this herbal looks at the Cinderella of their gifts – fragrance. Delicious air, made potent with benevolent herb aromas, can flow like a balm through our thoughts and feelings, and in this book we explore the myriad ways in which the range of scents – from light and sparkling through to rich and earthy – can be used to create desirable moods.

The word 'herb' is used in its broadest sense – that of a useful plant. This is an ancient concept from earliest tribal communication, which long precedes the development of botany and the second meaning given to 'herb' or 'herbaceous' – plants that die back to the ground each autumn and regrow the following spring. The scents discussed come from a wide range of herbs including annuals

like Basil, biennials like Evening Primrose, grasses like Sweet Grass, shrubs like Roses and trees like Bay, as well as a many 'herbaceous' plants.

The fragrance of herbs affects us in many ways, some subtle, some obvious. As irresistibly as music, scent can evoke a range of emotions to enhance our lives. As something unseen, uncontainable, seeping through boundaries and affecting our moods, it becomes a bridge between the world of matter and something more abstract. There are broad categories of aromatic effects: many herbs are stimulant, others are relaxing. This much is confirmed by tests on the brain when scents are inhaled. But this branch of science is still in its infancy and cannot yet measure the subtle differences created by the unique scent of each variety within a plant group. For example, Mints are stimulating, but within that group Peppermint is particularly rousing, whereas Applemint provides a gentle nudge. These nuances can be discovered by personal experience, and this book provides guidelines and recipes to help you in your voyage of discovery.

## The Power of Scent

As the first of our senses to evolve, the olfactory system has a uniquely direct relationship with the brain: one end of the scent organ is in the nose and the other inside the brain. Messages from the other senses – sight, touch, taste and hearing – are passed along nerves to the blood-brain barrier, a protective

RIGHT AND BELOW:
*Fresh herbs delight the mind and the senses in the fragrant gardens of Wollerton Old Hall, Shropshire.*

membrane around the brain, where they are transferred to a different set of nerves inside the brain. This means that a degree of 'editing' can take place which cannot happen with the sense of smell, and this is why aromas are so powerful and evocative. A smell may instantly conjure up granny's garden, an old cutlery drawer, a father's leather coat – often with the attendant emotional connection.

## HOW WE PERCEIVE SCENT

The way in which scents register in the brain is only just beginning to be understood; progress is hampered by our limited vocabulary for describing scents, relying as it does on comparing one smell to other familiar ones. But human scent receptors, although much smaller and less perceptive than those of a dog or cat, are still remarkably sensitive.

BELOW: *At Congham Hall, Norfolk, different herbs offer scents for every mood, from bright and invigorating to relaxing, slumberous fragrance.*

The average person can distinguish around 10,000 different odours, detect vanilla at 0.000000005g in a litre of air, and perceive previously unknown odours newly created in the laboratory. In contrast, the taste buds recognize only four sensations (sweet, sour, salty and bitter) and the entire delectable range of food and wine flavours comes from 'smelling' the components.

A substance has a scent because aromatic molecules readily escape from its surface. Some of these molecules pass into our noses and reach the receptors in the upper back of the cavern. Sniffing brings many more into this contact, and as the shaped scent molecules connect with matching nerve endings, they trigger a reaction which vibrates their scent message to the brain. Because our sense of smell was once our most important protection, our olfactory nerves are constantly replaced whereas damaged nerves in the eye, ear or brain are not repaired.

BELOW: *Modern herb gardens owe a debt to the Elizabethans, who first added beauty to gardens divided by use.*

RIGHT: *The fresh, soothing scent of Lavender has been a household favourite for centuries.*

## PERSONAL SCENT RESPONSE

Our personal response to scent depends on the arrangement of receptors in our nose and each of us may have a different combination When we sniff a Rose, we are inhaling a complex mixture of scented compounds. One person's nose may pick up more of the lemon component, another more of the tea scent and a third the hint of cinnamon, so we may each experience the same scent as slightly different sensations.

Reactions to scent are also governed by cultural norms. Something like Gorgonzola cheese, for example, will delight those who have acquired the taste but disgust others. Finally, scent reactions are influenced by memory association: if a frightening schoolteacher wore a particular perfume, this unpleasant association could defeat even the most seductive advertising.

As each person's fragrance reactions are specific to them, the only way to discover your own is through the enjoyable activity of experimenting.

## Historic Fragrances

The aromatic trail begins with the earliest campfires, where burning resinous woods created an uplifting incense which harmonized the tribe. It continues with the legend of Venus, who was credited with being the first to use perfumes for allure, and many aromatic names have come from Greek legends of transformed nymphs or lovers such as Mentha, Narcissus and Artemisia. The Queen of Sheba brought exotic resins and spices to King Solomon to persuade him to allow her trade routes to continue through his land; the Magi brought the infant Jesus the enlightenment fragrances of

Frankincense and Myrrh; and Cleopatra had the sails of her Nile barge soaked in Cyprinum, her favourite perfume, to create an aromatic envoy of her arrival to meet Antony.

Archaeological sites confirm the importance of aromatics. Pyramid temple reliefs depict the preparation of fragrant oils and the extensive use of incense and perfumes in daily rituals – Egyptian extravagance required daily caravans of imports along the famous Incense Trail. In the Roman city of Capua an entire street was occupied by manufacturers of perfumes. At En Gedi in Israel, the remains of a temple complex have been found to contain a sixth-century AD perfume laboratory. Among the 'Odours of Paradise', the followers of Mohammed so favoured Saffron and Musk that they mixed them with the mortar of temple walls to give a lingering perfume still noticeable today.

## The Still Room

The use of herbal fragrances in England reached a peak in Elizabethan times, and the still room was the domain of the mistress of the house. Here, in undisturbed peace, she gathered and dried fragrant herbs and flowers from the garden, woods and hedgerows to make comestibles, liqueurs, scented candles and soaps, potpourri, linen sachets, sleep pillows, perfumes, medicines, cosmetics, garlands and tussie-mussies. She might follow a familiar recipe or try new ideas passed on by a respected visitor. The best recipes were passed from mother to daughter in a 'receipt book', a prized family heirloom. In parts of North America and Australia the family recipe books remained important for much longer, as geography and distances meant many communities remained isolated and self-reliant.

The pleasurable range of activities can be repeated today with a few simple tools and ingredients in a cool, dry space.

## Essential Oils

The most significant difference now is the modern availability of essential oils – wondrous substances that are extracted from aromatic plants.

ABOVE: *The delicate scent of luxuriant Peonies can be enjoyed only from the flowers. The essential oil is one of those which so far has proved too difficult and too expensive to extract.*

## WHAT IS AN ESSENTIAL OIL?

If a plant is aromatic, and any part can be for example, Bay leaves, Lilac flowers, Cinnamon bark, Dill seeds, Valerian roots, Cedar wood – it means that it contains one or more essential oils. The Orange tree contains three: Neroli, the flower oil; Petitgrain, the twig and leaf oil; and Orange, from the fruit peel. The oils are self-contained compounds which may travel around a circulatory system within the plant. Their role is not fully understood but they are all antiseptic, some are antifungal and antiviral, they deter pests and attract pollinators, and they evaporate into the air in hot weather to create an envelope of protection around the plant. More ethereal ideas propose that they are a plant's communication system or that the oils are the soul of the plant.

Essential oils are extremely concentrated: it takes 30,000 Roses to make 15 g ($^{1}/_{2}$ oz) of Rose oil. They do not feel 'oily' but are more like water, and are called volatile oils (from the Latin *volare* – to fly) because their molecules evaporate rapidly. Each oil is made up of many components, with a tiny molecular structure which allows them to pass through the skin. By contrast, mineral oils have large molecules which form a barrier on the skin.

Essential oil molecules have been proven to reach our internal parts in four ways. First, through smell, the scent-vibration impulse reaches the brain, where it affects the limbic system, emotions and hormone production; second, through nasal mucous membranes into the circulation system; third, inhaled into the lungs and from there into the bloodstream; fourth, through the skin via the lymph and capillary blood systems. Skin-applied oils take from 20–70 minutes to reach the bloodstream.

RIGHT: *Rose oil is still the perfumer's favourite, despite being one of the most expensive.*

## ESSENTIAL OIL EXTRACTION

Oils are extracted from plant parts in several ways.

DISTILLATION Using heat and water or steam, this is the most common process and produces flower water as a by-product. A new, quicker system of distillation, called hydrodiffusion or percolation, is little used at present. Therapists prefer distilled oils as no other chemicals are involved, but perfumers prefer solvent extraction or enfleurage as the oil is closer to the original plant scent.

EXPRESSION The oils are pressed by hand or mechanically from the peels of citrus fruits.

SOLVENT EXTRACTION This is used for plants (mainly flowers) too delicate for distillation. The solvent, usually hexane, dissolves the essential oil and any waxes or resins from the plant material. The solvent is then vaporized to leave a 'concrete' or 'resinoid'. The essential oils are removed from these with pure alcohol, which is then evaporated off to leave the final 'absolute'. These absolutes are very expensive.

ENFLEURAGE Flowers are laid on layers of fat successively until it is saturated with essential oils, which are then extracted with alcohol. Now largely replaced by solvent extraction.

GAS EXTRACTION This expensive method involves nitrogen or carbon dioxide gas solvents and high pressure, and avoids alcohol.

PHYTONICS This new, expensive process uses room temperature heat and 'environmentally friendly' solvents to produce oils of excellent aroma.

## OIL SCENT AND QUALITY

Many factors influence the scent of an essential oil, so oil from a single species may display a range of subtle scent differences. Geographic and annual climate differences, soil type, plant variety, the skill of the grower, harvester and distiller, the quality of extraction equipment – all have an impact.

The resulting subtle differences in composition also have potential life-saving consequences. Tiny differences in the antiseptic qualities of each batch are enough to prevent bacteria from mutating and becoming immune to them, as is presently happening with antibiotics.

## Fragrant Herbal

In this book we investigate the spectrum of responses that can be invoked with scents: the stimulating odours we can choose to arouse our system in the morning; sharp, clean-scented herbs to help us concentrate and work; relaxing aromas for their stress-reducing balm; and, when we want to entertain friends, we can discover the warm, welcoming environment made possible with congenial fragrances. Romantic perfumes hold potent promise for affairs of the heart, and finally, when we want to still our thoughts for quiet reflection or sleep, rich resinous herbs will lull us into peaceful meditation or contented dreams.

The chosen herb and essential oil fragrances can be woven into the fabric of our day through a variety of pleasurable activities: tasting delectable dishes, from refreshing breakfasts to seductive dinners; applying body treatments, from wake-up shower gels to relaxing dream baths; using aromatic sachets, potpourri and oil vaporizers to enhance every room; and finally fragrant garden vignettes to reflect different times of the day and allow us to inhale the precious scents directly at source.

### THE PERFECT SCENT

Living plants give us fragrance in its most perfect state, and this is often at its richest after rain. The air seems lighter when storm tension has been released, and this eases the diffusion of fragrances after raindrops have broken up and dispersed the envelope of perfumed air that surrounds each flower. Chill night air is less fragrant, because cold checks the diffusion of perfumes and frost halts them altogether. But then the morning sun warms the leaves and flowers to give a special fragrance to start the day, called 'incense breathing' by the writer Thomas Gray. Indeed, the symphony of sun-warmed oxygenated plant fragrances we call 'fresh air' must be the most precious perfume of all.

ABOVE: *Sweet Peas are easy and decorative to grow, and their delicate fragrance will create a welcoming mood in your home.*

LEFT: *From friendship to passion, every aspect of love can be matched by a different Rose scent.*

# CHAPTER ONE

# Wake up, Refresh & Invigorate

*The sparkling, zesty concerto of herb fragrances selected for their stimulating and energizing effects is invaluable for rousing the body in the morning and providing a spirited pick-me-up during the day.*

These refreshing aromas will infuse you with a generous burst of optimism with which to engage in the adventures of the day.

Top of the invigorating list is the Mint family – Spearmint, Peppermint, Applemint and many more – which provide cool, clean, tingling flavours with waterfall freshness. People who work with Mint plants report a light-hearted exhilaration which can last for several hours. Next comes the glorious range of sun-kissed Citrus aromas. Think of the attention-catching zest when someone in a crowd begins to peel an Orange and heads turn, smiling, as the refreshing scent reaches each nose in turn. The jovial orange, yellow and lime-green peels and their tart tonic juices, rich in Vitamin C, are just waiting to release your vitality in the morning.

The equally delicious fresh-air fragrance of crisp Apples revives the mind and perks up the taste buds while the fruit works to detoxify the body. With the apple-scented leaves of perennial Chamomile and the Sweet Briar Rose, they are champagne for the spirit.

A classic experience of stimulating aromas is a forest walk. Breathe deeply among the spires of resinous evergreens like Pine, Cedar, Cyprus and Eucalyptus to rejuvenate both body and mind. Even in winter, these trees energize the spirit as their branches sparkle with crystallized snow, until they give way to the energy of spring, heralded by the cheery flowers and light, airy perfume of Snowdrops, Primroses and Cowslips.

This chapter offers many ingenious ways of using these invigorating scents.

INVIGORATING HERBS & OILS •
AROMATIC HERBS FOR CONTAINERS INDOORS
& OUT • HERBS IN THE CONSERVATORY •
SMALL HERB GARDEN DESIGNS • REFRESHING
COSMETIC RECIPES • DELICIOUS LIGHT
BREAKFASTS & BRUNCHES

*The stimulating effect of Mint and Citrus aromas is widely enjoyed through Peppermint in our toothpaste and Orange in our marmalade. Here we expand the list of refreshing herbs and explore energizing applications for the plants and their essential oils.*

# Invigorating Herbs & Oils

## Mints

For a refreshing sense of exhilaration, Mint is hard to better. Enjoyed world-wide in toothpastes, mouthwashes, chewing gum and sweets, it is the most popular tea in the heat and dust of Arab countries for its refreshing flavour and cooling effect, and for imparting the clean, tingling sensation of freshly brushed teeth.

Mint is named after Menthe, the Greek nymph crushed by Pluto's jealous wife but transformed by him into this lively scented herb. Hebrews strewed it on their temple floors to radiate its clear, renewing perfume as they worshipped, while in ancient Athens the men chose infused Mint oil to massage on their arms for its clean and energizing effect. The leisured Japanese wore pomanders of Mint suspended from the sashes of their silk kimonos, to waft up freshly scented air as they moved and to maintain their mental alertness as they pursued poetry and the arts.

With over 600 Mint varieties in existence, you have plenty of choice when selecting one with a crushed leaf aroma that pleases you. Concentrate on strongly scented forms such as Moroccan Mint, with the cleanest sharp spearmint flavour, and Red Raripila Mint, which has a clear, sweet spearmint flavour excellent for desserts and confectionery.

### SPEARMINT AND PEPPERMINTS

The leaves of these Mints have strong flavours and a mild anaesthetic action which produces the cool, refreshing taste for a myriad of culinary applications including teas, confectionery (especially with chocolate), sauces, drinks, ice-cream, cakes and liqueurs. They are stimulants and an aid to digestion. The various Peppermints – 'black', 'white' and 'crinkle leaf' – and Corsican Mint (*Mentha requienii*) all have strong, clear flavours, but Pennyroyal's medicinal peppermint scent and pondside Watermint's pungent peppermint are for household use, not consumption.

### FRUIT-AND-SPICE-SCENTED MINTS

Culinary Applemint blends the delights of a soft mint scent with a hint of apple. The cream variegated form has a similar but less intense fragrance. The attractive gold-splashed Ginger Mint and two forms of Watermint – the dark-stemmed Basil Mint (*M.* x *aquatica*) and Lemon or Citrus Mint (*M.* x *aquatica* 'Citrata') – each has a different spicy or citrus overtone. For perfume, the scent

LEFT: *Of all the Mints, this Moroccan Spearmint has the cleanest, sharpest pure mint flavour. Its lively green colour and healthy growth are an outward reminder of the lively, stimulating effect of its excellent fragrance.*

of Mint blended with sweet, light Bergamot is the winning combination found in the young purple-brown leaves of Eau-de-Cologne Mint, an elegant flavouring for fruit salads.

## ESSENTIAL OILS

The essential oils of the stimulating Mints not only delight our noses with their freshness but offer extra benefits: some boost circulation, improve energy and build up resistance to fatigue, while others have a cleansing action and aid the respiratory system. The scent of Peppermint is considered a general tonic for the young, elderly and convalescent. During periods of sluggishness or lethargy, sniffing a drop of Peppermint or Spearmint oil increases cheerfulness, clarity, optimism and the sense of being fully alive. These oils are also used in subtle aromatherapy to encourage emotional regeneration and positive change.

## Other Mint-scented Herbs

Alecost has debonair daisy flowers and balsamic, spearmint gum-scented leaves with a sharp tang, which were once used in brewing to clear, flavour and preserve ale and now in strong infusions to fragrance hair and linen.

The Australian Mint Bush (*Prostanthera* species) sports a head-clearing, camphorous, mint-scented leaf with bactericidal and fungicidal properties used by Aborigines to relieve colds. The leaves of the peppermint-scented Blue Gum (*Eucalyptus coccifera*) offer similar qualities in steam inhalations and room fresheners and, like Peppermint Geranium (*Pelargonium tomentosum*), can be added to zesty potpourris.

## Green Apples

The scent and texture of crunchy green Apples work wonders for cheering the mind and reviving the spirits, while the fruit clears body toxins. Dr John Caius, Tudor physician to Queen Elizabeth I, advised patients to 'smele an old swete apple to recover… strengthe' In the Scandinavian saga the *Edda*, Iduna keeps a box of fragrant Apples to feed the gods, thereby renewing their youth. Perhaps the Vikings already knew what recent studies have confirmed – that Apples can reduce blood cholesterol levels.

## Chamomile

The fresh apple fragrance of perennial Chamomile leaves also has a tonic effect. It is most useful in the garden for its scent and carefree daisy flowers. A manual of 1638 states that 'Large walks, broad and long, like the Temple groves in Thessaly, raised with gravel and sand, have seats and banks of Camomile.' Try gathering a handful of leaves, tying them in a muslin square and then swish it through the water for a truly reviving bath.

ABOVE: *The early morning mist rises to reveal a bed of refreshing Mints among the roses at Congham Hall.*

19

# Citrus

The Citrus family provides a range of universally popular 'wake-up' flavours and fragrances. The freshly squeezed juices of Orange, Lemon, Grapefruit and Lime offer a perfect fuel with which to ignite buoyant spirits. Pomelos – the large precursor of the Grapefruit – Tangelos, pip-free Minolas and Ugli (pronounced oo-gli) fruit offer further Citrus choices. With a different 'zing' from each juice, they can be mixed together to create the perfect blend of sharp and sweet for any palate. Traditional Orange juice diluted two-thirds with water boosts carbohydrate levels, making it an ideal revitalizer after exercise.

The most powerful citrus scent lies in the fruit peel, which gives flavour and tang to marmalades, another stimulating breakfast tradition. The tenderizing acid in the juice and peel makes an excellent marinade, while Citrus sauces are a sharp foil to rich meats and oily fish. The refreshing aspect of Lemon is popular in sorbet palate cleansers, taken to revive the taste buds between courses.

The celebratory feel of citrus colours and flavours is most evident at Christmas. A display of bright Tangerines, Mandarins, Satsumas and Clementines promotes cheerful thoughts of summer sun. Winter recipes highlight the excellent blending quality of refreshing Orange, with dark chocolate in a rich mousse, and with exotic spices in Clove pomanders and party punches. Liqueurs traditionally flavoured with Orange include Cointreau, Grand Marnier and Curaçao.

## LEMON

Drinking a cup of warm water mixed with the juice of a freshly squeezed Lemon is a cleansing and purifying wake-up routine. It also improves the skin by helping to eliminate toxins, as does a bath with quartered Lemons, Tangerines or Oranges tossed in. Externally, diluted Lemon juice is an astringent skin tonic; it reduces broken capillaries, whitens teeth and bleaches hair. Soap and body lotions with zesty Lemon are mildly antiseptic as well as invigorating, while the essential oil is a stimulant, improving circulation and boosting confidence. When travelling in hot, dry areas, buy a Lemon and rub it periodically to provide instantly refreshing air.

## GRAPEFRUIT AND LIME

Grapefruit juice is a tonic antidepressant and encourages weight loss, while an extract of Grapefruit seed is a fungicide, antibiotic and disinfectant. Grapefruit essential oil is used to reduce cellulite and work-related stress.

Lime juice is drunk in Sri Lanka to increase metabolism and prevent obesity. It adds an intriguing flavour to refreshing fruit salads, especially Papaya, which make excellent breakfast fare. Like Lemon, Lime essential oil is energizing, as it improves circulation and boosts the immune system.

## ORANGE

Research reveals that the seed oil of Bitter Orange contains linolenic acid, which reduces excess blood cholesterol. The oil of Sweet Orange peel is suitable for

treating obesity and dull complexions, and that of Mandarin peel stimulates poor digestion and reduces insomnia. The peels of unripe *Citrus reticulata blanco*, a Chinese tangerine, and of Bitter Orange are used to mobilize Chi (basic body energy) and tone the whole organism. In Japan they are powdered as a bath additive, or a whole citron (*C. medica*, an elongated, knobbly-skinned, highly aromatic fruit) is floated in the bath to promote glowing, silky skin.

### SCENTS AND OILS

Energizing citrus scents are now the rising stars of the perfume industry as the clean, lively notes of unisex fragrances are promoted. The sharp, clean scent of Grapefruit (the French *Pamplemousse* fragrance), along with Lime and Tangerine, will make you feel bright and breezy throughout the day. Bergamot Orange peel has a clean eau-de-Cologne scent used to flavour Earl and Lady Grey tea; the refreshing citrus-floral-green fragrance lifts depression and is featured in many light, stimulating perfumes enjoyed by both men and women. The almost universal appeal of citrus scents has been demonstrated by hospital ward tests, where room sprays of the cheerful oils were shown to relieve patient depression.

The untreated essential oils of some citrus fruits, especially Bergamot, increase skin photosensitivity and require cautious use, avoiding direct contact of oiled skin with sunlight, although some citrus oils with the offending compound removed are now available, labelled FCF (furocourmarin-free). All Citrus peel oils should be used within six months of opening, but fortunately they are among the least expensive, and more FCF-labelled oils are becoming available.

## Lemon-scented Herbs

The refreshing lemon scent that emanates from the leaves of several non-citrus herbs is due to the presence of citral in their essential oils.

### LEMON VERBENA

The most aromatic of these herbs is Lemon Verbena, a shrub brought from Argentina and Chile to Europe in the seventeenth century to be grown for perfume oil. The leaf scent has enormous staying power, and years later dried leaf crumbs still exude the lemon boiled-sweets fragrance. Position a pot-grown plant where you will brush past it in the morning for an instant pick-me-up. Infuse the leaves for an uplifting but soothing tea which fills the kitchen with its sweet lemon aroma, or add a few leaves to sparkling cold water to impart a refreshing, light lemon flavour to sip on hot summer days. Great armfuls of leaves can be harvested to make welcome gifts of their powerful fragrance.

ABOVE: *Lemon trees are the easiest citrus to grow. Here, one is grown in a pot as a summer focal point and moved into the conservatory before the first frost.*

RIGHT: *The strongest Orange scent is in the peel from which Orange essential oil is expressed. The leaves and twigs yield Petitgrain essential oil and the flowers give Neroli essential oil.*

### LEMON BALM

Lemon Balm (also called Bee Balm, Melissa and Heart's Delight) has a relaxing, welcoming effect, in addition to being refreshing. It is as attractive to bees as to people, and rubbing it on an empty hive helps to attract new tenants. Being easy to grow, Lemon Balm is often among the first plants acquired by herb enthusiasts, and if later neglected is a delight to rediscover, because regular pinching of the leaf tips both replenishes the teapot and maintains a tidy plant. Then, just like the 108-year-old Prince of Glamorgan in the thirteenth century, we will attribute our 100-plus years to the regular sipping of fresh Lemon Balm tea. The cheering essential oil is a general tonic and excellent antidote to Monday morning blues.

### OTHER LEMON-SCENTED HERBS

Light, spicy and delicious, the perky flavour of Thai cuisine often comes from Lemon Grass. Leaves and stems chopped into a sizzling wok full of ingredients infuse the whole dish with a fresh lemon flavour and release an irresistible tastebud-rousing aroma into the air. Lemon Grass is used in Mexico as a tea to settle an upset stomach.

Originally from the Cape of South Africa, Scented Geraniums (*Pelargonium*), whose leaves retain their fragrance well when dried, are available in both orange and lemon models. *Pelargonium citronellum* and *P. crispum* are lemon scented, *P.* 'Prince of Orange' has a spicy orange scent, *P. radens* a lemon-rose scent and *P. tomentosum*, peppermint. There are many variable hybrids, so smell the leaves and choose whichever appeals.

Lemon Mint, a refreshing bath herb, and Lemon Basil, a 'zingy' salad leaf and chicken flavouring, each offer an interesting lemon form of a popular culinary herb. Their wholesome fragrance is used to scent Mediterranean churches and in potpourri. Lemon Thyme has a clean, sharp scent combining the freshness of lemon and the antiseptic aroma of thyme – perfect for a morning kickstart. Lemon Eucalyptus leaves can be enjoyed placed in a pocket, in potpourri or in a humidifier.

ABOVE: *Pine has a bracing resinous forest fragrance which invigorates both body and mind. Long valued for its energizing scent, it was one of the plants cultivated in the ancient Benedictine monastery of St Gall, Switzerland. It stimulates deep breathing and is used extensively in inhalations to help breathing and as a powerful antiseptic for respiratory infections.*

## Stimulating Trees

Resinous evergreen trees, especially in their forest setting, offer an invigorating experience both from their clean, sharp, woody-green fragrances and the abundant fresh oxygen they exhale. Add new snow glittering under blue skies and the exhilaration is complete. Each type of tree offers a different facet of vitality.

### PINE

The clean green fragrance of Pine stimulates deep breathing, improves the circulation and metabolism, reduces mental fatigue and encourages a positive self-image. For a reviving tea, woodsmen collect young spring needles and sweeten the drink with Birch sap or honey. The tree resin gives Greek retsina wine its characteristic refreshing tang.

The antiseptic leaf oil from Pine is used extensively in inhalations for the respiratory system and is a popular deodorizing additive for domestic cleaning and bath products. Sprinkle the needles from any species on log fires or barbecues, and add them to herb pillows or hot soak tubs to relieve muscular and rheumatic pains by stimulating cell regeneration, toning the skin and speeding the elimination of toxins. Because a Pine bath is so refreshing and invigorating, it makes a good start to the morning or before a party as an energy booster.

### CEDAR

The magnificent Cedar is famed for its aromatic, durable wood. The scent is strengthening and uplifting, and builds self-confidence with which to tackle the day. These qualities were valued by the ancient builders, and the extravagant use of Lebanon Cedar to build the Hanging Gardens of Babylon and Solomon's Temple nearly caused the tree's demise. Chests made of its insect-repelling wood provide the opportunity to enjoy the sweet, balsamic scent for many years.

### JUNIPER

The sharp yet warm, resinous fragrance of Juniper is both stimulating and emotionally cleansing. Juniper oil refreshes the body through its detoxifying action, giving it a 'gin and tonic' kick-start. It has powerful connections with legends of protection, and some healers rub a drop around each wrist to protect themselves from absorbing a client's negativity. It is also a recommended barrier to black witches, as they apparently have a compulsive need to count its myriad tiny leaves – a task they realize they can never complete before being caught!

To many tribes, Juniper is a sacred tree, and Native Americans burn the needles. Vita Sackville-West described collecting dead Juniper branches to use 'as smouldering pokers to push into a wood-fire on my hearth, waving them about the room as one would wave old stalks of lavender or rosemary, redolent as incense but far fresher and less heavy on the air.'

### FIR, SPRUCE AND THE TREE OF LIFE

Silver Fir (*Abies alba*) and Norway Spruce (*Picea abies*) exude the nostalgic, invigorating forest scent of the Christmas tree, truly 'sprucing up' our mood. The Trees of Life or Arbor-Vitae (*Thuja* species) offer an intriguing range of refreshing fragrances. The flat leaf sprays of *T. occidentalis* have a fruity apple-resinous scent, while *T. plicata* adds a light grapefruit note over the resinous evergreen.

### EUCALYPTUS

In warm, dry countries the strong, clean, balsamic camphor-scented Eucalyptus thrives. There are more than 500 species with an array of stunning barks and aromatic leaves, gums and oils, including peppermint and lemon forms. The aromatic oil is not only stimulating, protective and cleansing but also antiseptic, antiviral and expectorant, and is an aid to the respiratory system. One of the safest of oils, no household should be without it in the season of colds and flu. Even invalids can sprinkle a few drops on their beds to refresh and cleanse.

ABOVE: *As spring sap rises, all life responds to the renewed energy. Emerging aromatic leaves refresh the air while the baby-breath fragrance of Primroses and Cowslips, enhanced by their bright green leaves and sunny yellow flowers, encapsulates the buoyancy of the season.*

*Aromatic herbs are the ideal plants for containers. The pots can be moved around with the changing seasons, placed next to a visitor to be stroked and inhaled, or brought indoors to decorate a room.*

ABOVE: *Pots of refreshing Rosemary, Bay, Santolina and cut-leaf Wormwood are beautiful, useful and aromatic.*

# Herb Gardening in Small Spaces

## Container-grown Herbs

A collection of healthy pot-grown herbs and fragrant flowers conjures up the friendly image of an attentive gardener lovingly tending his or her plants and engaging in a neighbourly chat to exchange ideas and cuttings.

Growing herbs in containers extends both the choice of plants and the growing season. Mobility makes them useful for filling seasonal gaps with extra colour and fragrance, or concealing eyesores. The containers can also be repositioned to catch the sun or the eye of the barbecue chef. Tender plants can be brought indoors for protection over the winter, and decorative aromatics used as table decorations or to enliven a convalescent's room.

When designing an aromatic balcony or patio garden, consider all three dimensions, positioning fragrant plants at foot level (Pennyroyal, Corsican Mint, Lawn Chamomile and creeping Thymes); at fingertip height (Bergamot, Sweet Myrtle and Artemisias); at nose height (Angelica, Fennel, Dill and Roses); and above, with hanging baskets and climbers (Akebia, Roses, Honeysuckle and Jasmine). When checking for areas that are in sun and shade, remember to look up. Higher areas may catch the sun even when lower parts of a balcony or terrace are in shade. Multiple heights can be achieved with tiered blocks, tall pots, interlocking pots which form a wall, cantilevered brackets or beams, or trellis which gives the opportunity to grow scented climbers in a trough at the base. Both trellis and trough can be on castors to create a movable wall.

## THE PLANTS

Given the correct conditions, most aromatic plants can be grown successfully in pots. Tall plants like Angelica and Fennel will require deep or weighty containers, or wall support, to prevent them from toppling over. Herbs like Parsley, Mints and Chervil, which prefer cooler soil, should not be allowed to dry out in hot sun; if possible, provide dappled sunlight for the plants or shade for their soil. Soft-leaved herbs like Basil and tall plants will be damaged by winds, so provide windbreaks with dense netting, trellis or evergreen shrubs, and avoid placing tall plants or hanging baskets on exposed roof gardens or in the 'wind tunnels' which can occur between buildings and walls.

## THE CONTAINERS

Clay pots are aesthetically pleasing, stable and allow excess water to evaporate though their surface, but they also cause plants to dry out more quickly. Soak new clay pots in water for 24 hours before use. Plastic pots are cheaper, easier to clean and store, and lighter, which is useful for balconies and roof gardens. All types of containers need drainage holes, and all plants will benefit from a layer of gravel or broken crocks in the bottom to prevent waterlogging. Consider using interesting and unusual outer containers for your herb collection: try wicker baskets and wooden trugs, ornamental bird cages, copper kettles, tureens, brightly painted tins and modern pottery.

In general, the larger the pot, the better the crop, especially with lush-leaved plants like Basil. Annuals grown for their leaves, such as Rocket and Coriander, may bolt to seed if their growth is restricted and, like taprooting herbs such as Borage and Dill, will perform better in deep pots. Herbs can be started in 8–11.5 cm (3–4½ in) pots and moved in stages to 15–30 cm (6–12 in) pots. Subshrubs like Lavender and Rosemary should finish in 25–30 cm (10–12 in) pots. Roses, clipped Bay, Citrus trees, Lovage, Fennel and Angelica will grow well in a Versailles box or half-barrel, and in these Lemon Verbena will develop to its full 3m (10 ft) magnificence.

Herbs can be grown in a variety of containers and in pleasing combinations for different uses. Here a blend of cottage herbs including Marjoram, Thyme and Sage, tumble 'in sweet profusion' out of a strawberry pot (top left); the bright green of curled Parsley and Mint, the lively green and gold of Variegated Lemon Balm leaves and the cheerful orange-gold flowers of Calendula enliven a breakfast patio (top right); for convenience a selection of herbs including flat-leaf Parsley, green and Tricolour Sage, Mint and Marjoram are grown at hand height near the kitchen and barbecue with Golden Feverfew to supply a year-round splash of gold (bottom left); a painted two-tier stand houses culinary herbs including Parsley, Purple Sage, Chives, Basil and Mints (bottom right).

A window herb garden. This living aromatic screen is a creative gardening outlet for even the tiniest town house. The close proximity of the plants encourages aromatic experiments as each herb offers its unique flavourful leaf or pretty flower. Most herbs thrive in this light sunshine and the easy access allows the herbs to be turned every two or three days, giving even light to all sides of the plants. Here a collection of culinary herbs including Sweet Cicely, Golden Lemon Balm, Coriander and Bay, reflect the enthusiasms of a keen cook while the Pennyroyal discourages ants in the kitchen. The window herb garden can easily accommodate a range of potpourri, tisane or cosmetic herbs, or those featured in favourite legends.

# Care and Cultivation

### COMPOSTS

Herbs – especially shrubby Mediterranean plants such as Rosemary, Sage, Thyme, Savory and Lavender – prefer an open, slightly alkaline soil with excellent drainage, so incorporate extra grit into their compost. A soil-based compost will suit most plants, is easy to water, holds nutrients well and is relatively heavy, which is good for keeping a tall herb upright but a disadvantage in a hanging basket or balcony pot.

Peat or peat-substitute composts are lighter but lose nutrients more quickly and dry out faster – if the compost dries out completely, submerge the pot in water to the base of the rim overnight. Peat is not a renewable resource, so alternatives are to be encouraged; specially treated coir, a coconut by-product, and composted barks are available, usually mixed with soil or peat. Mix granulated charcoal with the lower one-third of the compost (1 tbsp in a 11.5 cm/4$^{1}/_{2}$ in pot) to keep the soil sweet.

### REPOTTING

When roots protrude from the base of a container, repot into a pot one size larger, using the same compost mix. Remove the plant carefully, clear surface weeds and loosen the outer roots. Place a little compost in the new pot and test that the herb will sit at the same level as before, then fill loosely with soil, firm gently and water well. When the maximum pot size is reached, remove the top layer of soil each spring and replace with fresh compost laced with a slow-release fertilizer.

Place very large containers in position before filling, or on a sturdy base with castors. For balcony pots, fill the bottom one-third with a potting compost mixed half-and-half with perlite to reduce the weight. Add compost up to the bottom of the pot rim, or 7cm (2$^{1}/_{2}$ in) below the top of a barrel.

### WATERING AND FEEDING

Water in dry weather, usually daily in summer. Proprietary compost contains enough nutrients for 4–6 weeks, after which you can use liquid comfrey or another organic fertilizer every 2–3 weeks in spring and summer, monthly as growth slows, and none at all in the resting season. Frequently harvested herbs like Basil, Chives and Parsley require more feeding than others. The compost will settle and the level will drop every season as rain and watering leach out soil and nutrients, so perennials will need a regular topping up each year with fresh fertilized compost.

### PLANT COMBINATIONS

When growing several herbs together, try to choose plants with contrasting heights, leaf colours, shapes and textures. Grow more of the herbs you use most often. For each container, select varieties which have the same sun, soil and water requirements.

Grow sun-loving seedlings of Sweet Basil, Lemon Basil and Sweet Marjoram in one 30 cm (12 in) pot and Chervil, Coriander and Parsley in another, as these prefer dappled light and a cooler and wetter environment. A sink or small barrel of dryish, well-drained compost in full sun could house a Golden Sage, blue-green Tarragon, dwarf Rosemary, bright green Marjoram, gold variegated Lemon Thyme, purple Basil, Garlic Chives and orange-flowered Calendula. Several varieties of Mint could be grown in separate plastic bags in the compost around a statuesque Angelica, as all these plants enjoy sunlight but cool, damp soil. Bay, Rosemary and Lemon Verbena make excellent single specimens.

## Growing Herbs Indoors

Most herbs share the need for a sunny or light area, some humidity, and freedom from extremes of temperature and draughts. When growing herbs indoors, consider their positioning. Plants in groups look more generous, are easier to water, and create greater fragrance and a beneficial mini-climate.

ABOVE: *Holidays, even afloat, need not be without fresh aromatic herbs to create memorable meals shared with friends. This travelling collection of salad herbs includes the punchy summer flavours of flat leaf Parsley, Basil, Marjoram, Mizuna Mustard Greens* (Brassica japonica) *and Purple Orach* (Atriplex hortensis).

### LIGHT AND WARMTH

Maximize the growing space around windows by placing hanging baskets near the top, fixing up side brackets or glass shelves for pots, adding supports for climbers and positioning shelves on nearby sunny walls.

Sun-lovers like Basil need at least 6 hours of direct sun a day in order to thrive. Thyme, Sage, Marjoram, Scented Geraniums and dwarf Lavender are also happy in direct sunshine. Dill, Savory and Chives enjoy full sun but prefer a cooler temperature. Rosemary enjoys a bright situation (this can mean reflected light) but prefers a temperature of 15°C (60°F) to produce flowers in spring. Coriander, Salad Burnet and Parsley also prefer this bright-cool combination. Tarragon and Lemon Balm will take full sun but also tolerate light shade. Mint and Chervil will take some sun but prefer dappled light and a cool, moist compost. Lemon Verbena and Bay both prefer filtered sunlight with rich compost in a cool spot.

A decorated tea trolley creates the perfect solution for moving herbs around to catch the sun. Herbs on a windowsill should be turned a little each day so that all parts receive the same amount of sunshine. The reflective properties of glass can reduce light by 30–50 per cent; outside walls opposite a shady window can be painted white to reflect light and pale, glossy interior paints also help.

### ARTIFICIAL LIGHT

As a top-up during winter months, for fast seed germination, or if your house is quite shaded, you can use artificial light. You will need two fluorescent light tubes – one 'daylight' or 'cool white' (high in blue wavelengths) and one 'natural white' or 'warm white' (high in red wavelengths) – in order to provide the spectrum of light that the plants will require. To avoid scorching and spindly growth, stand the plants on blocks so that the lights are 15–23 cm (6–9 in) above small herbs and 30–45 cm (12–18 in) above larger ones, raising the lights or lowering the herbs as they grow.

### TEMPERATURE

Herbs prefer temperatures of 15–21°C (60–70°F) with a 5°C (10°F) drop at night, as would occur outside. During warm weather they will appreciate fresh air from an open window, but they dislike cold draughts in chilly weather – these can be caused by open fires which will draw cold air through any cracks or openings.

Herbs will tolerate temperatures of 7–24°C (45–75°F) but will not thrive, especially at the lower temperatures. With single glazing in cooler climates, windowsills will become too cold on winter nights especially if trapped behind curtains or shutters, and tender herbs will need to be moved further into the room.

When bringing plants indoors at the end of summer, do so before the central heating is turned on. If the heating is on in the evening only, making it warmer than in the daytime, it will be very confusing to a herb!

RIGHT: *A sophisticated blend of Sweet Violets, Lemon Thyme, Lavender and Rosemary wafts a welcoming balm over the entrance way.*

BELOW: *Pick a sweet Alpine Strawberry as the first refreshing taste of the day from this colourful basket of edible flowers and piquant leaves.*

## WATERING

Seedlings, and herbs under lights, growing in hanging baskets or in small pots, with large, soft leaves, positioned in hot sun or experiencing active growth, will require frequent (usually daily) watering. Reduce this in winter. Use tepid water from a kitchen filter jug to avoid excess lime, a watering can with a long neck and fine rose or a teapot, and water directly on to the soil, not the leaves. A mist atomizer, or open bowls of water, will help to maintain humidity, particularly with central heating.

Stand pots on a drip tray lined with clean gravel, to encourage humidity and hold the plant above excess water to avoid rot – overwatering is the most common cause of problems. Basil appreciates daily watering or leaf misting by midday to avoid wet nights and possible 'damping-off'. Large-leaved herbs grown in the kitchen will need the occasional wipe to remove the fine 'grease' build-up.

## Hanging Baskets

There are a number of prostrate or trailing herbs which are both decorative and suitable for growing in hanging baskets.

In a sunny position, grow a range of creeping Thymes with different leaf and flower colours, trailing Nasturtiums, Catmint or Ground Ivy (*Glecoma hederacea*). Choose the Prostrate Rosemary and balsamic blue-leaved Prostrate Sage. The smaller Winter Marjoram, golden Creeping Jenny (*Lysimachia nummularia*) and purple or gold-variegated Bugle (*Ajuga*) will dangle down in an attractive way.

For a shady location, use pungent Pennyroyal, Sweet Woodruff and the blue-flowered Periwinkle (*Vinca major*). Salad Burnet (*Sanguisorba minor*) trails its leaves, and Lady's Mantle (*Alchemilla mollis*) has long, arching flowering stems which will drape prettily over a pot or basket.

# In the Conservatory

A garden room maintained at a minimum of 10°C (50°F) provides a wonderful opportunity to extend the range of mood-enhancing aromatic plants. Make the most of it with plant stands, tiered shelving, wall-mounted pots and hanging baskets.

In a sunny breakfast corner, place pot-grown Lemon Verbena, Lemon Grass, Australian Mint Bush and Lemon and Peppermint Geraniums within stroking distance. Add bright green Lemon Thyme, minty Alecost and golden Feverfew with their pretty white daisies, plus a few glorious orange Calendulas or vibrant Nasturtiums to complete a picture of sparkling morning cheer.

The small citrus trees are a delight indoors with tangy fruit, smooth, elegant, aromatic foliage and sensuously spicy white blossoms. Recommended evergreen forms include two Lemons: *Citrus meyeri*, 1.2 m (4 ft) tall, and the hardy *C. limon* 'Eureka', plus the famous Seville Orange (*C. aurantium*), suitable for growing in a large pot. All three respond well to pruning. Also fun are the mini Oranges: Calamondin (x *Citrofortunella microcarpa*), 1.5m (5ft) tall, with its variegated cultivars 'Tiger' and 'Variegata', and the easily trained Otaheite Orange (*Citrus* x *limonia*), with tiny mauve fragrant flowers and sweet but insipid fruits.

BELOW: *The warmth of a greenhouse extends the range of herbs that can be grown and the sensuous Grapevine provides welcome dappled shade in the heat of summer.*

RIGHT: *A summer house or garden room becomes a welcome aromatic haven in cooler months, of benefit to both gardener and plants, as favourite pot-grown specimens are brought indoors. This range of containers offers opportunity for fragrant herbs both large and small. The formal symmetry of two standard Bays balances the casual exuberance of their companions.*

# Small Herb Garden Designs

A design of strong, simple shapes created by paths and edging near the house will make the whole garden look structured and well kept. This is ideal near the breakfast area, to provide an uncluttered space in which to sit with a clear mind to start the day. It also gives year-round form and an interesting view from upstairs windows. Planting can be simple or flamboyant – low maintenance for those with little time, or a divided pattern of culinary, craft and tisane aromatics for the herb enthusiast.

A herb garden site should be at least three-quarters in sunlight, and a breakfast area should bask in the morning sun while enjoying shelter from winds. The chosen shape need not be complicated, but it should be clear. Knot garden plants such as Box, Lavender, Santolina, Hyssop, Upright Germander, Curry Plant, Winter Savory or Dwarf Rosemary can serve as path edging, or be used in geometric or curving lines to add extra pattern. The formality can be emphasized by in-planting with herbs in a limited range of colours, or contrasted for a softer effect using a relaxed, sweet profusion of plants which trail on to paths.

Paths form the framework of these gardens, so interesting materials are important and give an opportunity for individual creativity. Grass, stone, brick and gravel can be used singly or in combination; pebbles, tiles, broken china or metal cogs can be laid into concrete, while lightly trodden areas could be planted with creeping Thymes or Lawn Chamomile. Plain concrete slabs make the design 'flat' on their own, but they can be lined with narrow-gauge bricks or alternated with other materials to great effect (and to reduce costs). Beds between the paths should not exceed 1.2–1.5m (4–5ft) in width for a maximum 75cm (2$^{1}/_{2}$ft) stretch to plant, weed and harvest.

RIGHT: *Strong geometric shapes create interest even in a new garden.*

# Design Ideas for Small Spaces

These patterns show the range of possibilities for even a tiny space. Inspiration can come from a Celtic cross, a Persian screen, a Hindu Mandala, a snowflake, or a computer chip. Try to avoid a straight-through path which draws the eye away.

ABOVE LEFT: A traditional design delineating beds of herbs by use, with dwarf box edging.

CENTRE LEFT: The two interlocking 'V's create a knot effect by the direction of path edging bricks.

BELOW LEFT: A circular path with four circles of edging plants. Where the planting circles would cross the path, the colour of the path pebbles changes to create the illusion of interlocking knotted shapes.

BELOW CENTRE: The diamond path uses 10cm (4 in) cobbles, creating four beds to feature collections of Thymes, Sages, Rosemaries and Marjorams.

BELOW RIGHT: The abstract geometry is created with 30 cm (12 in) slabs and would suit a modern situation. Choose slab colours carefully. Many become garishly bright when wet, so test with water.

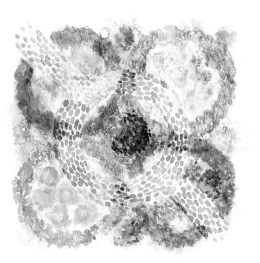

## List of Plants in Plan

1. Dwarf Box
2. Golden Lemon Balm
3. White Musk Mallow
4. Primrose
5. Calendula
6. Sunflower
7. Green Fennel
8. Variegated Ginger Mint
9. Corsican Mint
10. Lawn Chamomile
11. Golden Feverfew
12. Pennyroyal
13. Climbing Rose 'Gloire de Dijon' (yellow-apricot)
14. Climbing Rose 'Mme. Alfred Carrière' (white)
15. Variegated Applemint
16. Alecost
17. Cowslip
18. Pots of Lemon Verbena
19. Espaliered Apple tree: 'Worcester Pearmain' – attractive in flower and fruit, and does well in cooler climates, or Crabapples: 'Dartmouth' or 'Montreal' for scented flowers and fruits for delicious preserves.
20. Climbing Nasturtiums

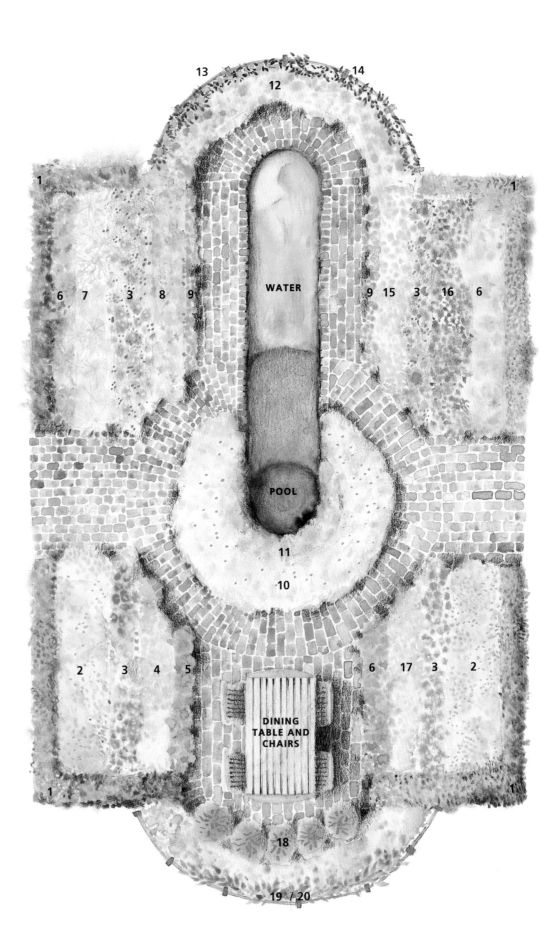

# A Garden of Refreshing Morning Plants

A delightful way to start the day is to breakfast in a bright refreshing garden space. This simple design, suitable for town or country, is enriched with decorative pebble path patterns and a mosaic of jewel-like pool tiles. The invigorating Mint, Lemon and Apple scents are amplified by bright gold and green leaves, butter-yellow Primrose, golden-orange Calendula and the embodiment of sunshine – the tall friendly Sunflower (*Helianthus annus*). The morning brightness is reflected in white Musk Mallow (*Malva moschata alba*), which flowers continuously all summer. Classical screens of vertical bamboo add to the feeling of lightness, provide privacy and complement the sparkling light and refreshing sound of the miniature tumble of water along the water channel.

Design with clean lines and open spaces to encourage a sense of clarity, and plant easy-maintenance herbs in simple shapes – restrict intricate patterns. Then take deep exhilarating breathes and enjoy the new day.

BELOW: *The Geffrye Museum herb garden, designed by the author, provides an enclosed oasis of calm in London's busy East End.*

*Use the stimulating herbs and their essential oils in cleansing routines to awaken the senses in the morning and provide a refreshing burst of energy at any time of day.*

# Refreshing Body Recipes

## Shower Power

A fragrant, invigorating bath or shower provides the perfect start to the day.

### BATH AND SHOWER OILS

For a stimulating bath, add a total of 4–6 drops of Grapefruit, Bergamot FCF, Lemon FCF, Eucalyptus or Cypress, or up to 4 drops Rosemary or 2 drops Peppermint essential oil, alone or combined with others, to warm water. The oils can be pre-mixed with nourishing Almond or Grapeseed oil (1 drop per ml of the vegetable oil) and used as a traditional bath oil. Add 1 tsp to the bath to leave the skin soft with a subtle sheen. Enjoy a 10-minute soak and breathe deeply.

The oils can also be used in the shower by adding them to a scentless shower gel at 1 drop per ml (stir with a chopstick), or by applying them directly to a wet body cloth after cleaning the skin. Massage the cloth over your skin as you stand under the running water and inhale the fragrance.

### GRAPEFRUIT BODY SHAMPOO

This rousing 'wake-up' recipe for bath or shower makes enough body shampoo for two showers. Blend 3½ tsp Almond oil with 4 drops Grapefruit, Rosemary or Petitgrain essential oil in a screw-topped glass jar. Add ½ tsp lecithin (to aid absorption through the skin), ¾ tsp Witch hazel and 4 tsp Grapefruit juice (or Pineapple, Orange or Apple) and shake well. Apply to wet skin, massaging over your body as you stand under running water or lie in the bath, to leave your skin nourished and smooth. Refrigerate the remainder of the shampoo and use within a week.

### MATSUBA-YU (PINE NEEDLE BATH)

This invigorating, forest-fresh soak improves circulation and helps to eliminate toxins. Wrap a few handfuls of fresh Pine branch tips in a muslin or cotton square and suspend under the running hot tap, then swish it around in the bath.

### YIN AND YANG TONIC BATHS

In hot weather, choose Cucumber tonic for a cooling bath or facial. Juice a Cucumber and add the juice to a basin of warm water. Stand in the bath or shower and pour cupfuls over your body repeatedly. Pat dry with a towel or allow to evaporate. This tonic also helps to reduce the pain of sunburn, soothe inflammation and reduce oiliness.

In cold weather, choose a warming, stimulating Ginger bath to boost your circulation. Grate a walnut-sized piece of fresh Ginger into a muslin bag, place under the running hot tap and then slosh it through the bath water.

### BILINGUAL BODY SPLASH

This speaks 'invigoration' to both mind and body. Mix together essential oils as follows: 7 drops Bergamot FCF; 2 drops each Lemon FCF, Petitgrain and Lavender; 1 drop each Rosemary and

ABOVE AND RIGHT: *Forest-fresh Pine Needle Bath.*

OPPOSITE: *Inhale the sharp scents of freshly cut Spearmint and Gingermint, Calendula, Feverfew and Marjoram for an early morning boost.*

Black Pepper. Allow to mature for 2 days. Add the mixture to 1 tsp gin and 10 tsp cider vinegar in a screw-topped glass jar and leave for a week. Add 1 cup spring water and shake well. Splash over your body after a bath or shower or use as a tonic reviver on a hot day.

## Body

Use these talcum powders in the morning for silky, aromatic skin throughout the day.

### EAU-DE-COLOGNE BODY TALC

This talc has a truly refreshing scent. Place 2 tbsp Arrowroot powder, or 1 tbsp Arrowroot and 1 tbsp unscented talc, in a screw-topped glass jar. Cut 5 wands of unsized blotting paper, each 8x1 cm (3x$^{1}/_{2}$ in), and drop a different essential oil on each one as follows: 10 drops Bergamot, 5 drops Lemon, 3 drops Lavender, 2 drops Neroli, 1 drop Rosemary. Bury the wands in the powder, seal, and leave for 1–2 weeks. Remove the wands and use the talc.

BELOW: *Watermelon and Lemon Skin Refresher.*

### PEPPERMINT FOOT TALC

Help keep your feet fresh and cool throughout the day with this soothing talc. In a screw-topped glass jar, mix 2 tbsp Arrowroot, or 1 tbsp Arrowroot and 1 tbsp unscented talc, with 2 drops each essential oils Peppermint and *Eucalyptus citriodora*. Both are cooling and deodorizing.

## Teeth and Mouth

Producing a clean-tasting, refreshed mouth is an essential morning ritual.

### MINTY ORANGE MOUTHWASH

Boil 10 Cloves and the zest of an organic Orange in 1 cup water for 5 minutes. Cool, strain and add 4 drops Orange essential oil, or 3 drops Orange and 1 drop Peppermint or Spearmint. Store in a screw-topped glass jar in the refrigerator. Shake well before use and use within a week.

### THREE-HERB MOUTHWASH

Steep 4 tbsp fresh Mint leaves, 1$^{1}/_{2}$ tsp Aniseed and a pinch fresh or dried Rosemary in 0.5 litre (1 pint) boiling water. Cool and leave overnight in the refrigerator. Strain and store in a screw-topped glass jar in the refrigerator. Use within a week.

## Face

Refreshing face treatments for days when you have time to spare, or need a little extra glow.

### FRESH-FACE PASTE

This mixture removes dull, dead skin cells and the cereal contains vegetable hormones which condition the skin. Mix 1 tsp Oatmeal and 1 tsp ground Almonds with $^{1}/_{2}$ tsp Apple juice (for normal skin) or $^{1}/_{2}$ tsp cider vinegar (for oily skin). Add 1 drop skin-balancing Geranium essential oil, if liked. Apply the mixture to your damp skin and with damp fingers massage once over your face very lightly, without pulling or scrubbing, and avoiding the eye area. Splash off with warm water.

### WATERMELON AND LEMON SKIN REFRESHER

For this cooling and freshening mixture, cut an average slice of Watermelon, remove the skin and seeds, and mash the flesh with a fork, pouring the excess juice into a glass for a refreshing drink. Squeeze half a Lemon or Lime over the fruit pulp. Place a cool damp face cloth or damp cotton pads over your eyes to relax them and protect them from the citrus juice, lie down and apply the fruit pulp to your face and neck, and then relax for 10–20 minutes. Rinse with cool water.

### SPRITZ MASK

Place 2 handfuls fresh herbs in a liquidizer with 2 tbsp spring water. Blend and strain off any excess liquid (or add more if necessary). Apply to clean, damp skin in a thick layer and relax for 20 minutes. Rinse with warm water. For your herbs, choose from Fennel, Mint, Nettle and Lime blossom. For dry skin, choose Houseleek or Marsh Mallow root, and for oily skin try Sage.

## *Shaving Surprise*

Prepare for a pleasant surprise with an individual shaving oil, an aftershave and a face splash that are both refreshing and healing.

### SMOOTH SHAVING OIL

Mix together essential oils as follows: 10 drops Frankincense; 6 drops each Lavender, Bergamot FCF; 3 drops Eucalyptus; 1 drop Tea Tree, and leave to mature for 1–2 days. Blend with 10 tsp Grapeseed oil. Massage 3 drops over the beard or other area to be shaved, then shave as normal. The essential oils smell good, leave the skin soft and supple, and are antiseptic, antiviral and antifungal, speeding the healing of any skin problems or cuts.

### SPICY AFTERSHAVE

Mix together essential oils as follows: 5 drops each Lavender and Bergamot FCF; 4 drops Frankincense, 3 drops Petitgrain; 2 drops each Grapefruit and Lime; 1 drop each Black Pepper, Patchouli and Basil; leave to infuse 2 days; add 2 tsp Lemon Vodka and infuse another 2 days; mix in 4 tsp Orange flower water. Leave 1 week. Shake before use.

### GRAPEFRUIT SEED FACE SPLASH

Grapefruit seed extract has many healing qualities including antibiotic, anti-viral, anti-fungal and deodorizing properties. Add 3 drops to 1tbsp of pure water and apply daily to the face, avoiding the eyes and broken skin. For scalp health, add 5–10 drops of extract to a portion of shampoo, massage on wet scalp and hair, leave 2 minutes, then rinse thoroughly. Repeat twice in the first week, then once every 2 weeks.

## *Eyes*

Make tired eyes bright and sparkling with these herbal refreshers.

### DARK CIRCLE BANISHER

To reduce tired circles under the eyes, make Mint or Chamomile tea with tea bags, remove and cool the bags. Drink the tea, place the bags over your eyes, lie back and relax for 5–10 minutes.

### WAKE-UP ICE

Freeze Mint or Chamomile tea in an ice-cube tray. Give the eye area a refreshing massage with a cube.

ABOVE: *Morning freshness with Surprise Shaving Oil and Spicy Aftershave.*

ABOVE: *The spirit of a warm summer morning captured in a Rose and Citrus potpourri.*

## Hair

Clean, fragrant hair has the dual benefit of making you look as well as feel full of zest for the new day.

### WAKE-UP SHAMPOO

This shampoo will leave your hair subtly fragranced, fresh and clean. Place 1 tbsp unscented or baby shampoo in a cup. Stir in a total of 3–4 drops of one or a mixture of the following essential oils: Bergamot FCF, Chamomile (Roman or German, for blond hair), Eucalyptus, Geranium, Mint, Petitgrain, Rosemary (for dark hair), Tea Tree or Thyme. Wash your hair as normal. Rosemary and Thyme help prevent dandruff and will condition greasy hair. Chamomile helps soothe scalp irritation. All these oils are stable in shampoo if you wish to make up larger quantities.

### FRAGRANT VINAIGRETTE RINSES

This rinse adds shine and subtle fragrance, and will also soothe itchy scalps. Mix $1/2$ cup cider vinegar with 3 drops Rosemary or Geranium essential oil, then add $1/8$ cup Apple juice and 3 cups spring water. Pour repeatedly through your hair, catching the rinse in a bowl. Or, infuse 4 tbsp fresh (or 2 tbsp dried) Rosemary, Lemon Balm or Sage in 3 cups boiling water for at least 10 minutes. Strain, add the Apple juice and vinegar and use as above. A final rinse of cool water encourages the outer hair cells to lie flat, adding to the smooth, lustrous finish.

### DEEP-CLEANSING FRUIT-DROP SODA

Dull, lifeless hair can be the result of residue built up by commercial hair products. Used once a month, this treatment removes them to reveal shiny, revitalized hair. Mix $1/4$ cup bicarbonate of soda with 1–2 drops Lime or Lemon essential oil. Dissolve in $1/2$–1 cup warm water and stir thoroughly. After shampooing and rinsing, gently massage the mixture through your hair for 1–2 minutes and then rinse.

## Dressing Scents

For fresh, clean, scented clothes in the morning, make instant sachets from a square of fabric. Fill with dried herbs chosen from Spearmint, Peppermint, Ginger Mint, Basil Mint, Applemint or Eau-de-Cologne Mint; Lavender, Southernwood, Lemon Verbena, Scented Geraniums, Alecost, Roman Chamomile, Lemon Thyme or Basil; Angelica seed, Citrus peels, Eucalyptus, Thuja, Juniper, Pine needles or Cedar chips; crushed Star Anise, Allspice, Cardamom, Cloves or Cinnamon. Tie with a ribbon or rubber band. Place sachets inside socks, gloves, purses and shirts on hangers, and in drawers, linen cupboards and storage boxes.

Thyme, Mint, Peppermint and Pennyroyal herb sachets are good deodorizors for use in trainers, shoes and boots. Store winter scarves with spice and citrus peel sachets. Wrap them around yourself in cold weather and inhale the cheering, 'warming' scent. Store summer scarves and handkerchiefs with Mint, Alecost or Lemon Verbena for a light, lively fragrance.

### MINTY-CITRUS ZESTY POTPOURRI

Mix equal quantities of Lemon Verbena, Alecost, Spearmint, Peppermint, golden Lemon Balm, Lemon Thyme, and young Bergamot leaves; dried Orange, Lemon, Citron and Lime peels; a sprinkling of Calendula petals, daisy-like Feverfew flowers and Juniper berries; 2 drops each Lemon, Lime, Grapefruit and Bergamot essential oils per 3 cups of mixture. Display in prettty bowls or add to clothes sachets.

RIGHT: *Slipper sachets filled with the refreshing leaves of Peppermint and Alecost.*

FAR RIGHT, TOP: *Sachets and hangers padded with Lemon Verbena for fresh morning shirts.*

MIDDLE: *Larger sachets will scent an entire wardrobe.*

BOTTOM: *Store winter scarves with warm spicy mixtures.*

# Light Breakfast

*The gentle singing flavours of some herbs, like Mint, Lemon Balm and Lovage, are well suited to stirring the early-morning palate.*

## Breakfast Fruit Salad

*A pretty plate of sliced fresh fruit decorated with mint is a deliciously healthy way to start the day.*

Try segments of different kinds of melons, pink grapefruit, grapes, kiwi fruit slices, mango, cherries and plump dried apricots. Use a few drops of Lemon or Lime juice to keep apple, pear and other similar fruit from browning. Top with toasted hazelnuts, pine nuts or pecans, yoghurt, a dribble of honey, a few drops of juice from a Lime and ribbons of its zest, and small sprigs of variegated Apple Mint.

## Apricot and Ginger Fromage Frais

*Try using Ginger Mint instead of root ginger for a wonderfully subtle flavour.*

preparation: 10 minutes

6 ripe apricots
several sprigs of one of the following: Peppermint,
    Lemon Balm, Sweet Cicely
225 g / 8 oz low-fat fromage frais
1 tsp grated root Ginger
unrefined caster sugar, to taste

Bring enough water to the boil to cover the apricots together with a handful of your chosen herbs. Poach the apricots in simmering water for 3–4 minutes until just tender. Drain, let cool and skin the fruit, then halve and stone. Discard the herbs.

Put the apricots in the food processor with the fromage frais, Ginger and sugar to taste. Snip in a few more sprigs of the herb and blend. Serve chilled.

**YOGHURT DRINKS**

**Try these delicious concoctions as quick breakfasts or for refreshment at any time of the day.**

**Use low-fat yoghurt, thinning it down with water or semi-skimmed milk and flavouring it to your liking. For creamier, thicker and more luxurious drinks, first drain the yoghurt in a sieve lined with muslin.**

**SWEET YOGHURT DRINK WITH LEMON BALM**
**Blend together 600 ml/1 pint yoghurt, 6 tbsp iced water, 4 tbsp honey and 1 tsp orange flower water, then snip in several leaves of fresh Lemon Balm.**

**SAVOURY YOGHURT DRINK WITH LOVAGE**
**Blend together 600 ml/1 pint yoghurt and 6 tbsp iced water, then snip in 6–8 Lovage leaves. Season to taste with sea salt and black pepper.**

# Moroccan Mint Tea

*Moroccan mint tea is traditionally sipped sweet and hot from tall glasses, but can be served chilled.*

### makes 600 ml / 1 pint

1 scant tbsp loose green tea
2 packed generous tbsp Moroccan Spearmint leaves,
 or other Mint as available
sugar or honey to taste

Bring 600 ml/1 pint water to the boil. Warm a tea-pot. Put the green tea and Mint leaves in the pot. Pour in the boiling water. Stir in sugar or honey to taste if you wish. Leave to infuse for 3–5 minutes, strain and serve, preferably in tall glasses or fine china cups.

If serving iced, strain through a muslin-lined sieve after 5 minutes, leave until cold and then chill.

LEFT: *Breakfast Fruit Salad and Sweet Yoghurt Drink with Lemon Balm*

ABOVE: *Moroccan Mint Tea*

**HIVE**
**ROUILLADE**

rouillade simply
eans 'a mixture' in
rench, but the term
most often used of
crambled eggs.

reparation:
minutes, toasting
read and cooking
ggs 10 minutes,
minutes to finish

or each serving
**extra-fresh large**
**eggs at room**
**temperature**
5 g / ³/4 oz butter
a salt and freshly
**ground black**
**pepper**
tbsp cream cheese
**small bunch fresh**
**Chives**
in slices of lightly
**toasted baguettes,**
**to serve**

ghtly scramble 2
esh eggs with the
tter, take off the
eat and season. Stir
the remaining egg
d the cream cheese
d snip in plenty of
ives. Spread over
e toast and serve at
om temperature.

# Breakfast & Brunch Dishes

*The role of eggs, cheese and cream in these meals brings to the fore those herbs like Chives, Chervil, Parsley and Tarragon which help develop the full flavours of dairy products.*

## Tomato and Tarragon Omelette

*Creamy egg, sweetly sharp tomato and pungent Tarragon make this simple omelette irresistible.*

**preparation and cooking: 10 minutes**
**for each serving**

*2 small-to-medium ripe vine tomatoes*
*about 15 g / ¹/2 oz unsalted butter, plus more to finish*
*1 scant tbsp snipped Tarragon*
*2 fresh free-range eggs*
*1 tsp milk*
*few drops of Tabasco sauce*
*sea salt and freshly ground black pepper*

Halve the tomatoes, squeeze out the seeds and extract the white pulp. Coarsely chop the flesh.

In a small non-stick frying pan over a moderate heat, melt half the butter and stir-fry the chopped tomatoes with one-third of the snipped Tarragon until soft. Season lightly and reserve.

Whisk the eggs until frothy. Wipe the pan clean and replace it over a moderate heat. Add half the remaining butter. Whisk the milk and a few drops of Tabasco into the egg and pour into the pan. Cook for 2–3 minutes, then sprinkle with most of the remaining Tarragon, reserving a little to finish.

Using a spatula, slip the rest of the butter under the omelette. As soon as it looks almost set, turn up the heat for 30 seconds, then slide on to a warmed serving plate. Season lightly.

Spoon the tomatoes over half the omelette, fold the

other half over, allowing a little tomato to show. For a glossy finish, swirl a very little butter over the top. Scatter over the rest of the Tarragon.

## Mushroom Brioches with Chervil

*Both mushrooms and brioche are texture treats as well as full of flavour. For a more pungent effect, you can use Chives instead of Chervil.*

**preparation: 10 minutes; cooking: 15 minutes**

*4 individual brioches*
*1 garlic clove, halved*
*¹/2 tbsp sunflower oil*
*350 g / 12 oz mixed mushrooms, preferably including some wild, sliced if large*
*45 g / 1¹/2 oz unsalted butter, plus more for the brioche (optional)*
*¹/2 shallot, finely chopped*
*2 heaped tbsp finely snipped Chervil, plus more sprigs to finish*
*1 heaped tbsp fromage frais, mascarpone or double cream*
*sea salt and freshly ground black pepper*

Warm the brioches in a cool oven.

Rub a sauté or frying pan with the cut sides of the garlic clove, then lightly coat it with oil. Add the mushrooms, season lightly and sauté for 5 minutes. Alternatively, spread the mushrooms on a microwavable plate, cover and cook on high for 4 minutes. Tip the mushrooms onto a plate lined with a double layer of paper towel to drain.

In the pan, melt half the butter. Add the shallot and a tablespoon of chervil. Stir for 2 minutes, then spread in the mushrooms. Turn up the heat and sauté for 3–5 minutes. Stir in the fromage frais, mascarpone or cream, the rest of the butter and chopped Chervil. Adjust the seasoning.

Halve the brioches. If you like, lightly butter the cut sides. Spoon the mixture over the bottoms, allowing it to spill over. Decorate with Chervil sprigs, loosely replace the tops at an angle and serve.

CHAPTER TWO

# Home, Work & Focus

*When it's time to work, aromatic herbs can make your tasks easier, safer and more pleasurable.*

In this chapter aromatics are used in two ways: some plants help the mind to focus and concentrate efficiently, while others have aromatic qualities which deter pests, increase hygiene or reduce pollution.

During demanding mental activity, an aromatic reprieve will clear the mind, ease the body and marshal the brain cells. Herbs like Angelica, Hyssop and Oregano, with refreshing green herbaceous scents and a slight pungency or sharpness, rather than a sweet or floral fragrance, work well. The leaf scents will refresh, relax or stimulate your mind, and some fragrances will also enhance memory and creativity. Research confirms the ancient reputations of Rosemary and Basil for improving memory, and their power is most potent in their essential oils. These can be placed on a handkerchief to sniff periodically for the sensation of a waft of oxygen straight to the brain, or incorporated into a room spray with other mind-focusing oils.

Aromatic herbs to help with household chores have been the focus of still-room activity since Elizabethan days. Many, such as Pennyroyal, Tansy, Santolina and Southernwood, are insect repellents, while Thyme, Sage and Rosemary are all powerful disinfectants.

For offices, modern research now offers specific houseplants to grow to reduce interior air pollution, computer radiation and noise levels. Essential oils like Grapefruit, Geranium and Lavender can reduce the polluting effect of fire retardants and commercial cleaning products, while everyone benefits from a refreshing spray of antiseptic oils such as Bergamot, Juniper, Eucalyptus, Tea Tree and Thyme. A blend will deodorize a room, protect against many bacteria and viruses, and impart a light, clean, efficiency-enhancing fragrance.

CRISP SCENTS FOR CONCENTRATION • HOUSEHOLD HERBS & OILS • USEFUL GARDEN HERBS • TRADITIONAL ELIZABETHAN HERB GARDEN DESIGN • HARVESTING & DRYING • POTPOURRI TECHNIQUES & RECIPES • AROMATIC PET CARE • OILS, VINEGARS & PRESERVES • SAVOURY SOUPS & SANDWICHES

*A new area for the use of aromatics is to help the mind work and focus. This is especially useful for those working at a computer, microscope, cash desk or air traffic console, who can double the value of rest breaks for their eyes by pinching and inhaling the scent of sharp, stimulating fresh herbs.*

# Scents for Concentration

## Fresh Herbs

The vibrant green colours of fresh herbs are calming, and as the volatile aromatic oils evaporate they oxidize and provide a refreshing atmosphere similar to standing beside a waterfall. Each herb has a slightly different effect on the mind, depending in part on personal memories and preferences. Experiments will show which are most effective for you.

For a mind-focusing break make up a vase of fresh herbs and place within arms reach of your work area. Pinch and inhale a different leaf at each break. Chose available sprigs from Alecost, Angelica, Basil, Bay, Calamint, Catnip, Cedar, Citrus leaves, Cyprus, Fennel, Germander, Hyssop, Lavender, Lemon Balm, Lemon Verbena, Marjoram, Mint, Oregano, Pine, Rosemary, Santolina, Savory, Thyme, Wax Myrtle and Wormwood.

### PLANTS TO REDUCE POLLUTION

For optimum health, efficiency and concentration the various pollutants exuded by many modern home and office fixtures and fittings need to be reduced. Certain plants, including *Dieffenbachia* species, are known to filter out a variety of building pollutants, especially if grown in soil with plant-pot carbon. Several houseplants reduce pollutants that are common in homes and offices. To reduce formaldehyde, grow Spider Plant (*Chlorophytum elatum*), Heart Leaf Philodendron (*Philodendron oxycardium*), Azalea (*Rhododendron indicum*), Mother-in-Law's Tongue (*Sanseveria laurentii*), Poinsettia (*Euphorbia pulcherrima*) and the Fig tree (*Ficus moraceae*). To reduce benzene, grow English Ivy (*Hedera helix*), Marginata (*Dracaena marginata*) and Goldon Pothos (*Scindapsus aureus*). To reduce TCE (trichloroethylene), grow Peace Lily (*Spathiphyllum* 'Mauna Loa') and Dragon Tree (*Dracaena deremensis* 'Janet Craig' and 'Warnecker'). Add Rosemary, Thyme or Lavender, as they tolerate dry air and add antiseptic aromas.

The Peruvian cactus *Cereus uruguayanus*, with scented white flowers, appears to reduce the electromagnetic pollution of computers and is being grown in the New York Stock Exchange. Place this slow-growing houseplant near the television or computer.

LEFT: *The clean, vibrant scent of Rosemary can aid concentration.*

RIGHT: *The lively sharp scents of Rosemary, Rue and Artemisia, planted outside a study window, freshen the air and focus the mind.*

## Essential Oils

The power of scent to aid mental work is strongest when using essential oils. Put 5 drops on a handkerchief and sniff periodically, keeping the handkerchief enclosed at other times to maintain the scent. Rosemary oil is the first choice for concentration and has an invigorating fragrance acceptable to almost everyone. A sniff of Basil oil is like fresh air to the cerebellum. Other brain focusers include Peppermint, Black Pepper and Grapefruit. To maintain sensitivity, alternate these with other stimulant oils that facilitate concentration: Eucalyptus, Lemon Eucalyptus, Thyme, Lemon, Fennel, Bergamot, Cedarwood, Cypress, Juniper, Lemon Grass, Ginger, Cinnamon, Clove, Lime Blossom, Nutmeg, Cardamom, Coriander, Petitgrain, Lime and Orange. Alternatively, these oils could be diluted in an air spray or used in a head-clearing bath or massage.

### TO REDUCE FATIGUE

For overwork, inhaling the scent of Rosemary, Basil, Peppermint, Black Pepper or Eucalyptus oil will reduce mental fatigue, while oils of Geranium, Thyme, Sweet Marjoram, Pine and Nutmeg will help overcome general fatigue. However, neither group should be used excessively in place of rest breaks.

### AIDE-MÉMOIRE

When studying, place a drop of a different essential oil inside each text book to provide memory links, avoiding oils that already have other strong associations for you. To reinforce the memory, you could dab the same oil on your sleeve to sniff discreetly during an exam. For a double function, choose from the group of general memory-enhancing oils: Basil, Black Pepper, Cardamom, Coriander, Ginger, Grapefruit, Lemon, Rosemary or Thyme.

### COMMERCIAL APPLICATIONS

Japanese firms have taken these ideas seriously following the work of Dr Shizuo Torii, who illustrated the relaxing or stimulating effects on the brain of different essential oils, and other research which showed that lemon-scented air increased office efficiency and reduced keyboard errors by 50 per cent. Two giant construction firms now incorporate integral aroma systems into their 'intelligent' buildings, using different scents in different areas. Reception areas may have a subtle injection of Lavender or Rose; computer rooms might receive Rosemary or Eucalyptus to maintain alertness; and general office space could be given Lemon or Mint in the morning to stimulate, Lavender in late morning for stress reduction, Grapefruit after lunch to reinvigorate, woody scents in the afternoon to encourage relaxation, and a boost of Lemon at the end of the day to cope with homeward traffic. Essential oils are combined according to male-female staff ratios and changed periodically to maintain aroma sensitivity.

As these practices become more widespread, it is important that staff are involved in selecting the aromas and that everyone insists that true, safe essential oils, not synthetics, are used, so that they add to our health benefits and not to the general air pollution.

*Most aromatic leaves contain natural antiseptics and many incorporate insect-repellent compounds, while their fragrance makes household tasks more enjoyable.*

# Household Herbs & Oils

Herbs with insect-repellent properties include traditional Lavender, the pleasantly balsamic Southernwood and spicy Sweet Gale. Useful Thyme aromas range from the sweet *Thymus* 'Fragrantissimus' and pine-scented *T. azoricus*, through Lemon Thymes, fruity *T. odoratissimus* and pungent Caraway Thyme, to the familiar common Thyme. The clean smell of Peppermint, pungent scent of Santolina, Tansy, Mugwort and Wormwood, spiciness of Lemon peel, Cinnamon bark and Cloves, and woody fragrance of Sandalwood chips, Cedar and Camphorwood, will repel moths, ants and other pests. Try rubbing the leaves of Bush Basil, Chamomile, Elder, Mint, Peppermint, Mugwort, Rue, Shoo Fly (*Nicandra physaloides*), Tansy, Wormwood and Pennyroyal on to window and door frames to deter flies. (A powerful cleansing herb, Pennyroyal was once added to kegs of water to keep them sweet on long sea voyages.)

Two potent plant insecticides are the powdered flowerheads of Pyrethrum (*Tanacetum cinerariifolium*), which can be sprinkled (wearing gloves and away from pets and humans) to deter flies, ants, cockroaches, bedbugs and fleas, and the seed oil of India's Neem Tree (*Azadirachta indica*), purchased ready-made, which destroys over 200 insect species.

A few Bay leaves placed in storage bags of flour, rice or dried pulses will deter weevils. Place Pennyroyal sprigs where ants appear and pinch them frequently to release the scent. Rub fresh leaves across ant routes, along skirting boards and table legs, and in cupboards, which will force them to look elsewhere. The smells of Peppermint and Tansy leaves are repellent to mice. Use these herbs dried indoors and grow them around hen houses and duck or rabbit pens.

## FUMIGATION

The bitter-scented common Fleabane (*Pulicaria dysenterica*), greater Fleabane (*Inula conyzae*), Mugwort and Wormwood kill fleas and lice. First, clear the room of people and pets; then, wearing a mask to avoid inhaling the fumes, burn the leaves over low embers and encourage the fumes to fill the room. Keep the room sealed for several hours or overnight. The smouldering dried leaves of Hemp Agrimony (*Eupatorium cannabinum*) will repel flies and wasps.

## BOOK PROTECTION

Small sachets of insect-repellent herbs can be placed among books for scent and protection. Sweet Woodruff dispels the mustiness of old or unaired books – press the star-shaped leaf whorls between the pages. Cedar shelves or boxes can become heirlooms for the safe storage of books, linen and trousseaux. The antiseptic leaves of the Neem Tree are used in India to protect library books.

ABOVE: *Both Purple and Green Sage leaves have a bold form and scent, which benefits from slow drying to preserve their flavour. Smouldering dried leaves helps banish unwelcome cooking smells.*

Above) Dramatic squares of Box-edged silver Santolina featured as a new rarity and elegant moth-repellent in Tudor herbals.
(Below) The stunning silver-green leaved *Artemisia ludoviciana* is the most decorative of the Artemisias.

*Pungent herbs are a boon to the organic gardener, as their chemical make-up can reduce or eliminate many potential horticultural problems. Some herbs supply fertilizer and green manure, while others deter pests and diseases or encourage beneficial insects.*

# Useful Garden Herbs

## Herbal Fertilizers

To brew a general fertilizer with extra potash, pack chopped Comfrey or Nettle leaves into a container, cover with water, add a lid (it will smell dreadful) and soak for 4 weeks. Use the liquid fertilizer as needed by diluting 20:1 with water. It is especially good for tomatoes, potatoes and houseplants. Yarrow, another good general fertilizer, also provides extra copper.

Dill tops are rich in minerals, potassium, sulphur and sodium; Fenugreek sprouted seeds provide nitrates and calcium; Tansy leaves supply potassium and several minerals; and brewed Tea leaves yield nitrogen, phosphoric acid, manganese and potash.

To use as fertilizer in the garden, pour 1 litre (2 pints) boiling water over 1 cup fresh or $1/2$ cup dried herb, cover and steep for 10 minutes, then strain and water needy plants.

### GREEN MANURE
Growing a green manure crop for one season will increase fertility and improve the texture of the soil. Phacelia (*Phacelia tanacetifolia*) is an excellent blue-flowered annual to use; scatter seed thinly over the area to be treated and dig in at the flowering stage.

### COMPOST ACTIVATOR
When adding fresh greenery to a compost heap, Yarrow works homoeopathically to activate decomposition. Use one finely chopped leaf for each wheelbarrow-load of compost material.

## Herbal Insecticides

Among plants which eliminate harmful insects, the Neem Tree is destined for world importance. Following its crop of fragrant white flowers are seeds which yield the potent but non-toxic, garlic-scented Margosa oil that can destroy over 200 insect species including locusts, grasshoppers, cockroaches and rice pests, plus mites, nematodes, fungi, bacteria and some viruses. When purchasing, ask suppliers for Neem products.

Derris powder (from *Derris elliptica*, and best purchased with instructions) is used to control biting and sucking insects, especially aphids, but must be kept away from ponds as it is harmful to frogs and fish. Pyrethrum powder, from the pretty, mildly pungent white daisy, is another to use on sucking insects. Buy it ready-made, or grow your own plants, dry and powder the flowerheads, and sprinkle where required (wearing gloves) to deter flies, ants, cockroaches, bedbugs and fleas. For garden use, steep 55 g (2 oz) powder in 75 ml ($1/8$ pint) methylated spirit, dilute with 27 litres (6 gallons) water and spray.

When using herbal insecticide treatments, aim to do so late in the day, preferably in the evening, to cause the least possible harm to beneficial insects, bees and butterflies.

BELOW: *Comfrey provides an excellent potash fertilizer with calcium, potassium, phosphorus and trace minerals. Yarrow makes a good general, copper-rich version.*

## APHID CONTROL

To control aphids, pour 1 litre (2 pints) boiling water over 4 crushed garlic cloves, cover and steep for 10 minutes. Strain, cool, add 1 tsp washing-up liquid to help it stick to the leaves and use it as a spray the same day.

## GREENHOUSE PESTS

Sprinkled prunings of antiseptic herbs like Thyme, Rosemary, Sage, Wormwood, Hyssop, Savory and Bay will discourage pests from the greenhouse.

## 'BIOLOGICAL' CONTROL

Hoverfly larvae consume enormous quantities of greenfly. To encourage them in your garden, grow Phacelia, Buckwheat, Geranium (*Geranium* species), Chamomile, Dill, Fennel, Heliotrope, Marigold, Mint, Nasturtium, Parsley, Poppy, Sunflower, Sweet Rocket and Yarrow.

## Antifungal Herbs

To prevent damping-off mould in seedlings, pour 1 litre (2 pints) boiling water over 1 cup fresh (or ½ cup dried) Chamomile flowers, cover and steep for 10 minutes. Strain, cool and water over seedlings the same day.

To combat mildew and fungal diseases, prepare a mixture as above but using Couch Grass rhizomes instead of Chamomile flowers.

## Companion Planting

Chamomile is called the 'Physician Plant' as it improves the health of most plants grown nearby, possibly by exuding a plant tonic through its roots. Foxglove has a similar effect.

Some smells confuse or deter aroma-sensitive insects. The female carrot fly can smell bruised carrot leaves 6.5 km (4 miles) away and home in to lay her eggs, but stems of pungent Wormwood left next to a carrot row will mask the carrot scent as they are stepped on while the gardener tends the crop. Garlic will deter many pests, as will the *Tagetes* Marigolds, which are excellent grown between tomato plants, while Tansy benefits orchards.

(Above) Tread strongly scented Wormwood clippings while weeding to deter carrot fly. (Below) Root secretions from *Tagetes* deter potato eelworms.

# Herb Companions

*When planting your crops, refer to this table. Friends will either encourage plant growth or deter pests. Enemies are detrimental to healthy growth.*

### Angelica
FRIEND Parsley
ENEMY Celery; Lovage

### Apple
FRIENDS Mint; Nasturtium – *grow up and around trunks to deter woolly aphids*; Alliums (especially Chives) – *help protect against scab*; Penstemon – *can repel sawfly*; Tansy – *discourages moths*

### Artichoke
FRIEND Parsley
ENEMY Garlic

### Basil
FRIEND Parsley
ENEMY Rue; Tansy; Artemisias

### Beans
FRIENDS Savory; Borage; Buckwheat, Phacelia – *attract hoverflies*; Elder – *leafy twigs deter blackfly*
ENEMY Alliums

### Bergamot
FRIEND Mint; Parsley; Brassicas

### Brassicas
FRIENDS Mint, Hyssop, Sage, Thyme, Dill, Caraway – *strong scents help confuse predatory insects*; Bergamot – *strewn between young brassicas deters flea beetles*; Nasturtium – *deters whitefly*
ENEMIES Beans; Tomato

### Carrot
FRIENDS Onion; Garlic; Wormwood; Sage; Rosemary; Chives; Coriander; Tomato; Radish; Lettuce – *strongly scented herbs confuse carrot fly, others improve carrot health*

### Catmint
FRIENDS Thyme; Radish

### Chamomile
ENEMY Rue

### Chervil
FRIENDS Radish; Beans
ENEMY Rue

### Courgette
FRIENDS Nasturtium; Borage; Fennel
ENEMY Rue

### Cucumber
FRIEND Borage
ENEMIES Thyme; Sage

### Dill
FRIEND Brassicas
ENEMY Carrot

### Fennel
FRIENDS Courgette; Marrows
ENEMIES Most other plants

### Fig
FRIEND Rue

### Garlic
FRIEND Beetroot; Strawberry
ENEMY Legumes

### Grape
FRIENDS Blackberry; Sage; Mustard; Hyssop – *increases yields*

### Hyssop
FRIEND Brassicas

### Lavender
FRIENDS Thyme; Marjoram
ENEMIES Rue; Parsley

### Lemon Balm
ENEMIES Rue; Fennel

### Lettuce
FRIEND Chervil – *deters aphids, ants and possibly slugs*

### Marjoram
ENEMY Alliums

### Mint
FRIEND Nettle

### Parsley
FRIEND Lavender

## Peach

FRIENDS  Alliums – *also for apricot*; Strawberry – *host to parasites which feed on oriental fruit moths*

## Pear

FRIENDS  Tansy; Mint; Nasturtium

## Plum

FRIENDS  Legumes – *help maintain mineral levels*; Garlic – *aids general tree health*

## Potato

FRIENDS  Beans; Maize; Nasturtium; Summer Savory; Flax; Comfrey – *wilted leaves planted with seed potatoes prevent scab*; Horseradish – *buried in perforated pots to contain its vigour, deters eelworms*; Marigold – *Tagetes deters eelworms.*
ENEMIES  Black and Woody Nightshade

## Radish

FRIENDS  Nasturtium; Chervil

## Raspberry

FRIENDS  Garlic; Rue; Tansy; Marigold (*Tagetes*)

## Rose

FRIENDS  Chives – *control blackspot, but can take 3 years to become effective*; Sage, Garlic, Parsley – *deter aphids (do not allow Garlic to flower)*; Spearmint – *deters aphid 'owners', ants*

## Rosemary

FRIENDS  Sage; Brassicas; Beans

## Sage

FRIENDS  Brassicas; Carrot; Rosemary

## Southernwood

FRIEND  Brassicas

## Strawberry

FRIENDS  Borage; Catnip – *can reduce bird damage, but a sacrificial clump in sun is needed if there are cats in the area.*
ENEMY  Brassicas

## Summer Savory

FRIEND  Beans
ENEMY  Radish

## Sweet Pepper

FRIEND  Basil

## Tarragon

FRIEND  Potato
ENEMIES  Fennel; Rue

## Thyme

FRIENDS  Rose; Brassicas
ENEMY  Rue

## Tomato

FRIENDS  Mint; Basil, Onion, Chives – *deter insects*; Tagetes Marigold – *deters white fly, and roots excrete a nematode-killing substance. Grow with Basil*; Asparagus – *root secretions kill tomato root nematodes, while tomatoes deter asparagus beetles. Grow with Parsley*; Dandelion – *exude cichoric acid which protects tomatoes from fusarium wilt disease*; Nettle – *helps tomatoes keep longer*; Borage – *can reduce attacks of tomato hornworms*; Horehound – *stimulates fruiting*; Nasturtium – *deters whitefly from greenhouses and acts as a sacrifice to black aphids.*
ENEMIES  Brassicas; Potato

## Winter Savory

FRIEND  Beans
ENEMY  Radish

## Wormwood

*Plant Wormwood and other Artemisias in their own bed, as they inhibit the growth of many plants and can even discourage earthworms*

## Yarrow

ENEMY  Rue

# Herbs for Bees & Butterflies

Following the practical monastic format, a herb garden can be divided into areas for bees and butterflies, flavouring herbs, dye plants, cleaning herbs, flower arranging and so on. Choose aromatic varieties to increase the pleasure.

## A Bee Garden

Encouraging bees into the garden benefits plant pollination, honey production and reduces stress as their pleasant, lazy drone drifts around. Although scent is important to bees, colours are more so. They prefer yellow, blue-green to blue, mauve, purple, and red containing ultraviolet. Grow bee plants in a sheltered spot (holly or ivy trellises are effective), in full sun in groups of 5 or more, and include a range to flower from early spring through to late autumn, which is especially helpful to the vanishing bumblebees. Beehives look pretty but are better suited to large gardens, as bees ignore plants within about 15 m (50 ft) of their hives which may be contaminated by the bees' own cleansing flights.

BELOW: *Encourage the busy drone of pollinating bees by planting their garden favourites.*

### AROMATIC PLANTS

Anise Hyssop, Allium, Basil, Lemon (Bee) Balm, Borage, Catmint, Chamomile, Clover, Cowslip, Fennel, fruit tree blossom, Lime blossom, Marjoram, Meadowsweet, Melilot, Mignonette, Mint, Mustard, Nasturtium, Sage, Savory, Thyme, Valerian, Violet, Woodruff.

### NON-AROMATIC PLANTS

Calendula, Crocus, Flax (*Linum usitatissimum*), Forget-me-not (*Myosotis sylvatica*), Ivy (*Hedera helix*), Jacob's Ladder (*Polemonium caeruleum*), Mullein (*Verbascum thapsus*), Poppy, Sunflower (*Helianthus annuus*), Teasel (*Dipsacus fullonum*), Woad (*Isatis tinctoria*), Winter Aconite (*Eranthis* species).

## Plants for Butterflies

Butterflies and moths also help to pollinate the plants in our gardens and often display stunning wing colours and patterns. Concern is growing about their numbers as wild areas diminish, so providing nectar herbs in gardens is helpful. Butterflies respond to scent more than bees do, but they also have preferred colours – saffron-yellow, mauve, crimson, deep pink and blue. Moths respond to pale-coloured scented flowers, such as Lily-of-the-Valley, which show up in moonlight. Include plants on which they can lay their eggs and which provide food for their caterpillars. The most useful are Nettles, Thistles, Dog Violet (*Viola canina*) and Lady's Smock (*Cardamine pratense*). Butterflies and moths also need overwintering areas and attractive butterfly boxes are available to fix to a sheltered, sunny wall. Alternatively, allow a thick patch of Ivy to grow nearby.

### AROMATIC PLANTS

Buddleia, Honeysuckle, Hyssop, Jasmine, Lavender, Lilac, Narcissus.

### NON-AROMATIC PLANTS

Sedum, Leopard Plant (*Ligularia* species), Aster (*Aster* species).

RIGHT: *Herbs divided by use make a decorative and educational garden for schools, museums and public parks. Here, at the London Museum of Garden History, sixteenth and seventeenth-century plants form a living memorial to the Tradescant family – naturalists, plant collectors and gardeners to the King.*

# A Traditional Elizabethan-Inspired Garden

The newfound peace of Elizabeth I's reign allowed gardening in England to flourish. The gentry had more time to create and enjoy gardens, and the subject entered a glorious new era. The important food and medicinal herbs were still grown, but now herbs for beauty and fragrance were included, a sense of aesthetics developed, and the period has given us an archetypal image of the herb garden.

This design reflects the enthusiasm for gardening that was released in the Elizabethan period. Gardens were often created to support the needs of a large household, and for convenience, plants were grown in beds dedicated to a particular use. This allowed the mistress of the household to see, for example, which colouring plants in the 'dye' bed or which first aid plants in the 'medicinal' bed had reached their optimum growth and should be harvested. She would then ensure they were properly dried and added to the treasures of her still room for future creative endeavour.

The range of plants expanded enormously. Seeds were exchanged with travellers from Europe and new species began to filter in from North America and the Orient.

The garden was generally enclosed for privacy and protection. Here the Yew hedge has a gentle curved shape along the top which makes the space feel lighter and less enclosed. The south or sunny boundary has posts supporting thick rope horizontals which repeat the gentle curves. They provide a framework for climbing Roses, Honeysuckle and Clematis and yet allow sunlight to filter through. The Rose-covered pergola over the entrance adds significance and heightens the sense of stepping into a special fragrant space.

## List of Plants in Plan

### Central Knot
1. Topiary Ball Bay Tree
2. Box  (*Buxus sempervirens*)
3. Dwarf Box (*B. s.* 'Suffruticosa')
4. Silver Santolina (*Santolina chamaecyparissus*)
5. Willow green Santolina (*S. c.* 'Lemon Queen')
6. Bright green Santolina (*S. viridis*)
7. Sweet Violets (infill)
8. Topiary Rosemary 'Miss Jessop's Upright'

### Entrance Way
9. Lavender, Old English
10 Honeysuckle (*Lonicera caprifolium* & *L. japonica* var. *repens*)
11 Old Roses with 'New Dawn' and 'Evelyn'

### 12. MEDICINAL HERBS including:
Calendula; Chamomile; Coltsfoot (*Tussilago farfara*); Comfrey (*Symphytum officinale*); Feverfew; Elecampane (*Inula helenium*); Houseleek (*Sempervivum tectorum*); Self Heal (*Prunella vulgaris*); Spearmint; Rosehips; Sage; Wood Betony (*Stachys officinalis*); Yarrow. Virginia Scullcap (*Scutellaria lateriflora*): Valerian (*Valeriana officinalis*); Vervain (*Verbena officinalis*)

### 13. HOUSEHOLD HERBS including:
Alecost; Horsetail (*Equisetum arvense*); Mint; Pennyroyal; Rosemary; Soapwort; Sweet Cicely; Sweet Marjoram; Tansy, Thyme, Wormwood

### 14. DYE PLANTS
including: Alkanet (*Anchusa officinalis*); Dyer's Chamomile (*Anthemis tinctoria*); Dyer's Greenweed (*Genista tinctoria*); Lady's Bedstraw (*Galium verum*); Madder (*Rubia tinctorum*); Weld (*Reseda luteola*); Woad (*Isatis tinctoria*)

### 15. POTPOURRI HERBS including:
Applemint; Eau-de Cologne Mint; Lavenders; Lemon Verbena; Mignonette; Orris Iris; Pinks; Roses; Southernwood; Sweet Myrtle; Sweet Woodruff; Thymes

### 16. TISANE HERBS including:
Agrimony; Anise Hyssop; Bergamot; Betony; Catmint; Chamomile; Lemon Balm; Peppermint

### 17. SALAD HERBS including:
Chives; 'Cut-and-come-again' Lettuces; Dandelion; Jack- by-the-Hedge (*Alliara petiolata*); Lawn Daisy (*Bellis perennis*); Mustards (*Brassica nigra* & *B. hirta*); Nasturtium; Orach (*Atriplex hortensis*); Red Clover (*Trifolium pratense*); Salad Burnet (*Sanguisorba minor*); Summer Purslane (*Portulaca oleracea*)

### 18. CULINARY HERBS including:
Angelica; Basil; Borage; Chervil; Fennel; Garlic; Hyssop; Juniper; Lovage; Marjoram; Mints; Oregano; Parsley; Saffron; Sage; Savory; Skirret (*Sium sisarum*); Sorrel; Tarragon; Thymes; Tree Onion

### 19. COSMETIC HERBS including:
Calendula; Chamomile; Dill;

**20**

**20**

**15**

**2**

**HIGH-BACKED SEAT**

**2**

**3**

**3**

**18**

**2**

**2**

**20**

**3**

**2**

**3**

**2**

**6**

**4**

**6**

**7**

**7**

**18**

**5**

**7**

**5**

**6**

**6**

**16**

**5**

**5**

**3**

**3**

**4**

**7**

**7**

**7**

**4**

**17**

**8**

**1**

**5**

**5**

**5**

**6**

**7**

**6**

**5**

**5**

**18**

**7**

**6**

**4**

**6**

**7**

**2**

**2**

**3**

**3**

**20**

**9**

**9**

**19**

**ENTRANCE**

Eau-de-Cologne Mint;
Fennel; Lady's Mantle
(*Alchemilla mollis*); Madonna

Lily; Marshmallow (*Althea
officinalis*); *Rosa gallica* var.
*officinalis*; Wild Strawberry

20. YEW HEDGE

ABOVE: *In the Elizabethan period, divided herb gardens
provided the household with all the herbs it needed.*

*Enjoy the aromatic bounty of your herb garden throughout the year by careful harvesting and drying of the best specimens for use in home and office, for potpourri, and for pet care.*

# Harvesting & Drying Herbs

## Harvest Time

### LEAVES

Herb leaves are generally best harvested just before the plants flower, but can be picked for immediate use at any time during the growing season, with evergreen leaves available throughout the year. Collect undamaged leaves after the morning dew has evaporated. Cut whole stems of small-leaved herbs such as Thyme and Marjoram.

### FLOWERS

Harvest undamaged flowers in their prime – that is, when they are just fully open. Collect them in an open basket late in the morning in dry weather, when the dew has evaporated and the sun has begun to warm the blooms. Take care not to bruise the petals as you pick. Cut Lavender stalks whole.

### SEEDS AND FRUITS

Ripe seed is papery dry and buff to black. Collect seed on a warm, dry day – the trick is to catch it when fully dry, but before it disperses. Collect pods directly into paper bags for carrying back to the house, keeping species separate and labelled. Pick ripe fruit before it is overly soft. Collect berries and hops on their stalks and fork off when half dried.

### ROOTS AND RHIZOMES

Dig up roots and rhizomes in autumn, after the aerial parts of the plant have begun to wither and die. Perennial roots are harvested in their second or third year. Always check the legality of harvesting the roots of wild plants – in Britain, it is illegal to harvest roots from any land except your own without the owner's permission.

## Drying

Herbs should be dried slowly, away from sunlight and humidity, to preserve their properties. Use a well ventilated cupboard, ideally with a drying temperature of 32°C (90°F) for the first 24 hours, followed by a reduced temperature of 24–26°C (75–80°F); cooler temperatures lengthen the drying time. Store in dark-coloured, airtight glass jars labelled with the name of the herb and the date, placed out of direct sunlight. Most herbs are best used within a year.

### LEAVES

Try to wipe, not wash, soil from leaves. Hang stems of small-leaved herbs in small, loose bunches tied with string. For larger leaves, stretch muslin or pierced brown paper over wire cooling racks and spread the leaves thinly over the top. Dry pungent herbs away from others to avoid tainting. Remove

ABOVE: *Fragrant Thyme in generous flower.*

BELOW RIGHT: *After the dew has evaporated, spend a leisurely morning harvesting Lavender and Marjoram.*

Hang loose bunches of abundantly fragrant herbs about the house for friends and family to enjoy on week-ends and holidays, before removing them to a dark, damp-free and well-ventilated spot for drying.

dried leaves from their stems and store them whole in airtight jars. Condensation indicates that the leaves are not fully dried and should be removed and dried further, or that the lid is not airtight.

### FLOWERS

Dry small-headed flowers such as Chamomile whole, but separate the petals of larger flowers and dry as for leaves. Small quantities can be dried in a microwave oven – place a single layer in a dish and dry on low to medium power for 2–3-minute periods, turning them gently at intervals. This can take 6–20 minutes, depending on the thickness of the petals. It is a useful way to test petals intended for potpourri to see how they hold their colour.

### SEEDS AND FRUITS

Remove seeds from their pods and place them in a drying cupboard or warm, dry room, spread out in

shoebox lids with identifying labels. Umbels of seeds can be hung up by their stems to fall into boxes, or tied loosely in paper bags. Seeds will usually dry within 2 weeks, ready to store in airtight jars. Seed for sowing should be kept in labelled paper envelopes in a cool, dark, frost-free place. Rosehips and other fruits are best dried in an airing cupboard, turning them frequently.

### ROOTS AND RHIZOMES

Clean the roots or rhizomes and cut large ones into smaller pieces. These need temperatures of 50–60°C (120–140°F) to dry and can be dried slowly in a low oven, turning regularly until they are fragile and break easily. Store in dark-coloured, airtight containers, and discard if the roots become soft. Orris root needs to be turned occasionally, but must be left in a drying cupboard for at least 3 years to develop its proper scent.

# Potpourri

Capturing the fragrance of summer in your own potpourri is one of the great pleasures of herb gardening. Even a small space can provide a wide range of raw materials, from the luxury of Rose petals and hay freshness of Sweet Woodruff leaves, to the incense of Balsam Poplar buds and the pungency of Eucalyptus seed pods. Flower-colour choices fill the spectrum and leaf shades range from cream-splashed Applemint and golden Thyme to rich ruby Basil; from bright green Moroccan Mint to glossy, dark green Bay. Turning and stirring the chosen elements until they are bone dry is an aromatic treat.

Then comes the creative part: experimenting with a symphony of aromatic ingredients to create potpourris for different moods, from zesty and refreshing to sweet and soothing. Dry potpourri is the easiest to make and can be put to use in clothes sachets, sleep pillows and sofa sacks, but to release its scent it needs regular handling plus reviving with essential oils after a few months. Moist potpourri is purely an aromatic, not a visual, delight, but its perfume lasts for years.

BELOW: *Sweet-scented Roses, Lavender and Sweet Pea petals from an English country garden.*

## FLOWERS

In classic potpourris, Rose petals and Lavender make up most of the volume as they retain their perfume well. Nowadays the choice of materials is enormous, but flowers should still dominate the mixture. Scentless flowers chosen for their colour can be fragranced by sealing them for several weeks in a container with a strip of paper dotted with an essential oil.

## LEAVES

Because leaf scent is often stronger than the fragrance of flowers, smaller quantities are used, and they should be chosen to harmonize with each other and with the flowers. Crush some for extra fragrance and leave others to be broken up later to prolong the life of the potpourri. Autumn leaves can be pressed and dried to add extra colour.

## STORE CUPBOARD EXTRAS

Spices can be used sparingly in potpourri in a ratio of about 1 tbsp to 4 cups of flowers and leaves. These will impart a musky or oriental quality, and suggest a 'masculine' or warm 'winter' aroma. Citrus peels are both fragrant and decorative: cut thin strips with a zester or peeler and air-dry or oven dry them quickly. Unused herbal teas can also be added to the potpourri bowl.

## FIXATIVES

Fixatives prolong the life of potpourris by capturing and retaining some of the fragrance molecules. Each has its own scent, which enters the aromatic equation. Most easily available is Orris root from *Iris florentina*, popular for its subtle violet scent which does not influence a blend too strongly. Use 1 tbsp per 2–4 cups of potpourri mixture.

## DRY METHOD

Select a mood or theme and choose the scents, colours and presentation bowl accordingly. Blend the ingredients, fixative and essential oils and store in an airtight container in a dry, dark, warm place for 6 weeks, shaking gently at intervals to blend and intensify the mix.

## MOIST METHOD

This is the original method and begins with highly fragrant Rose petals. These are only partly dried, until they are leathery and their volume halved. For every 3 packed cups of petals use 1 cup of salt (half coarse sea salt, half finer, non-iodized salt) and sprinkle it over successive 1cm ($^1/_2$ in) layers of petals, filling a crock or bowl two-thirds full. Stand this aside for 10 days in a dry, dark place which is well ventilated to avoid mildew. The petals and salt will usually form a cake; break this up and mix with a fixative and other dried aromatic ingredients, place in an airtight container and leave to 'ferment' for at least 6 weeks, stirring at intervals. The finished potpourri should then be transferred to an opaque container with a tightly fitting lid. Remove the lid to release the scent as liked, but remember to close it when not in use to retain the scent. Stir occasionally.

## *Potpourri Ingredients*

### FLOWERS FOR SCENT

Acacia, Broom (*Cytisus battandieri* is pineapple scented), Carnation, Cottage Pink, Elder, Freesia, Heliotrope, Honeysuckle, Hyacinth, Jasmine, Jonquil, Lavender, Lilac, Lily-of-the-Valley, Lime blossom, Madonna Lily, Meadowsweet, Mexican Orange Blossom (*Choisya ternata*), Mignonette, Musk Mallow, Narcissus, Nicotiana, Orange blossom, Philadelphus, Rose (petals and whole buds), Stock, Sweet Pea, Sweet Violet, Wallflower.

### FLOWERS FOR COLOUR

Bergamot, Borage, Calendula, Chicory, Cornflower, Delphinium, Feverfew, Forget-me-not, Foxglove, Hound's Tongue (*Cynoglossum officinale*), Larkspur, Lawn Daisy, Lobelia (*L. syphilitica*), all red Poppy, Sage, Tansy, Tulip, Viper's Bugloss, Zinnia, any of the small 'everlasting' flowers, plus Pussy Willow catkins and Sweet Myrtle buds for texture.

### AROMATIC LEAVES

Alecost, Balm of Gilead, Balsam Poplar (buds), Basil, Bay, Bergamot, Lady's Bedstraw, Lemon Balm, Lemon Verbena, Melilot, Mints (Applemint, Peppermint, Spearmint, and especially Eau-de-Cologne), Nasturtium, Patchouli, Pine needles, Rosemary, Sage (especially Pineapple), Scented Geraniums (Rose, Lemon, Apple, Orange, Pine, Nutmeg, Peppermint), Southernwood, Sweet Briar, Sweet Cicely, Sweet Marjoram, Sweet Myrtle, Tarragon, Thymes (Lemon and Pine), Wild Strawberry, Woodruff.

ABOVE: *Vibrant blue Cornflowers: a decorative ingredient of potpourri*

### SPICES, SEEDS, ROOTS AND WOOD CHIPS

Alexanders (seed), Allspice, Aniseed, Cardamom, Cinnamon, Cloves, Conifer cones (small), Coriander, Dill (seed), Eucalyptus (pods), Ginger (root), Juniper (berries), Nutmeg, Star Anise, Vanilla (pods), Citrus peel (Orange, Lemon, Lime, Bergamot), aromatic roots of Angelica, Elecampane, Sweet Flag, Cowslip, Vetivert and Valerian, raspings of Cedarwood and Sandalwood, Cassia chips.

### FIXATIVES

Orris root – violet scent (1 tbsp per 2–4 cups potpourri); Gum Benzoin – sweet vanilla scent (15 g / $^1/_2$ oz per 4–6 cups); Tonka Bean (*Dipterix odorata*) – pungent vanilla scent (1–2 beans per recipe); Storax (*Liquidambar orientalis*) – use as Gum Benzoin. Sweet Violet root, Angelica root gum, crushed seed of Sweet Cicely and Ambrette/Muskseed (*Abelmoschus moschatus*), Sandalwood, Cinnamon, Cloves, Patchouli, Vetivert, Frankincense and Myrrh 'tears' and Oakmoss also act as fixatives.

### ESSENTIAL OILS

Essential oils extend the range of scents available and can replace a missing ingredient or revive a flagging potpourri. However, they are intense, so only a few drops are used and should be added one at a time to avoid dominating the subtler scent of the flowers.

## Potpourri Recipes

### FAMILY HEIRLOOM (DRY METHOD)

Start with a traditional mix of Rose petals and Lavender flowers with Bay leaves, ground Allspice and powdered Orris root. At each family celebration with flowers – first bouquet, wedding flowers, birth of a baby and so on – dry the best petals and add them to the potpourri. If the scent fades, enliven it with more Rose petals or essential oils. The fragrance will develop with the family history and each blossom will have a story to tell.

### TRADITIONAL SPICY ROSE (MOIST METHOD)

4 cups 'fermented' Rose petals; 1 cup Rose buds; $^1/_2$ cup Sweet Myrtle leaves; $^1/_4$ cup each crushed Bay leaves, mixed Orange, Lemon and Lime peel, and powdered Orris root; 2 tbsp each ground Cinnamon, Mace and Allspice; 1 tbsp ground Cloves; 1 grated Nutmeg.

### CONNOISSEUR'S SWEET JAR (MOIST METHOD)

4 cups 'fermented' Rose petals; 1 cup each Lavender, Cottage Pinks and Jasmine; $^1/_2$ cup each Wallflower and Rosemary; peel of $^1/_2$ Orange stuck with 20 Cloves and dried; 3 tbsp powdered Orris root; 1 tsp each ground Cinnamon, Allspice and Star Anise; essential oils: 4 drops Bergamot, 3 drops each Neroli, Rose and Lavender.

### FOREST BLEND (DRY METHOD)

$^1/_2$ cup each Pine needles, Thuja sprigs, Cedar chips, Eucalyptus leaves, Balsam Poplar buds, Wild Strawberry leaves, Sweet Violet flowers and Sweet Woodruff flowering tops; $^1/_4$ cup each Bay and Rosemary; $^1/_8$ cup each Angelica root and Sweet Violet root; 2 tbsp crushed Juniper berries. Add a few small Pine cones sprinkled with essential oils: 2 drops each Cedarwood, Cypress, Hyssop, Juniper, Frankincense and Oakmoss.

### ENGLISH GARDEN (DRY METHOD)

2 cups each Rose petals and Lavender; 1 cup each Rose buds, Sweet Myrtle leaves, Philadelphus, Violet, Honeysuckle and blue Delphinium; $^1/_2$ cup each Cottage Pink 'Mrs Sinkins', Peony petals, Madonna Lily petals, Meadowsweet florets, and Chamomile, Gypsophila or other tiny white flowers; $^1/_8$ cup powdered Orris root; 1 tbsp mixed ground Cloves, Cinnamon and Allspice.

RIGHT: *This Family Heirloom Potpourri is rich with memories made with petals from a wedding chaplet, a christening posy, Valentine Rosebuds and a graduation bouquet.*

# Aromatic Recipes for Home & Office

A room spray of essential oils can perform 4 functions: the oils can be selected to disinfect against a wide range of bacteria and viruses, deter insects, deodorize rooms or fragrance a space in order to enhance a specific mood.

## Disinfectant Air Sprays and Room Fresheners

A combination of several essential oils will kill most known harmful bacteria. Eucalyptus, Rosemary, Tea Tree and Juniper are valuable for combating most bacteria during epidemics and they are also said to strengthen the body's immune system.

### PROFESSIONAL ROOM SPRAY

This mixture will help to eliminate most harmful bacteria, many viruses and a few fungi. Bergamot and Eucalyptus are the best room deodorizers; Bergamot, Lavender, Peppermint, Lemon and Mandarin all deter insects; and ants dislike the scent of Cloves. The first 4 oils listed below are the main ingredients of classic eau-de-Cologne, echoing this famous refreshing scent.

The recipe is for a 50 ml (2 fl oz) spray bottle and uses 200 drops essential oil per 50ml (2 fl oz) finished volume. Use essential oils as follows: 60 drops Bergamot; 20 drops Lavender; 15 drops each Lemon, Rosemary, Thyme, Tea Tree and Lemon Eucalyptus; 10 drops each Eucalyptus, Juniper and Mandarin; 5 drops each Clove, Sandalwood and Peppermint. Any combination should kill most harmful germs. Measure the oils into a clean glass bottle, replace the lid, swirl to bind the oils and leave for 24 hours to amalgamate. Add 25 ml (1fl oz) isopropyl alcohol or vodka. Replace the lid and blend, swirling and tipping the bottle several times, then leave for 24 hours. Add 25 ml (1 fl oz) distilled water and blend again. Decant into in an atomizing bottle and spray as required. This spray will keep fresh for many months in a cool, dark place and will transform any interior into a clean, refreshing space.

### INSTANT ROOM SPRAY

For immediate use, you make a spray of one or more essential oils and water without alcohol, but you will need to shake the atomizer vigorously before each use and the keeping time will be greatly reduced. You can use as few as 5 drops oil per 50 ml (2 fl oz) to refresh a room or deter insects, or 10 drops per 50ml (2 fl oz) if treating infectious diseases. A clean plastic bottle is acceptable for dispensing but not for storing, as plastic can contaminate the oils.

### ANTI-POLLUTION SPRAY

Preliminary research suggests that a spray which includes Lavender, Patchouli, Petitgrain, Geranium, Clary Sage, Grapefruit, Lemon, Rosemary and Tea Tree can reduce the effects of harmful chemicals given off by cigarette smoke, cleaning solutions, fire retardants and furniture polishes, especially in office blocks. Follow the spray instructions above.

The positive-ion problem created by enclosed air-circulation systems, VDUs and some metals and fibres used in modern construction are likely to be reduced by a spray of tree essential oils including Cypress, Citrus, Pine, Cedar, Sandalwood and Juniper, as they increase the effectiveness of the beneficial negative ions.

### FAT-BUSTING KITCHEN SPRAY

To remove grease smells, mix a total of 5–6 drops Eucalyptus, Rosemary, Lavender, Lemon or Lime essential oils with 50ml (2fl oz) water.

ABOVE: *Room sprays create a refreshing atmosphere and combat viruses and bacteria.*

# Enhancing Freshness

For general freshness, use any fragrant dried herbs in places where they can be disturbed to release their perfume.

## FRAGRANT POLISH

Perfumed furniture polish was popular with the Victorians. To make a quick version, melt a wax-based polish in a double boiler, stir in several drops of Lavender, Sweet Marjoram or other essential oil and return it to its original tin to solidify.

## MAGIC CARPETS

Create a clean, sweet scent with a calm, uplifting effect in the living room or guestrooms using the Georgian technique of brushing lavender flowers with a stiff brush over the carpet and back to the skirting board where they are stored. Repeat each day while the flower fragrance lasts (about 2 weeks).

Carpet fresheners leave a subtle fragrance, particularly good for using after entertaining to refresh a room. To 100 g (4 oz) bicarbonate of soda, add 20 drops of essential oils. Seal in a plastic bag overnight or longer, sprinkle over the carpet, brushing it into deep piles, and leave for an hour before vacuuming.

## PEPPERMINT CUSHIONS

Fill sachets with dried Spearmint and Peppermint leaves to tuck into cushion covers. When touched, they will release a cool, refreshing scent and discourage flies from settling.

## LINEN SACHETS

'I long for an Inn where the sheets smell of lavender', wrote Izaak Walton in *The Compleat Angler* (1653). No shop-bought product can compare to the deliciously fresh fragrance of linen dried in the sun and then stored in a warm airing cupboard with fragrant bundles or a swag of sweet insect-repellent herbs like Lavender and Southernwood. To these, add Rosemary, Alecost, Elecampane root, Orris root, Roseroot (*Rhodiola rosea*) and Sweet Flag. For a spicy alternative, use Nutmeg, Cinnamon, Caraway seed, Cedar shavings or Vetivert roots,

ABOVE: *A linen swag containing Lavender, Sweet Gale, Southernwood and Mint can be hung in airing cupboards and wardrobes to perfume the air and discourage insects.*

ABOVE: *Simmer antiseptic Rosemary sprigs in water for a fresh floor rinse.*

with dried Citrus peel or Gum Benzoin powder for a vanilla scent. Sprigs of herbs can be tucked between the linen or placed in muslin bags.

### KITCHEN POTPOURRI

This mixture will banish kitchen smells and help to deter ants, flies and weevils. Using the dry method described on pages 64 and 65, mix 2 cups Lemon Verbena; 1 cup each Basil and Bay; $1/2$ cup each Southernwood, Pennyroyal, Rosemary, Santolina and Mugwort (leaves); $1/4$ cup each Nasturtium and Tansy (leaves and flowers); a sprinkling of Tomato calyces; $1/4$ cup Cedarwood or Cinnamon chips; 1 tsp crushed Cloves; 1 tbsp Orris root powder. Add 3 drops each Bergamot and Eucalyptus oils. Handle the potpourri frequently to release its cleansing scent.

### HOUSEHOLD HYGIENE

Thyme, Rosemary, Hyssop ('purge me with Hyssop and I shall be clean'), Juniper, Eucalyptus, Pine, Sage and the roots of Angelica all have disinfectant qualities. If you have abundant prunings, simmer a quantity in a lidded pan for 30 minutes with just enough water to cover them. Strain, and use the liquid for washing kitchen counters, floors and bathroom fixtures. A little added washing-up liquid will remove grease from surfaces. Store the excess in the refrigerator for up to a week. Alternatively, add 20–30 drops of the essential oil of one of the herbs listed above to a bucket of water. Wear gloves while using the liquid to avoid sensitizing your skin.

# Herbs for Pets

Interest is growing in natural treatments for domestic animals, but please remember that pets are sensitive and often small in size, with limited ways of communicating. This makes the margins for error slight when treating pets, so unless you are very experienced it is best to refer problems to an holistic or traditional vet.

## Dogs and Cats

Lavender, Pennyroyal (avoid with young and pregnant pets) and Rose Geranium essential oil repel fleas. Tuck herbs or sachets into pet baskets.

### FLEA COLLARS

For an indoor flea collar: make a tube of thin cotton fabric and fill it with Pennyroyal leaves (some pets may reject the strong smell) or Lavender flowers and 2 drops Rose Geranium essential oil.
For an outdoor flea collar: mix 1 tsp cider vinegar with 3 drops Lavender and 1 drop Rose Geranium or Cedarwood essential oils. Place the mixture in a plastic bag with a shop-bought soft collar, shake, seal and infuse for 24 hours before fitting the collar.

### FLEA INFESTATION

To a bowl of warm water, add essential oils of Lavender, Cedarwood or Pine – 4 drops for large dogs, 2 drops for small dogs or cats. Dip a cloth or comb into the water, then groom the animal gently both with and against the direction of the coat. Wipe over with a clean, wet cloth. Avoid larger quantities of oil because pets will ingest this when grooming. Adding 1–2 Garlic capsules (depending on the pet's size) to the daily diet will make the blood unpalatable to fleas.

### TRAUMA

Catnip will help cats through the trauma of house moving. Keep your cats confined for a day or two before moving and then for a week in your new home, reassuring them with attention and a dried Catnip toy sachet in their new bed.

RIGHT: *Use a cat's natural love of Catnip to reduce the trauma of moving house and increase the appeal of scratching posts.*

BELOW: *On hot days Mint discourages flies from settling, while Lavender is a constant companion to discourage fleas.*

## SCRATCHING POST

Delight your cat and at the same time save your furniture by rubbing Catmint leaves or Valerian root on a scratching post.

### Small Animals

Wash rabbit and hamster cages with a disinfectant made from 1 drop Tea Tree, Lavender or Eucalyptus essential oil per 1 litre (2 pints) water. Placing dried leaves of Tansy, Rosemary or Thyme in amongst the bedding will help to discourage flies from breeding.

### Horses

In hot weather, wipe a damp cloth infused with 2 drops Lemon Grass, Peppermint or Lavender essential oil over your horse's coat to discourage flies. To reduce the number of stable mice, grow Peppermint or Pennyroyal outside the door and add a strong Peppermint infusion or 10 drops Peppermint essential oil to a bucket of water when rinsing the floor after cleaning out the bedding.

# *Flavoured Butters, Vinegars & Oils*

*Flavoured butters, vinegars and oils, although so simple to make, provide you with a wonderful way of having the full potency of fresh herbs to hand at all times in your store cupboard and refrigerator.*

## *Flavoured Butters*

*A 'sausage' of herb butter wrapped in cling film and frozen is a versatile freezer ingredient. Just slice off discs as required. Always use unsalted butter.*

## *Chive Butter*

*Use the same method to prepare Tarragon and Parsley butters.*

100 g / 3¹/₂ oz soft unsalted butter
2 tsp lemon juice
3 heaped tbsp finely snipped Chives
sea salt and freshly ground black pepper

Using a fork (or your food processor, particularly if it is equipped with a small bowl), mash together the soft butter, lemon juice and Chives. Season lightly with salt and more generously with pepper. Chill.

To store the butter, spoon it over microwavable cling film, shape into a long sausage shape, wrap and chill for up to 2 weeks or freeze for up to 2 months. Cut off butter discs as needed.

## *Oregano Butter*

*Mediterranean herbs, such as Oregano, Marjoram, Sage and Rosemary, respond well to this 'hot oil' approach.*

¹/₂ tbsp vegetable oil
100 g / 3¹/₂ oz soft unsalted butter
2 tbsp finely snipped fresh Oregano
1 garlic clove, crushed
sea salt and freshly ground black pepper

Heat the oil and 2 teaspoons of butter in a small frying pan. Over a low heat, stir-fry the Oregano and the garlic for 1 minute. Drain on paper towels.

Using a food processor with a small bowl or a fork and a mixing bowl, combine the Oregano, garlic and the rest of the soft butter. Season lightly with salt and more generously with pepper. Cover and chill for at least 1 hour or up to 2 weeks.

## *Montpellier Butter*

*This is traditionally served with grilled meat and fish.*

1 shallot, chopped
85 g / 3 oz of a wide variety of the following: young
    spinach or Sorrel leaves, Watercress, Parsley,
    Chervil or fresh Coriander, Tarragon or Chives
4 anchovy fillets, drained and chopped
2 small gherkins, chopped
1 tbsp drained capers
1¹/₂ garlic cloves, smashed, peeled and crushed
100 g / 3¹/₂ oz soft unsalted butter, cut into small
    pieces
1 hard-boiled egg, shelled and chopped
3 tbsp olive oil
1 scant tbsp wine vinegar (Tarragon-flavoured, if
    using fresh Tarragon in the herb mix)
sea salt and freshly ground black pepper

In a pan, cover shallot, leaves and herbs with boiling water and blanch for 1 minute. Drain, refresh in cold water and drain again. Spread between 2 double layers of paper towel and press dry.

Put the dried mixture in a food processor, together with the prepared anchovies, gherkins, capers, garlic and the butter. Season with pepper. Process and scrape down the sides of the bowl with a spatula. Add the egg and process again to blend. Scrape down the sides of the bowl once again. With the motor still running, trickle in the oil. Stop processing once all the oil has all been incorporated.

Adjust the seasoning and stir in the vinegar. Cover and chill for at least 1 hour for flavours to develop. It will keep in the refrigerator for up to 2 weeks.

## FLAVOURED OILS

Mix fine-flavoured herbs with fine-flavoured or unflavoured oils, reserving gutsy olive oil for Basil, Rosemary and garlic. Prepare small amounts at a time : home-flavoured oils are best used within a few weeks. For a more pronounced flavour, try the `hot oil' method below.

## GARLIC AND MARJORAM OIL

*2 garlic cloves*
*several sprigs of fresh*
*Marjoram, snipped*
*125 ml / 4 fl oz fruity*
*olive oil*

Blanch the garlic in boiling water for 3 minutes. Drain and repeat. Refresh in cold water, then peel and pat dry. Put the Marjoram, garlic and oil in a pan and bring to a simmer. Push down the garlic and Marjoram well to extract as much flavour as possible. Swirl around, then strain into a sterilized bottle via a funnel. Try the same method with Oregano, Rosemary, Sage and Thyme.

## PERSILLADE AND GREMOLADA

Finely chopped Parsley and garlic added to casseroles at the end of cooking add a unique pungent herby freshness to the dish. Stir in lightly at the very last minute, after you have taken the dish off the heat just before serving. To make Persillade, the traditional French preparation, chop or snip a small bunch of flat-leaf Parsley and crush a clove of garlic. Mix lightly and use. For Italian Gremolada, add a generous teaspoon of grated unwaxed lemon (and/or orange) zest. For convenience's sake, you can replace the grated peel with ribbon-like fine strips extracted with a zester.

Persillade and Gremolada mixed with breadcrumbs make a wonderful topping for part-baked gratins and casseroles. Sprinkle over the dish, drizzle with olive oil or dot with butter and bake for a further 15–20 minutes.

## PARSLEY CONDIMENT

In a small bowl, just before serving, mix coarse sea salt and very well drained finely chopped curly Parsley. Good with boiled meat, poultry, and country soups and pretty on the table.

# Herb Salsas & Condiments

*When you are preparing a herb salsa, pesto or condiment, it pays to be generous. The trick is to use more herbs and seasonings than you think sensible. The flavour will be intense, the texture dense and the salsa packed with taste. Once you have mastered the basic method, experiment with variations. A little fresh Coriander or ground Fenugreek can be added to the Parsley and Walnut Salsa mixture. Hazelnuts and Chervil mix happily (use a mild-tasting oil) and so do Dill (or Tarragon) and almonds. A moderate amount of flat-leaf Parsley can safely be added to most combinations, including classic Basil pesto.*

## Parsley and Walnut Salsa

*You can replace the walnuts with 2 tablespoons capers, 2 drained and chopped anchovies and 2 teaspoons balsamic vinegar for an excellent canapé topping.*

**preparation: 10 minutes**

large bunch of flat-leaf Parsley (the equivalent of a
    well-packed cup of leaves)
1 or 2 garlic cloves, smashed
45 g / 1½ oz fresh shelled walnut kernels, chopped
½ small unwaxed lemon
30 g / 1 oz Parmesan cheese, shaved into slivers
3 tbsp walnut oil
2 tbsp groundnut or sunflower oil
sea salt and freshly ground black pepper

Snip the Parsley leaves and some thinner stalks into the bowl of your food processor. Add the garlic and walnut kernels. Using a zester, prepare ribbons of lemon zest and add to the bowl, then squeeze in the juice. Process until coarsely puréed.

Add half the Parmesan and process again. Then, with the motor still running, trickle in the oils. Stop while still quite coarse. Adjust the seasoning.

Cover and set aside until ready to use — chill if working several hours ahead (it will keep overnight in the refrigerator, but no longer than 2–3 days).

## Dill and Mustard Dip

*This dip and the Fromage Blanc with Chervil and Chives below both go well with hard-boiled eggs, smoked fish, cold chicken and pork.*

**preparation: 5 minutes, plus chilling**
**makes about 250 ml / 9 fl oz**

200 ml / 7 fl oz good mayonnaise
2 tbsp crème fraîche or sour cream
1 tbsp coarse-grain mustard
several Dill fronds

Stir the cream and mustard into the mayonnaise. Snip in the Dill, stir and chill until ready to serve.

## Fromage Blanc with Chervil and Chives

*Serve as a cool dessert or as a 'cheese course' with a mixed leaf salad, or with baby new potatoes to accompany poached fish.*

**preparation: 10 minutes, plus chilling**
**makes about 300 ml / ½ pint**

100 g / 3½ oz fromage frais (with no less than 8
    per cent fat) or very fresh mild goats' cheese
100 g / 3½ oz ricotta
2 tbsp mascarpone
1 shallot, very finely chopped
2 tbsp finely snipped Chervil
2 tbsp finely snipped Chives
sea salt and freshly ground black pepper

Mix together the cheeses. Season with a little salt and more generously with pepper. Scatter over the shallot, Chervil and Chives a little at a time and gently stir in.

Chill for at least 30 minutes to allow the flavours to develop. Adjust the seasoning just before serving.

## GARLIC CREAM

Serve this hot with lamb, grilled fish or vegetables.
Preheat the oven to 190°C/375°F/gas 5. Brush or drizzle 4 unpeeled heads of garlic with olive oil. Bake for about 30 minutes, leave to cool a little, then squeeze out the pulp. Process or beat the pulp with a tablespoon each of olive oil, milk and single cream (or yoghurt) and, if you like, a scant tablespoon of breadcrumbs. Season to taste.

## SHALLOT CONFIT

Peeled shallots can be baked in the same way as garlic heads. Drizzle or brush with extra olive oil once cooked and season with a little coarse sea salt and fresh black pepper. Serve with pan-fried or grilled meats and roast chicken.

# Herb Preserves

Jams, jellies and compotes packed full of flavour are not only delicious on their own, but give you the opportunity of storing herbal flavours to give zip to everyday cooking. Try the Red Onion and Bay Leaf Marmalade with grilled duck breast or under the cheese on Welsh rarebit, and the Fruit Compote with Borage and Rum as a topping for a fresh fruit salad or as the base for crème brûlée. Prettily packaged, these preserves also make great gifts.

## Red Onion and Bay Leaf Marmalade

**preparation: 10 minutes; cooking: about 1 hour, plus cooling**
**makes about 450 g / 1 lb**

4 tbsp sunflower oil or 60 g / 2 oz unsalted butter
900 g / 2 lb red onions, thinly sliced
3 Bay leaves
75 g / 2³/₄ oz sugar
3 tbsp sherry vinegar
2–3 Sage leaves, chopped
sea salt and freshly ground black pepper

In a large sauté pan, warm the oil or melt the butter. Add the onions and Bay leaves. Season lightly and stir. Cover and soften over a very low heat.

After about 30 minutes, turn up the heat a little. Sprinkle in 2 generous tablespoons of sugar, the vinegar and the chopped Sage leaves. Season again, stir in 4 tablespoons of water and continue cooking uncovered for another 15 minutes, keeping the heat moderate.

To finish, sprinkle in the rest of the sugar and turn up the heat to high. Stir the mixture for a minute or two while it caramelizes a little.

Bottled in sterilized jars, this marmalade will keep for several weeks in the refrigerator.

## Fruit Compote with Borage and Rum

**preparation: 10 minutes; maceration: 2 weeks**
**makes about 850 ml–1 litre / 1¹/₂–1³/₄ pints**

450–575g / 1–1¹/₄ lb mixed fruit, including stoned and
    quartered peaches, apricots, nectarines, cherries,
    seedless white and red grapes, husked physalis
115 g / 4 oz caster sugar
few strips of zest from an unwaxed orange
several Borage leaves, finely chopped
about 400 ml / 14 fl oz rum

Put the fruit, together with the sugar, orange zest and Borage in a sterilized jar that will hold about 850 ml–1 litre / 1¹/₂–1³/₄ pints. Pour in the rum, making sure the fruit is entirely covered, and shake gently.

Cover and leave in a cool dark place for at least 2 weeks and up to 4 months. Gently shake the jar occasionally.

LEFT TO RIGHT: *Fruit Compote with Borage and Rum, Red Onion and Bay Leaf Marmalade, Bramley and Cider Jelly with Pineapple Sage, and Pear Preserve with Coriander*

## Bramley and Cider Jelly with Pineapple Sage

*If Pineapple Sage is not available, use ordinary Sage. Use the same recipe to make apple and cider jelly flavoured with Thyme, Rosemary or Mint.*

*preparation: 20 minutes; cooking fruit: 20 minutes; straining: 12 hours; boiling jam: 20 minutes, plus cooling; settling: 48 hours*
*makes about 1.5 kg / 3¹⁄4 lb*

*2 kg / 4 lb Bramley apples*
*15 leaves of Pineapple Sage, with stalks*
*600 ml / 1 pint still cider*
*about 1 kg / 2¹⁄4 lb preserving or caster sugar*
*juice of 1 lemon*
*juice of 1 orange*
*tiny spriglets of sage for decoration*

Chop the whole unpeeled apples. Put in a large pan with about 850 ml / 1¹⁄2 pints of water and 10 Sage leaves with stalks. Bring to the boil and simmer for 15 minutes, or until tender. Press the apple with a wooden spoon to extract the pulp.

Strain for 12 hours in a clean jelly bag over a large bowl. Do not squeeze the bag as this would make the jelly cloudy.

Measure out the strained juice and return it to the pan. Add the cider and bring to the boil. Put the sugar in a warm place (allow 450 g / 1 lb sugar per 600 ml / 1 pint of apple juice).

Add the lemon and orange juice and the rest of the sage leaves to the pan. Stir in the sugar and continue to stir until it has dissolved, bringing the liquid slowly to the boil.

Turn up heat and boil rapidly for about 15 minutes until setting point is reached (104°C/220°F on a sugar thermometer — the surface of the syrup will wrinkle when you put a teaspoon of it on a cold plate). Discard the sage.

Spoon into warm sterilized jars, and add sprigs of fresh sage to decorate. Keep in a cool place for up to 6 months, and use any time after 48 hours.

## Pear Preserve with Coriander

*preparation: 10 minutes; cooking: about 40 minutes, plus cooling; settling: 48 hours*
*makes about 1.5 kg / 3¹⁄4 lb*

*1 unwaxed Lemon*
*1 unwaxed Lime*
*1.3 kg / 2³⁄4 lb firm pears*
*1 kg / 2¹⁄4 lb preserving or caster sugar*
*2 tsp lightly crushed Coriander seeds*
*3 fresh Coriander stalks*

Using a zester, take off several strips of lemon zest and reserve. Halve the lemon, squeeze out the juice into a large pan. Chop up the lemon halves, reserving the pips. Repeat the procedure with the lime.

Peel and core the pears, reserving the skin and cores. Cut the pears into attractive wedges. Put the pear wedges in a large pan with just enough water to cover, then add the strips of lemon and lime zest. Put the sugar in a warm place.

Put the reserved lemon and lime pips and chopped pieces with the pear skins and cores, the Coriander seeds and stalks into a double layer of dampened muslin. Tie up the corners to make a bag and add to the pears. Bring slowly to the boil and cook gently for 12–15 minutes, until the pears are just tender. Carefully lift them out with a slotted spoon, allowing the juices to drip back into the pan. Reserve.

Turn up the heat and boil the liquid rapidly for about 15 minutes until reduced by half. Remove and discard the muslin bag.

Stir the warmed sugar into the liquid, reduce the heat and stir until the sugar has dissolved. Boil until setting point is reached (see left). Return the pears to the pan, bring the syrup back to the boil then take it off the heat at once.

Spoon into warm sterilized jars, cover and label. Keep in a cool place for up to 6 months, and use any time after 48 hours.

# Soups

Soups can benefit from both dried and fresh herbs. A last-minute sprinkling of chopped Chervil, Parsley, Mint or Sorrel can even make a store-cupboard soup taste homemade.

## Soupe au Pistou

*This is the French equivalent of minestrone, served with their own version of pesto.*

**preparation: 10 minutes; cooking: 30 minutes**

2 tbsp olive oil
1 Spanish onion, finely chopped
2 garlic cloves, crushed
850 ml / 1½ pints vegetable or chicken stock
575 g / 1¼ lb tomatoes, blanched, deseeded, skinned and chopped, or a large can of chopped tomatoes
2 tbsp chopped fresh Basil
1 tsp of one or more of the following dried herbs: Thyme, Sage, Oregano, Marjoram, Savory
1 large waxy potato, diced
4 small turnips, chopped
1 carrot, chopped
1 head of Fennel, trimmed and chopped
4 small courgettes, chopped
350 g / 12 oz shelled baby broad beans
sea salt and freshly ground black pepper

for the Pistou sauce:
1 egg
1 tsp hot mustard
1 garlic clove, crushed
1 tsp wine vinegar
175 ml / 6 fl oz light olive oil
3–4 tbsp snipped fresh Basil (or whole small leaves)
5 tbsp grated Parmesan or Pecorino cheese

Heat the oil in a large sauté pan and cook the onion and garlic over a moderate heat for 3–5 minutes. In a separate pan, bring the stock to the boil. To the sauté pan, add the tomatoes with any juice, half the Basil and the dried herbs. Season, then add the potato, turnips and carrot. Pour in the boiling stock, stir and return to the boil. Immediately reduce the heat, add the Fennel and courgettes and season lightly. Cover and simmer for about 15 minutes, stirring a few times. Throw in the broad beans and continue to cook until the vegetables are tender.

Meanwhile, prepare the Pistou sauce: boil the egg for 4 minutes, then scoop out the yolk and put it in a bowl. Reserve the white. Beat the yolk with a pinch of salt, the mustard, garlic and vinegar. Whisk in the oil as if you were making mayonnaise. Mash up the egg white and stir it into the sauce with the Basil and cheese. Season generously.

To serve, spoon some Pistou into a tureen or individual bowls and tilt to coat the insides. Ladle in the soup, spoon over the rest of the sauce and serve very hot, sprinkled with the remaining Basil.

## Tarator

*Tarator is a Middle-eastern walnut sauce for fish and vegetables, which thins down to a very refreshing soup.*

**preparation: 15 minutes, plus chilling**

handful of chopped walnut kernels
2 medium cucumbers, peeled, halved lengthwise, deseeded and cut into chunks
1 or 2 garlic cloves, smashed
600 ml / 1 pint Greek-style yoghurt
2 tbsp Boursin naturel, fromage frais or single cream
3 tbsp snipped fresh Mint leaves, plus a few whole leaves for decoration
2 tbsp snipped fresh flat-leaved Parsley, plus a few whole leaves for decoration
1½ tbsp strong-flavoured olive oil
sea salt and freshly ground black pepper

Process the nuts in the food processor until coarsely chopped. Add the cucumber and garlic, followed by the yoghurt, Boursin, fromage frais or cream, half the Mint, the Parsley and oil. Season, add the rest of the ingredients and process again. Chill.

Just before serving, add a little chilled water to thin the soup down. Adjust the seasoning. Sprinkle with Mint and Parsley, and float an ice cube in it.

Make the most of dried herbs in the winter months, when fresh herbs are scarce and expensive. Nowadays dried herbs are often unfairly neglected, when all that is needed is a little time to release their full flavours: Thyme, Rosemary, Oregano, Marjoram, Savory and Dill will all work wonders in soups, sauces, roasts and casseroles, if you add them at the beginning of cooking. Save any fresh herbs for finishing off dishes with clean vibrant notes.

ABOVE: *Soupe au Pistou; Avocado, Rocket and Coriander Soup*

## *Avocado, Rocket and Coriander Soup*

**preparation: 15 minutes, plus chilling**
**serves 2-3**

*2 ripe avocados*
*juice of 1 lime, plus a few thin strips of zest*
*large bunch of Rocket*
*several sprigs of fresh Coriander*
*few drops of green (Jalapeño) Tabasco sauce*
*about 300 ml / ½ pint chilled vegetable stock*
*sea salt and freshly ground black pepper*

Peel the avocados and stone. Chop the flesh coarsely and put in the food processor with the lime juice and zest. Snip in the Rocket and a few sprigs of Coriander. Season and add a few drops of Tabasco. Process until puréed. Scrape down the sides of the bowl, pour in the stock and process until smooth. Add about 150 ml / ¼ pint of cold water and process again. Adjust the seasoning. Chill.

Before serving, adjust the seasoning again. If you like, roll up 2 or 3 Coriander leaves together and snip them over. If the soup is not chilled enough or too thick, float a few ice cubes in it.

A snip of fresh herbs will help turn the humble sandwich into an impromptu treat:
• use very lightly toasted bread for texture.
• anoint with butter, olive oil or mayonnaise.
• smear with a touch of grainy mustard.
• cover with skinned and chopped left-over chicken, turkey, ham, etc, or with cottage cheese.
• snip over 1 spring onion, 4 Chives / 2 Basil leaves / sprig of Tarragon / a few Rocket, Sorrel or baby Spinach leaves.
• finish with ribbons of salad leaves and season.

# Salads & Sandwiches

Salads should be the best showcases for the fine strong flavours of fresh herbs. Don't be afraid to use them in quantity; the salad won't just taste memorable, it will be full of nutrients. An easy way of adding extra flavour to a sandwich is to use a flavoured butter, see page 72.

## Early Summer Salad

*The baby leaves used in this salad are packed with flavour. Sorrel in particular, with its deep taste, slightly lemony and gently bitter, makes the use of other herbs redundant. The strawberries may sound eccentric but, in fact, they do hit just the right note.*

*preparation: 10 minutes; cooking: 5 minutes*

*small bunch of thin asparagus tips*
*handful of baby Spinach leaves*
*handful of Rocket*
*small head of oak leaf lettuce, torn into shreds*
*small head of soft lettuce, cut into ribbons*
*handful of Sorrel, cut into thin ribbons*
*12 small strawberries, sprinkled with 1 tsp good*
*    balsamic vinegar*

*for the dressing:*
*2 tbsp sunflower or grapeseed oil*
*3 tbsp sour cream (or 2 tbsp single cream mixed with*
*    1 tbsp yoghurt)*
*1 tbsp white wine vinegar*
*sea salt and freshly ground black pepper*

Blanch the asparagus in lightly salted boiling water for 3–4 minutes. Drain and dry with paper towels.

LEFT: *Winter Salad*
RIGHT: *Pan Bagna with Marjoram*

Whisk the dressing ingredients in a small jug with salt and pepper to taste until combined.

Toss the various leaves together in a wide shallow bowl. Scatter in the asparagus tips and the small strawberries with balsamic vinegar. Toss very lightly. Dribble over the dressing, toss lightly and serve soon.

## Pan Bagna with Marjoram

*Alternative or additional ingredients for this gloriously messy sandwich include cooked green beans, anchovy fillets, black olives, flat-leaf Parsley, cooked broad beans, drained cooked tuna fish, hard-boiled egg. The herb flavour here is the fresh Marjoram which works with the cheese and marinade; try Savory with the beans, Dill or Fennel with the tuna, Tarragon with the eggs.*

**preparation: 10 minutes; standing: 20 minutes**

*4 large vine tomatoes*
*3 tbsp Garlic and Marjoram Oil (see page 73)*
*few sprigs of fresh Marjoram*
*60 g / 2 oz feta or dryish goats' cheese*
*1 large pale sweet onion*
*4 baps, rolls or mini-baguettes*
*few leaves of oak leaf lettuce*
*sea salt and freshly ground black pepper*

Halve the tomatoes, then squeeze them to press out the seeds and take out excess pulp. Cut into half-slices or wedges.

Sprinkle with the garlic-infused oil, spriglets of Marjoram, salt and pepper. Crumble over the cheese. Cut the onion into thin rings and scatter these over the tomato mixture. Leave to marinate at room temperature for at least 20 minutes.

Open up the baps, rolls or mini baguettes. Take out a little of the crumb if necessary. Spread the bottom halves with the marinade juices. Shred in a few salad leaves and spoon over the tomato mixture. Cover with the other halves and press gently.

## Winter Salad

*You can vary this salad by using red cabbage, orange, hazelnuts (use hazelnut oil), pecan nuts (use 50 per cent walnut oil) and Gruyère slivers instead of pancetta. The cream and yoghurt bring out the fine sharpness of the Chives.*

**preparation: 10 minutes; cooking: 5 minutes**

*2 heads of chicory*
*1 small head of radicchio*
*1 mini cabbage or ¼ Savoy cabbage*
*1 small head of Cos (romaine) lettuce*
*1 crisp apple*
*1 tsp lemon juice*
*handful of plump raisins or dried cranberries*
*½ tbsp oil*
*175 g / 6 oz cubed pancetta, lardons or diced bacon*
*2 heaped tbsp pine nuts*

*for the dressing:*
*2 tbsp groundnut oil*
*1 tbsp single cream or fromage frais*
*1 tbsp yoghurt*
*1 tbsp red or white wine vinegar*
*1 small soft-boiled egg (optional)*
*bunch of Chives*
*sea salt and freshly ground black pepper*

Trim the chicory into bite-sized pieces, shred the radicchio and cabbage, chop the lettuce. Thinly slice the apple and brush it with lemon juice. Mix all of these in a shallow bowl with the raisins or cranberries. Season lightly with salt and pepper.

Wipe a frying pan with oil and sauté the diced pancetta, lardons or bacon until crisp, adding the pine nuts a few moments before the end of cooking. Drain and scatter over the salad.

Prepare the dressing: mix the oil, cream or fromage frais, yoghurt and vinegar, then stir in 1 tablespoon of water. Spoon in the soft-boiled egg, if using. Snip in most of the Chives, reserving 6–8 stalks. Stir well and season to taste.

Pour the dressing over the salad and toss to coat. Snip over the rest of the chives and serve.

CHAPTER THREE

*Relax &*
*Unwind*

*To be surrounded by the sweet scents of herbs is the perfect antidote to overwork and stress.*

A walk in the herb garden after the bustle of a journey home through heavy traffic allows the cool green fragrances to calm your spirit; stroking the leaves and inhaling the perfume of the flowers creates a subtle symphony of soothing scents. The gentle unwinding effect of Lavender, the light, almond-scented froth of Meadowsweet and the innocent fragrance of Sweet Peas create an air of tranquillity that offers a path back to equilibrium. Their harmonizing effect is enhanced by their soothing pastel colours, velvet textures and the wildlife they attract, as they fill the garden with butterflies, dragonflies, bees and songbirds.

To enhance the experience of relaxation, find time to daydream or read, and sip Clover or Lavender tea 'to dispatch melancholy', or take a Sweet Violet wine cup for a stronger boost of good cheer. Enjoy a hazy summer afternoon in a hammock among the hay-scented leaves of Sweet Woodruff, Vanilla Grass and Melilot (Sweet Clover), with a Monet background of Cornflower blue, Poppy red and Chamomile daisies. Alternatively, unwind with a quiet stroll through the dappled shade of trees, breathing in the light spring fragrance of Apple blossom or the wafting honey perfume of Linden blossom.

At the end of the day, take a relaxing aromatic bath with essential oils of Lavender, Geranium or Sandalwood. For aching muscles, deeper stress, or simply to feel cosseted, a massage with aromatic plant oils reinforces the healing fragrance of nature. Different essential oils reduce physical, mental or emotional stress: for example, Bergamot helps lift depression, Clary Sage reduces nervous exhaustion and Sweet Marjoram soothes tension headaches. Oils can also be blended to suit individual needs and preferences.

At the first signs of stress, the fragrances of soothing herbs can restore a sense of balance. For more serious problems, they will provide a fragrant breathing space in which to chart the best way forward.

STRESSBUSTING HERBS & OILS •
THERAPEUTIC HERB GARDENS •
RELAXING RAINBOW HEALING
GARDEN DESIGN •
AROMATHERAPY • RELAXING
MASSAGE BLENDS • TRAVEL &
HOLIDAY HERBS & OILS • LIGHT
LUNCHES & AL FRESCO EATING

*Relaxing, balancing fragrances are the most accessible delight of aromatic herbs and can be enjoyed from a fresh bouquet, essential oils or directly in the herb garden.*

# Relaxing Herbs & Oils

## Lavender

The classic image of a herb garden includes Lavender with its silvery leaves, soft blue and purple flowers, and sweet-sharp fragrance which lifts the spirits and banishes anxieties. The flowers can be enjoyed in an elegant tisane or soothing bath, while a Lavender sachet is a gift of fragrant serenity for anyone confined to bed. Lavender's versatile and popular essential oil is reassuring, soporific and often the first choice of aromatherapists for treating emotional or mental stress. It also reduces muscular pain from both mental and physical effort.

## Chamomile

The feathery foliage of lawn Chamomile releases its apple fragrance to wriggling toes on a summer's day, while the earthy green-scented flowers provide a soothing tea to sip in the shade on hot afternoons. Used Chamomile teabags laid on resting eyes will reduce inflammation and dark shadows. The essential oils of three Chamomiles (German, Roman and Moroccan) are grounding, anti-depressant and sedative, reducing stress symptoms such as irritability, tension headaches and anxiety as well as helping to calm anger. Most of the other legendary Chamomile healing attributes are found only in the German and Roman oils and are due mainly to the presence of azulene, a compound which forms during distillation. This rich blue substance is not present in the fresh flowers (although possibly in dried) and is found in highest concentration in German Chamomile, with marginally less in the Roman oil.

Research gathered by medical chemists has found not only confirmation of the wide range of Chamomile's folk uses, but also discovered new applications. The stress-reducing properties of German and Roman oils help calm fractious, overtired children, reduce inflammation and soothe sporting aches; they also increase defences against stress-related ulcers and aid cell regeneration, especially in irradiated and sunburnt skin. German Chamomile oil has been shown to help liver cells regenerate and has an antihistamine-like action: a drop applied under each nostril can bring instant relief to hayfever sufferers, which lasts from 30 minutes to a lifetime for the lucky few.

German Chamomile oil has a strong, earthy green scent but only tiny amounts are used, which helps to counter its odd smell and high cost. It can be combined with Lavender or Clary Sage to soften the aroma, and reinforce its sedative qualities. Roman Chamomile oil has a slightly sweeter scent preferred by some; aromatherapists use it to help balance a person who has experienced emotional stress. Moroccan Chamomile (Ormenis Flower) is often considered a poor cousin because it is cheaper and has different constituents. Nevertheless,

LEFT: *Long, loose, aromatic spikes of dusty-rose and mauve Clary Sage flowers growing in the enclosed sanctuary of Chelsea Physic Garden, fronted by magenta-flowered Wood Betony whose leaves make a mildly sedative nerve tonic tea.*

through its rich balsamic scent it offers its own qualities for encouraging balance. It creates an unhurried state which helps an overactive mind deal with fear of change, allowing it to 'let go' and move towards composure.

## Clary Sage

The dusty-pink to mauve flowers and large, textured leaves of Clary Sage dispense a penetrating, warm, nutty pungency which once pervaded Roman courtyards. There it was nurtured as a medicinal 'wonder herb', echoed today in the use of its essential oil as a powerful relaxant with 'feel good' properties to relieve anxiety, nervous exhaustion and irritability. It is a soporific boon for those who are fatigued from overwork but unable to sleep. The oil can produce a mild feeling of inebriation and was once unwisely used in a brown food-colouring base to create a 'poor man's beer'. So relaxing is this oil that aromatherapists advise clients to avoid driving after undergoing a massage with it.

## Lemon Balm

The light freshness of Lemon Balm leaf provides a tea to calm depression and restlessness. Ancient texts speak of the plant as the heart's elixir, strengthening the vital spirits and chasing away black thoughts. It was traditionally imbibed in wine cups and cordials, and the famous sixteenth-century physician Paracelsus called it his 'elixir of life'. He believed it could completely revive a man, a view endorsed by the *London Dispensary* (1696): 'Balm, given in Canary wine, will renew youth, strengthen the brain and relieve a languishing nature.' This further enhanced its reputation for promoting longevity and dispelling melancholy. The herb's essential oil, called Melissa, is a tonic and antidepressant; it releases tension and is used in aromatherapy to cushion against emotional over-sensitivity. It offers a useful combination, being both calming and uplifting.

## Scented Geraniums

Scented Geraniums (*Pelargonium*) are tender plants with a range of perfumed leaves. The rose-scented *P. radens* and *P. graveolens* are a soothing delight in both garden and office. Their uplifting, antidepressant essential oil is effective in dealing with work-related tension, reducing anxiety and feelings of aggression.

ABOVE: *Early morning sun starts to warm the Lavender fields which by midday will be an intensely aromatic, shimmering haze filled with the gentle droning of bees.*

ABOVE: *Delicately fragrant orchard Apple blossom.*

## Lime Blossom

While sipping Lime blossom (Linden) tea and eating madeleines, Proust was suddenly transported in memory back to his childhood. The tea is a popular digestive in France, especially after elaborate meals, and is a treatment for insomnia and nervous tension. Linden water is a soothing bath tonic.

## Sweet Meadow Scents

The tranquillizing flowering tops of Sweet Marjoram have a spicy green scent enjoyed by both men and women; mix it with Lavender and wear it as a relaxing buttonhole sprig. The essential oil is painkilling and sedative, and helps prevent mental stress from manifesting as physical symptoms, but it is only for short-term use. Sweet Marjoram oil helps improve restricted breathing caused by stress, and as a bonus it is anti-oxidant in massage, reducing skin-ageing free radicals while improving local circulation and the dispersal of toxins.

Sweet Woodruff has a mildly sedative, new-mown-hay scent shared with Sweet Grass, Vanilla Grass, Lady's Bedstraw and Melilot, herbs that evoke the contentment of placid summer days and full harvests. The scent comes from coumarin, a compound formed a few hours after the herb is cut, and lasts when dried, making each of these herbs a delight in the linen closet. Sweet Grass is plaited and used in several Native American ceremonies.

## Year-round Equilibrium

Because natural fragrances link us to something deep and basic in nature, many herb and flower scents are relaxing. Spring offers sweetly aromatic Broom, Daphne and Wallflowers, plus the young eau-de-Cologne-scented leaves of herbaceous Bergamot. Late spring brings the rich honey-vanilla perfume of climbing Akebia's dangling purple flower clusters, the traditional fragrance of Lilac and the sensuous bounty of Peonies. Midsummer wafts us the orange-blossom scent of Philadelphus (Mock Orange), Sweet Myrtle and Choisya (Mexican Orange Blossom), the chocolate-clove scent of Pinks – source of the medieval nerve tonic 'sops in wine' – and the evocative fragrance of Sweet Peas. It also brings the soft almond perfume of Meadowsweet flowers with their wintergreen-scented leaves and the sweet Japanese Honeysuckle, both of which contain the pre-aspirin painkiller salicylic acid. In late summer, the soothing honey sweetness of Buddleia pleases humans and butterflies. Then, once more, winter-flowering Honeysuckle gives a fragrant start to the new year.

## Stress-reducing Essential Oils

The essential oils of several flowers can help reduce stress-related problems. The exquisite and expensive Rose oil offers a gentle anti-depressant for emotional stress and is used to balance male/female anxieties. Jasmine, expensive but powerful, has a calming and uplifting effect on the nervous system and is considered invaluable for anxiety and depression with a psychological origin. The less costly, voluptuous floral perfume of Ylang-Ylang is also antidepressant, calming and seda-tive. It has a regulating effect on the nervous system and reduces insomnia, tension and angry frustration. Some find its scent magnetic, others cloying, and for the latter it is best combined with a Citrus or Lavender fragrance to lighten the effect.

The refreshing aspect of several Citrus oils can pierce the gloom of disharmony. Neroli (Orange Blossom oil) has a hauntingly beautiful, clean, sharp scent, like green saplings in fresh snow but with a lingering floral richness. It is a natural tranquillizer with a remarkably calming effect for many kinds of stress including panic attacks, shock, over-work, insomnia, irritable bowel syndrome and pre-menstrual tension. It is also effective when used before a stressful event such as an examina-tion, interview or public performance.

The essential oil of Bergamot cuts through anxiety and tension, helps reduce the sense of being caught in mental or emotional traps, and is used by some professionals to aid drug withdrawal. Petitgrain oil, from the leafy twigs of the Orange tree, is a light, green, woody version of Neroli which reduces ten-sion headaches and neuralgia and, being less expensive than Neroli, can be used instead for less serious depression and anxiety.

Two rising new antidepressant stars are Mandarin oil, with a gentle, safe action used to bring equilibrium to stress-related anxiety and the recovery stage of emotional breakdown, and Grapefruit oil, with its cheerful, buoyant fra-grance that speaks of a fresh start, used for depression and mental exhaustion.

From Australia, the leaves of Lemon Eucalyptus yield the clean, sharp, refreshing fragrance now used by aromatherapists to treat depression, with-drawal and feelings of impending crisis. As Lemon Eucalyptus attacks many bacteria, viruses and a few fungi, strengthens the immune system, and has elec-trical properties similar to those of the human body, it is one of the best oils for dealing with the many potential side effects of stress.

At the end of a stressful day, the simplest way to use the soothing power of these essential oils is in a long soak in the bath. Unwind with 4–6 drops swooshed around in the water: choose from Lavender, Chamomile, Geranium, Neroli, Jasmine, Rose or Sandalwood. For a relaxing but reviving bath before an evening out, blend one of these oils with 2 drops of Grapefruit or Mandarin.

With such a wide range of soft, sweet, green and floral fragrances offering relaxing and balancing properties, your choice will depend on personal prefer-ence and may vary with changing circumstances. As always, let the pleasure of experimentation be your guide.

BELOW: *Relaxing soft scents and colours, with an accent of white standard Roses, seen in Congham Hall's walled herb garden.*

ABOVE: *Shakespeare's Eglantine Rose earned the name Sweet Briar for its sweet apple-scented foliage.*

*Perhaps the greatest gift a garden can give us today is to change our perception of time. If we feel rushed and overloaded, just stepping into the herb garden allows the plants to work their magic and dissolve the stressful sense of haste.*

# Aromatic Gardens for Relaxation

The first inhalation of soft, natural perfumes registers security and tranquillity in the brain. This counters any adrenalin-producing thoughts and breathing becomes slower and deeper. The soothing scents, colours and sounds help untangle the stressed jumble of thoughts, worries and muscular tension, until the mind moves into a neutral state of simple observation, noting cloud formations, a pair of darting butterflies in a counterpoint dance, a bee struggling to reach the nectar in a foxglove, or the intriguing drop of dew, beloved of alchemists, that collects in a Lady's Mantle leaf.

BELOW: *A harmonious aisle of Roses and Catmint.*

But this is only the first benefit of lingering in an aromatic garden. When the mind is relaxed and open it allows our creative energy to bubble through and we begin to experience new inspired ideas – philosophical light bulbs flash, mental adventures unfold and solutions to problems materialize. For me, the precise trigger is when the sun moves from behind a cloud and increases the light reflection on every leaf and petal, literally enlightening the garden. As the eyes readjust, a peculiar sensation occurs that feels like a shift of perception. This process disengages the anxious thought patterns, moves into neutral and then allows fresh energy – promoted by aromatic herbs – to flood the system, restoring internal balance and revealing new perspectives. These benefits increase each time we re-enter the garden, as the memory of previous relaxation returns us more quickly to a calm and harmonious state.

## Special Features

A distinct entrance, such as an arch clipped into Yew or a circular Chinese moongate, reinforces the idea of stepping into a special place. A well-positioned, comfortable seat is important; consider whether you prefer the morning light or the setting sun. Privacy and shelter are also significant: a hedge, fence or wall will help to contain the plant fragrances while reducing buffeting winds, outside noises and intruders. Yew is the classic material, because it clips beautifully and is a perfect dark green foil for the full range of herbal colours. Sweet Briar Rose provides a thick barrier with apple-scented leaves, while Willow plants can be woven together to create a living fence with planting pockets, seats, arches and even arbours fashioned into the structure.

To improve the views, you might wish to obscure irritating objects beyond your boundaries. This can be done by judiciously planting a tree, erecting trellis to be smothered by climbing Roses, Honeysuckle or Akebia, or careful positioning of a cantilevered hanging basket. Sit in the proposed garden area and experiment to see what can be blocked out.

## Harmonious Herbs

Most herbs have an easy, natural appearance that fits gracefully into a garden for relaxation. Traditional fragrances and images include Lavender, which is pleasing with Catmint in front or intermingled with scarlet Bergamot, white Musk Mallow and blue Borage, which flower at similar times. The pink of Roses is intensified by Geranium 'Johnson's Blue', and Rose perfume is intensified by Parsley beneath. Clove Pinks are set off by delicate blue Harebells, while the violet spikes of Anise Hyssop rise elegantly through pungent silver Roman Wormwood or sweet-scented, feathery Southern-wood. Clary Sage displays a unique range of colour and scent all on its own, and a collection of green-, grey-, silver- and gold-leaved Thymes, exuding aromas from common thyme to lemon, caraway, fruit, citrus and pine, and sporting white, pink or purple flowers, look splendid together. Tall spires of the Fairy Foxglove (*Digitalis lutea*) look glorious above the fern-like leaves of crisp Tansy, and the size of luscious Peony blooms is emphasized by neighbouring clouds of dainty white Queen Anne's Lace (*Anthriscus sylvestris*) or Sweet Cicely umbels. It is simple to experiment with different combinations because herbaceous herbs are easy to transplant.

ABOVE: *The innocent fragrance of Sweet Peas brings a smile to all who pass by.*

91

## Monastery Gardens

The eternal popularity of the cloistered garden reflects a widespread appreciation of secluded tran-

quillity. It was in monastic gardens that knowledge of herbs was preserved through the Dark Ages, as travelling clerics and pilgrims exchanged new plant seeds and gardening skills. In these self-supporting communities, sections of the garden were allocated to specific uses: beds for 'pot' herbs (vegetables), 'salet' herbs for salads, 'sweet' herbs for flavouring and the physic area for 'simples' (medicinal herbs used on their own or blended to form 'compounds'), plus sites for bee plants, dye plants, altar flowers and household herbs. The herb garden served as both spiritual and physical balm, as a place for contemplation and for convalescence, with the physic garden often planted beneath the infirmary windows so that patients could benefit from the healing aromas. Near the chapel, carpets of Thyme or Chamomile interspersed with pretty wild flowers were planted as fragrant 'Fields of Paradise'.

A less pious but equally relaxing aromatic aspect of monastery gardens was the monks' use of flavouring herbs to concoct world-

famous elixirs, cordials and liqueurs for use as balms, tonics and medicines. Although the blends of herbs which flavour Benedictine, Drambuie, Chartreuse and other liqueurs are still vigorously guarded secrets, many are known and can be grown to flavour your own relaxing wine cups. They include Alecost, Angelica, Anise, Balm, Caraway, Coriander, Elecampane root, Fennel, Hyssop, Lovage seed, Meadowsweet, Mint, Speedwell, Sweet Cicely, Sweet Flag root, Sweet Woodruff, Thyme and Violet.

## Physic Gardens

Physic gardens continue the disciplined growing of herbs in beds but this time in botanical divisions. Although their purpose is to provide material for research, the innate character of herbs still creates an atmosphere of harmony and balance.

## Other Aromatic Landscapes

Orchards with the delicate springtime blossom of Apple, Peach and Cherry, or the exquisite intoxicating fragrance of Orange blossom in warmer areas, followed by the sensuous summer scent of ripening fruit and musky, fermenting fallen fruits in the autumn, ooze a contentment guaranteed to melt away tension. Plant Honeysuckle, Cowslips, Meadowsweet, Evening Primrose, Soapwort, Agrimony, Elecampane, Sweet Cicely and any of the hay-scented herbs as additional fragrant plants which may survive in the rough grass, and then sling a hammock between trees for dreamy summer days of blissful relaxation as you weave your daisy chains.

For a profoundly relaxing experience, the aromatic and spatial qualities of an ancient woodland link back to the earliest human memories. Venerable trees generate a deep sense of peace and protection, and the sweet, clean smells of damp earth, leaves and moss, the fragrance of Primroses, Cowslips, Sweet Violets and Wild Strawberries, the gentle rustling of leaves, and the infinite shades of green, filtered light nourish the mind and spirit and provide a sense of continuation and unity that brings the deepest peace.

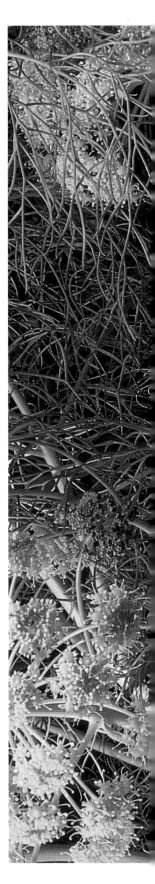

TOP LEFT: *Fennel in a monastery in Germany.*

LEFT: *Evening Primrose seed oil can lower blood pressure.*

RIGHT: *Giant Fennel* (Ferula communis)

# Relaxing Rainbow Healing Garden

The plan for this aromatherapy garden is an eight-petalled 'flower' with one 'petal' acting as the entrance and space for outdoor massage, and the other seven as mini gardens. There is a central seating area around an almond tree that allows a view of each segment. Each contains one or more aromatherapy plants plus others of the relevant colour. Plant tall plants on the outer edges, grading to smallest plants near the apex.

## Suggested Plants

### Code

**A** Plants which yield essential oils or pressed oils
**B** Other aromatic plants with appropriate flower or leaf colour
**C** Healing herbs and others with appropriate flower and leaf colour.

### Red

(SCARLET TO PINK)
**A** Old Roses: 'Guinée', 'Mme Isaac Pereire', 'Souvenir du Docteur Jamain', 'Empereu du Maroc', 'Prince Charles', 'Duke of Wellington'; Rose Geraniums, scarlet Clove Pinks; Honeysuckle *repens*; Lavender 'Hidcote Pink'
**B** Magnolia Vine (*Schisandra chinensis*); Soapwort; Bergamot; scarlet Peony; pink Musk mallow; pink Hyacinth. In warmer climates California Allspice (*Calycanthus occidentalis*).
**C** red Opium or Field Poppies; Crimson Clover

(*Trifolium incarnatum*); red Lupin; Wall Germander; Lady's Smock (*Cardamine pratense*); Gay Feather (*Liatris spicata*); Wood Betony (*Stachys officinalis*).

### Orange

(WARM GOLDEN ORANGES),
**A** Rose 'Elizabeth of Glamis'; Rose 'Alchemist', 'Sweet Magic', 'Geraldine', 'Heaven Scent', 'Southampton'.
**B** Honeysuckle (*L. x tellmanniana*); climbing Nasturtiums; *Buddleia globosa*; *Lilium henryi*; Madonna Lily; Edible Chrysanthemum; Mignonette; Tagetes 'Tangerine Gem'; Nasturtium; Wild Wallflower (*Cheiranthus cheiri*); Peony 'Souvenir de Maxime Cornu'.
**C** California Poppy (*Eschscholzia californica*); Calendula.

### Yellow

(SUNNY BUTTER YELLOWS AND YELLOW-SPLASHED LEAVES)
**A** golden Hop; Evening

Primrose; Gold variegated Lemon Balm; golden Lemon Thyme; Chamomiles; yellow Jasmine (*Jasminum humile*); Incense rose (*R. primula*), Rose 'Canary Bird', 'Fresia', 'Leverkusen', 'Cloth of Gold'.
**B** Japanese Honeysuckle; Ginger Mint; yellow Narcissus & Jonquils; Mignonette; golden Feverfew; variegated Applemint; Melilot; Agrimony; Tansy; *Paeonia lutea*; Elecampane (*Inula helenium*).
**C** Sunflowers; Foxglove (*Digitalis lutea*); Giant Cowslip (*Primula florindae*); Winter Jasmine (*Jasminum nudiflorum*); Lady's Mantle; Dyer's Chamomile; Mullein; Golden Rod (*Solidago virgaurea*); *Iris pseudacorus*; Arnica.

### Green

(GREEN AND WHITE FOLIAGE AND FLOWERS)
**A** Fennel; Peppermint; Lemon Balm; Geranium; *Lavandula viridis*; Sweet Marjoram; Mints; Basil; Rosemary; Thymes; Sweet Myrtle; Angelica; Hops.
**B** Dang Shen (*Codonopsis pilosula*); Sweet Cicely; Tobacco Plant (*Nicotiana alata* 'Lime Green'); Sweet Woodruff; Parsley; Corsican Mint; Lawn Chamomile 'Treneague'; Pennyroyal; Chervil; Solomon's Seal.
**C** Yam (*Dioscorea discolor*); Ivy 'Parsley Crested'.

### Blue

(GREEN AND BLUE FOLIAGE AND LIGHT BLUE FLOWERS)
**A** Borage; Rosemary; prostrate Sage; Lavender

'Munstead'; Flax.
**B** *Crocus thomasinianus*
**C** *Clematis alpina* 'Frances Rivis'; *Convolvulus* 'Heavenly Blue'; *Lobelia siphilitica*; *Camassia quamash*; Bluebell; Forget-me-Not; Scilla; Harebell; Flax; Virginia Skullcap; Soft/Blue Comfrey (*Symphytum asperum*), Love-in-a-Mist; Periwinkle (*Vinca major*); Jacob's Ladder (*Polemonium caeruleum*); Phacelia; Lungwort; Cornflower (*Centaurea cyanus*), Sea Holly (*Eryngium maritimum*); Rue 'Jackman's Blue'; Iris 'Mary Frances'.

### Indigo

(DARK BLUE FLOWERS AND GREEN FOLIAGE)
**A** Rock Hyssop; Dark blue Lavender ('Folgate', 'Twickle' or 'Sawyers Selection');
**B** Catnip.
**C** Clematis 'Jackmanii Superba'; Wisteria 'Violaceoplena'; Monkshood (*Aconitum napellus*); dark blue Delphiniums; *Lobelia syphilitica*; *Scilla siberica*; *Ajuga reptans* 'Atropurpurea'; Self Heal (*Prunella vulgaris*); Larkspur (*Consolida ambigua*); Alkanet (*Anchusa officinalis*); Balloon Flower (*Platycodon grandiflorum*); Iris 'Matinata'.

### Violet

(VIOLET AND PURPLE FLOWERS; GREEN AND PURPLE LEAVES)
**A** bronze Fennel; Clary Sage; Eau-de-Cologne Mint; purple Sage; purple-leaf Basil; Sweet Violets; Lavender 'Hidcote' & *L. stoechas*; dark-leaved Mints.
**B** Akebia; purple Sweet Peas;

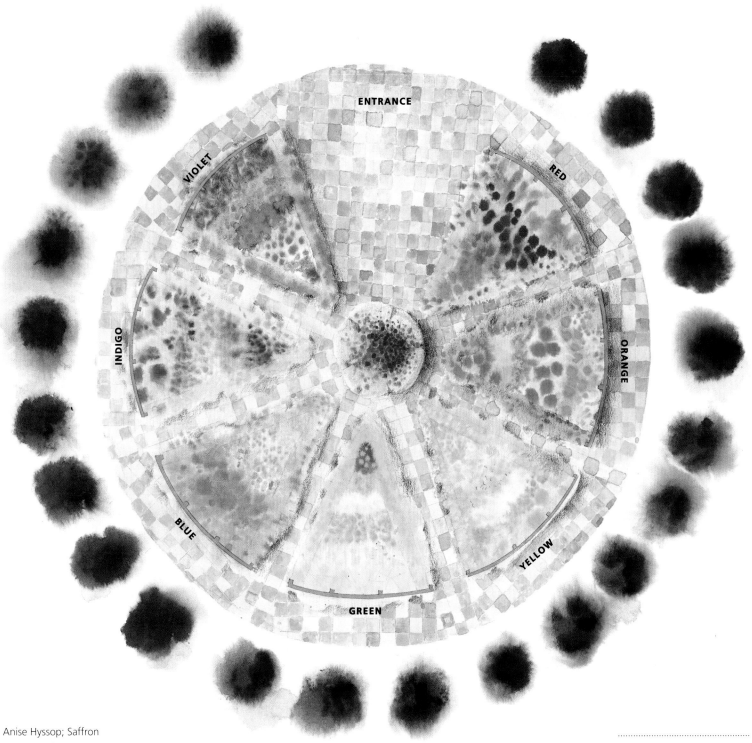

ENTRANCE

VIOLET

RED

INDIGO

ORANGE

BLUE

YELLOW

GREEN

Anise Hyssop; Saffron
Crocus; *Heliotropium
arborescens*; Lilac; Buddleia;
Sweet Rocket; Catmint;
Honeysuckle var. *repens*.
**C** purple-leaf Grape
'Teinturier'; Milk Thistle
(*Silybum marianum*); Scotch

Thistle (*Onopordum
acanthium*); *Echinacea*;
purple Orach; purple
Plantain; Globe artichoke;
purple-leaf Hazel; violet

Passion flower; dark purple
Hollyhock (*Alcea rosea*);
purple Columbine; purple

Penstemon; Iris 'Paradise
Bird'.

ABOVE: *This garden is
made up of seven segments,
to represent either the seven
days of the week, the seven
major chakras or the seven
colours of the rainbow.*

95

*The many techniques evolved to encourage relaxation and restore equilibrium, from Yoga to Meditation, all benefit from the presence of harmonizing fragrant herbs and oils.*

# Time for Relaxation

Sweet perfumes slow and deepen our breathing and encourage us to take time to relax. Inhaled aromatic molecules are registered in the brain next to the area which produces stress hormones and serve to counter messages of anxiety. The secret is to have your favourite fragrant remedies ready for immediate use in times of stress.

Research shows that the fragrance of Lavender sends a calming message to the brain which counters adrenalin-producing stress signals. Stroke a drop of essential oil over your temples to reduce tension headaches; massage a drop across your throat to calm tickly coughs; and place a drop on the pillow to relieve insomnia, especially in young children.

### MEADOW POTPOURRI

On dull, miserable days, enjoy sweet aromatics in potpourri. This recipe blends herbs scented of new-mown hay with meadow flowers for colour. Using the dry method (see page 64), mix 1 part each Sweet Woodruff, Melilot, Lady's Bedstraw, Meadowsweet leaves and florets and Sweet Marjoram; $1/2$ part each red Poppy and blue Cornflower; $1/4$ part Chamomile flowers. Add 1 tbsp Orris root per 2 cups potpourri.

# Aromatherapy

Without a garden, the most popular and useful way of restoring harmony and balance with fragrant herbs is through aromatherapy – massage with diluted essential oils. Although aromatherapists require considerable training, a very relaxing and beneficial massage can be given by friends.

Choose a warm, quiet, private space with soft lighting. In place of a massage table, which is upper-thigh height, choose a narrow, firm bed, a futon or padded blankets on the floor. Cover with towels to absorb oil drops and have extra towels ready to cover parts of the body which are not being massaged. Select oils for their appropriate qualities and by asking the person whom you are massaging about their preferences.

## Mixing Massage Oils

When essential oils are used in massage, they are always diluted in a base or carrier oil (see page 98). This is usually a pressed vegetable seed oil. Mix the oils in a clean dark glass bottle. The recipes given on page 98 are for drops of essential oils to be mixed with 50 ml (2 fl oz) carrier oil and this will be enough for 3–4 full body massages. Do not mix more than you will use in 2–3 months, as diluted blends will deteriorate.

First add the drops of essential oil(s) to the empty bottle. If you have selected more than one, replace the lid and roll the bottle sharply between your hands to mix the molecules. Then add the carrier oil up to the top of the bottle's shoulder. Replace the lid and roll again several times to blend the oils. Label and date the mixture. Keep the bottle tightly closed when not in use and store in a cool, dark place.

RIGHT: *Dappled orchard shade and soft meadow scents for a perfect daydreaming afternoon.*

ABOVE: *Sandalwood eggs release their pleasing aroma when held in the hand.*

## Carrier Oils

A good carrier oil is a smooth lubricant, is scentless, has penetrative properties to assist the essential oils, is 100 per cent pure (organically grown, pesticide-free and cold pressed if possible) and is reasonably priced. Some also have therapeutic properties of their own.

ALMOND  Very popular, almost odourless oil that is emollient, nourishing and slow to become rancid. Apricot Kernel and Peach Kernel oils share the same properties but are more expensive.

GRAPESEED  Another very popular oil that is fine, light and odourless, gives a satin-smooth finish, contains vitamin F and is inexpensive.

HAZELNUT  Deeply penetrating oil that stimulates circulation and nourishes the skin.

AVOCADO  Nourishing and deeply penetrating oil, especially in fatty areas, but sticky when massaged so best as an addition to other carrier oils. Add 1 tsp to 30ml (1fl oz) massage mix to increase oil penetration. Rich in vitamins A, B, D and lecithin, it also helps skin to heal. Do not chill, as some compounds will precipitate.

OLIVE  Calming oil that is emollient and good for rheumatism, stretch marks and itchy skin, but has a strong aroma.

CORN, SOYA AND SUNFLOWER  Acceptable as carrier oils: Soya has a pleasant feel and does not become sticky with pressure; Sunflower contains vitamin F but does not keep particularly well.

JOJOBA  Liquid wax that is very stable (it is indigestible to bacteria and humans). It dissolves sebum so is good for acne, and gives a satin-smooth feel to the skin.

MACADAMIA NUT  Newer and expensive oil that is nourishing and smooth in application It contains palmitoleic acid, a skin component responsible for moisture retention and suppleness which decreases rapidly after the age of 20. It is valued in facial massage for use on dry and ageing skins as it softens facial lines.

## Dilutions

Normal dilution is 0.5–3 per cent essential oil to 99.5–97 per cent carrier oil; this is roughly 5–30 drops essential oil in a 50 ml (2 fl oz) bottle. For children and face-only massage, use 5 drops per 50 ml (2 fl oz). For pregnant and lactating mothers, people with sensitive skin, and those who are on medication or are addicted to drugs, tranquillizers or alcohol, use 5–10 drops per 50 ml (2 fl oz). For emotional conditions, start with 10 drops, as a lower dose can be more successful. See Safety, pages 250–1 for oils to avoid with certain conditions.

## Massage Recipes

The recipes below are for drops of essential oil to be mixed with 50 ml (2 fl oz) of carrier oil.

DEEPLY RELAXING
For unwinding after a stressful or frustrating day: 7 Bergamot FCF; 6 each Lavender and German Chamomile; 5 Clary Sage.

RELAXING AND REFRESHING
Antidote to a stressful day: 7 each Petitgrain, Geranium and Mandarin; 5 Lavender.

RELAXING AND ENERGIZING
To prepare for an evening out: 9 Bergamot; 7 each Geranium and Lemon Eucalyptus; 4 Jasmine.

TO BRING BALANCE
After emotional stress: 8 Bergamot; 7 Geranium; 5 Rose; 4 Sandalwood.

ANTI-ANXIETY CONFIDENCE BOOSTER
Before an examination or interview:
10 Grapefruit; 7 Lavender; 5 Neroli; 4 Ylang-Ylang.

## OIL ESSENTIALS

Most essential oils are sold in 10 ml or 20 ml bottles. Expensive oils are sold in 2.5 ml or 5 ml bottles.

When mixing small quantities, you should generally use:
1–3 drops in 5 ml (1 tsp) carrier oil
4–12 drops in 20 ml (4 tsp) carrier oil
10–30 drops in 50 ml (10 tsp) carrier oil, and so on pro rata.

## MASSAGE SAFETY

Amateurs should avoid massage on a person with heart trouble, acute back pain, cancer or infectious disease and avoid areas near fractures, wounds, burns, bruises, swelling, varicose veins, torn muscles or any-where that causes discomfort.

ABOVE: *Essential oils should be stored in tightly lidded, dark glass bottles, away from sunlight and extremes of temperature.*

## Giving a Relaxing Massage

In aromatic massage, the essential oils are absorbed in 3 ways: they are smelled via the nose and affect brain chemistry; they are inhaled into the lungs where they enter the blood stream; and they pass through the skin into the lymph system. Combined with the generous and healing act of massage, the effect is utterly relaxing.

## Basic Massage Strokes

You will need to know three basic strokes in order to carry out the massage techniques described here.

### STROKING

This is a long, even-pressured movement used to relax muscles at the beginning, middle and end of a massage. Use both hands in an open, relaxed way, moulded to the shape of the body. Over smaller areas, stroke rhythmically using your hands alternately.

### KNEADING

This slow, smooth, rhythmic action for tense muscles follows stroking movements. Lay your hand over the muscle with the thumb splayed, then gently 'pick up', squeeze or roll the muscle, bringing your hand towards your thumb. Use your hands alternately. This movement stimulates circulation and the elimination of toxins which contribute to muscle ache.

### PRESSURE CIRCLES

This is a deeper, static action for releasing tension. Position your hands with thumbs splayed, keep them still and move either the palms or the thumb pads in small circles with a little pressure.

## Starting to Massage

Have the person lie on their front with their arms comfortably at their sides or under their head. Warm your hands and breathe deeply to centre yourself. Massage one area of the body at a time, pouring 1/2–1 tsp massage oil into the palm of one hand, rubbing your hands together, and then stroking over the area you are about to massage.

### BACK

Place your open hands on either side of the spine, then stroke upwards, out to the sides, down and back to the centre, keeping continuous skin contact. Follow with dinner-plate-sized circles along the length of the spine, then careful small pressure circles on either side of the spine. Knead across the hips, the outer sides of the back and the shoulders. Finish with rhythmic stroking.

### LEGS

Move the towels to cover the back, then start with the backs of the legs. Begin with a light stroke away from the heart and a return stroke of deeper pressure to stimulate the circulation. Build up a rhythm, avoiding the backs of the knees. Use kneading on the thighs (especially on cellulite). Finish with stroking. Massage the feet, then loosen each joint and gently pull each toe. Turn the person over, using the towels to keep them warm. Massage the front of each leg, working firmly sideways and upwards, and lightly downwards.

### FRONT

Circle the navel gently clockwise with alternate hands. Place the heel of the hand on the Tan Dien point (2 finger thicknesses below the navel) and slowly rock the abdomen to release tension. Finish with stroking up the centre of the body, out over the ribs and back down the sides.

### ARMS

Knead the upper arm, then stroke the whole arm to the wrist. Support the hand on your fingers and massage it with your thumbs. Gently pull each finger in turn. Repeat for the other arm.

## HEAD

All actions should be gentle. Position yourself above the head, lean forward, place a hand on each shoulder and push down. Roll the head to one side and support with one hand; with the other, stroke the opposite side from shoulder to skull base. Repeat on the other side. Return the head to the centre, place your hands on the upper chest, slide out over the shoulders to the back of the neck and cradle the head to release tension. Repeat rhythmically. Wipe the oil from your hands, and using finger pads, massage all over the scalp, then run your fingers through the hair. Head and face massage is a relaxing treat for those for whom full body massage is not advisable.

## FACE

Stroke the forehead towards the crown, then lightly oil your hands and use gentle strokes from the chin up the face, circling the eyes in the direction in which the eyebrows grow. Use small circular movements on the chin along the jaw, then from the mouth to the ear, up each side of the nose, and along the brow and temples to the hair line. Finish with circular 'face-washing' movements. Work the ears with small circular movements, pinch the outer edges from the top down and gently tug the ear lobes 3 times. 'Palm' the eyes to reduce fatigue and hold this position for 20 seconds. Remove your hands slowly, leaving the person to relax in their cocoon of tranquillity.

## FOOT BATH

To make a foot bath, place smooth pebbles in a basin. *For a cooling effect*, add ankle-deep cool water with 2 drops Peppermint oil. *For a relaxing effect*, add 2 drops Lavender oil to hot water. Massage your feet over the pebbles.

# Herbs & Essential Oils for Holiday Use

## Travel Preparations

Easily portable herbs and essential oils, with their antiseptic, anti-fungal, anti-viral and insect-deterring qualities, will ensure your holiday is relaxing and reviving.

### BY CAR

Crush Angelica leaves to reduce nausea and keep the air refreshed. Passengers will enjoy 2 drops calming Lavender, Geranium or Frankincense oil on a personal hanky, but the driver should use only stimulating oils such as Peppermint, Cypress, Juniper, Rosemary, Eucalyptus or Citrus sprinkled on sleeves or near the air conditioning. These will also encourage alertness on arrival. In hot countries where Lemons are readily available, roll one in your hands to release the cooling scent.

### BY AIR

To minimize jet-lag, bathe before departure with 2 drops of Peppermint or Eucalyptus. Before night flights take a Lavender and Chamomile bath (and drops on a tissue on the plane) to encourage sleep. Chew crystallized Ginger to prevent nausea. Drink Peppermint tea for stress-related indigestion. Drink plenty of fruit juice and water, avoiding tea, coffee and alcohol. To minimize swollen feet and ankles on long flights, massage Lavender and Eucalyptus (5 drops in 1 tsp carrier oil or on a damp cloth) on legs and feet. A discreet pocket atomizer of 2 per cent Citrus oils in water will refresh and humidify your air space; alternatively, keep the oils on a damp cloth in a plastic bag to sniff or sponge on your neck when needed.

On arrival, to relieve the physical tension caused by cramped seating and to relax or sleep, use 1 drop each Lavender and Geranium oil in the bath or diluted over your neck and shoulders. Take a Lavender and Grapefruit (or Peppermint and Eucalyptus) bath in the morning.

To be alert after a long flight, mix 1 drop each Grapefruit and Lavender, or Rosemary and Lemon Grass, or Peppermint and Lemon Eucalyptus, or Mandarin and Lemon Geranium, in 2ml ($^1/_2$ tsp) carrier oil. Apply to the wrists and temples before landing and again before arrival at your destination.

## Hotel Hygiene

Use a small bottle of antiseptic room spray (see page 70) with Thyme, Eucalyptus, Tea Tree, Lavender, Bergamot and Lemon Grass, for bathroom, mattress, door handles and so on. Wipe Lemon juice around the rim of cold drinks glasses, squeeze over fish dishes and rub over your hands for hygiene. Use a few drops of Lemon essential oil in water to be used for washing fresh fruit.

### TRAVEL KIT ESSENTIAL OILS

Lavender, Chamomile, Lemongrass, Peppermint, Grapefruit, Geranium and Eucalyptus, plus optional Lemon, Tea Tree, Thyme, Cedar and Citronella.

### TEABAGS

Chamomile (for nerves and tired eyes), Fennel or Peppermint (indigestion), Black tea (diarrhoea), Elderflower (catarrh and tired eyes).

### ALOE VERA GEL

Cooling and healing for burns, sunburn, skin allergies and irritations.

## ROOM WELCOMING

Spray or use an oil burner with favourite oils to fragrance a hotel room, especially to help children settle into new surroundings.

## Insect Deterrents

For general use, choose from the following essential oils: Lemon Grass, Citronella, Geranium, Eucalyptus, Lavender (especially flies and bedbugs), Patchouli, Peppermint (mosquitoes and rodents), Cedarwood (also repels rats and leeches) and Rosemary.

## ROOM SPRAYS

All the general repellent oils can be used in room sprays (5–10 drops in 50ml (2fl oz) water), or applied neat to window and door frames and lightbulbs.

## BODY PROTECTION

For multiple use, blend 6 drops Lemon Grass, 4 drops each Eucalyptus, Lavender and Geranium, and 2 drops Peppermint essential oils. Put 5 drops near your bed or on a tissue. Add 4 drops to 1 tbsp body lotion or carrier oil for skin application.

## BITES

Apply 1 drop Lavender or Geranium essential oil, or Lime or Garlic juice, or a fresh Onion slice, and repeat later to prevent itching.

## Skin Care

To prevent sunburn, always use a high-factor sunscreen cream.

## AFTER-SUN BATH OR MASSAGE

Blend 3 drops Chamomile, 2 drops each Lavender and Geranium, and 1 drop Peppermint essential oils in 1 tbsp skin-nourishing Jojoba or Macadamia oil. Apply Aloe Vera gel.

## SUNBURN

Immerse the area in very cold water or apply cold compresses for 10 minutes to remove heat. Apply Aloe Vera gel or neat Lavender essential oil (1 drop covers a large area) to heal the burn; second choice is Eucalyptus. Later, take a cool bath with 7 drops Lavender, Chamomile or Eucalyptus oil. Pat dry and apply Lavender oil.

## PRICKLY HEAT RASH

To a warm bath, add 3 drops each Lavender and Eucalyptus essential oils, pre-mixed with 1 cup baking soda if available. Halve these quantities for children.

## First Aid

For serious problems, always consult a qualified medical practitioner.

## HANGOVER

Take 1 g Vitamin C and drink lots of water or Orange juice the same evening. Take 2 g Evening Primrose capsules the following morning and a bath with 5 drops Grapefruit or a blend of 2 drops Fennel and 1 drop each Juniper, Rosemary and Rose or Lavender essential oils.

## MINOR CUTS

Use essential oils of Tea Tree, Thyme, Lavender or Eucalyptus – 1 drop neat, or 8 drops in a bowl of water as a wash.

## REHYDRATION DRINK

After episodes of diarrhoea or heatstroke, dissolve 1 level tsp of salt and 8 tsp sugar or glucose in 1 litre (2 pints) boiled water. Adults should drink up to $1/2$ litre (1 pint) every hour. Add juice of 1 lemon to lower temperatures. Make fresh daily.

## HAYFEVER

Sniff 1 drop Chamomile or Melissa essential oil for temporary relief.

## ANTISEPTIC FOODS

Dishes flavoured with chilli and garlic can help prevent diarrhoea, colds and flu.

ABOVE: *Sweet Marjoram makes a digestive, nerve-soothing tea.*

103

# Light Lunches / Alfresco Eating

Snacks and light lunches, especially if they are to be eaten out-of-doors, benefit from sharp pungent flavours. Unusual combinations, like the Tarragon and Dill with the smoked salmon, bring new interest to favourite ingredients.

## Salmon Rillettes with Horseradish

*Serve this coarse-textured fish mousse with rye bread as this complements both the salmon and the Horseradish.*

**preparation: 10 minutes; cooking: 5 minutes, plus chilling**

225 g / 8 oz boned and skinned cooked salmon fillet
    (preferably poached or microwaved)
225 g / 8 oz smoked salmon off-cuts
30 g / 1 oz unsalted butter
few drops of Tabasco sauce
2 tbsp crème fraîche
2 tbsp yoghurt, preferably bio
freshly grated or creamed Horseradish to taste
few sprigs of flat-leaved Parsley, for garnish (optional)
sea salt and freshly ground black pepper

Shred the salmon and snip the smoked salmon off-cuts into a bowl. Melt the butter in a frying pan, add the salmon and stir to mix. Season with a little Tabasco and pepper. Take off the heat.

Stir in the crème fraîche and yoghurt. Adjust the seasoning and add Horseradish to taste – a very little at a time, until just piquant enough for your liking. Stir and chill until needed. Garnish with some flat-leaved Parsley if you like.

## Sweet Onion Tart with Oregano

*Adding fresh oregano towards the end of cooking gives this sweet onion tart a nicely sharp edge.*

**preparation: 10 minutes; cooking onions: 50 minutes; baking: 20 minutes, plus cooling
serves 6**

25-cm / 10-inch part-baked shortcrust pastry shell

for the filling:
1¹/₂ tbsp vegetable oil
1 kg / 2¹/₄ lb Spanish onions, thinly sliced
1 tsp dried Sage
1 tbsp flour
2 heaped tbsp finely snipped fresh Oregano
3 fresh medium eggs
125 ml / 4 fl oz evaporated milk
3–4 tbsp whipping cream
salt and freshly ground black pepper

Make the filling: in a large frying pan, heat the oil and add the onions. Sweat the onions for about 40 minutes over a very low heat until soft.

Season and sprinkle in the Sage, flour and half the Oregano. Turn up the heat a little and cook for 3 minutes.

Preheat the oven to 190°C/375°F/gas 5. Lightly whisk together the eggs, evaporated milk and cream. Season to taste, then stir this into the onion mixture.

Tip the mixture into the pastry shell, arrange with a spoon so that the onion is evenly distributed. Now bake for about 15 minutes. Take out of the oven, sprinkle over the rest of the Oregano and cover with foil if the tart is browning too much. Return to the oven for 5 minutes.

Serve at room temperature rather than chilled.

LEFT: *Sweet Onion tart with Oregano*

RIGHT: *Salmon Rillettes with Horseradish*

Pick the Thyme off the stalks. Reserve a tablespoon to finish and put the rest in a food processor with the lemon juice and zest and the garlic. Season and add a little olive oil. Blend until very coarsely puréed, then quickly whiz in the rest of the oil.

Spoon this over the dough rounds, spread it out evenly and bake for about 8 minutes until the dough is crusty and the topping is lightly browned. Scatter over the rest of the fresh Thyme. Serve hot.

## Griddled Potatoes with Smoked Salmon, Tarragon and Dill

*Using smaller potatoes for this dish produces bite-sized canapés.*

**preparation: 15 minutes; cooking: 12–15 minutes**

3 large waxy potatoes, peeled and cut into
    5-mm / ¼-inch thick slices
oil for brushing
3 tbsp good mayonnaise
1½ tbsp crème fraîche, sour cream or Greek yoghurt
1 tsp creamed Horseradish
several sprigs of fresh Tarragon
few fronds of fresh Dill
150 g / 5 oz smoked salmon, cut into strips
sea salt and freshly ground black pepper

Cook the potatoes in lightly salted boiling water for 8–10 minutes, until almost done but still firm. While the potatoes are cooking, preheat a lightly oiled griddle or grill rack.

Drain the potatoes carefully, put them on the prepared griddle or grill rack and cook for 1–2 minutes on each side until just a little charred.

Mix together the mayonnaise, crème fraîche, sour cream or yoghurt and the Horseradish. Season and snip in 3 or 4 sprigs of fresh Tarragon and a few Dill fronds. Spread the mixture over the charred potato slices and top with a mound of smoked salmon. Snip over a little extra Tarragon and Dill.

## Manakeish

*This gutsy Thyme bread is inspired by a Lebanese dish. Serve like pizza, with a green salad or sweet tomatoes.*

**preparation: 10 minutes; cooking: 10 minutes**
**makes 8 small rounds**

450 g / 1 lb ready-to-bake pizza dough
bunch of fresh Thyme (or 3 individual sachets)
juice and zest of ½ unwaxed lemon
1 garlic clove, chopped
175 ml / 6 fl oz extra-virgin olive oil
sea salt and freshly ground black pepper

Preheat the oven to its highest setting. Divide the dough into 8 pieces and shape these into balls. Roll each out into a 10-cm / 4-in round.

# Vegetables

*Add some herbal flavours to a vegetable dish and what might otherwise simply serve as a side dish could easily rank as a dish in its own right.*

## Baked Squash with Bay Leaves, Capers and Madeira

**preparation: 15 minutes; cooking: 50 minutes**

55 g / 1³/₄ oz butter, plus more for the baking pan
2 round winter squashes (gem, sweet dumpling or
    other)
5 large fresh Bay leaves, plus 4 small fresh Bay leaves
    or spriglets, to finish off the dish
1 small garlic clove, crushed
¹/₂ shallot, finely chopped
1 generous tbsp drained capers
1 tsp balsamic vinegar
5 tbsp Madeira
sea salt and freshly ground black pepper

Preheat the oven to 180°C/350°F/gas 4 and butter a baking tray.

Cut the squash in half lengthwise and scoop out the seeds. Season lightly and put in the pan, cut sides down, over 4 of the Bay leaves. Bake for around 40 minutes, or longer, until tender, depending on the type of squash you use.

While the squash are baking, over a low heat in a small pan, sauté the garlic and shallot in one-third of the butter for a few minutes, until softened but not coloured. Add the capers, remaining large Bay leaf, balsamic vinegar and Madeira. Bring to a simmer, then reduce the heat to extremely low and cook for 3 minutes. Cover and keep warm.

Remove the squash from the oven, but leave the oven on. Allow to cool a little, then scoop out the flesh in neat pieces, leaving the shells intact.

In a bowl, toss the soft squash flesh in the hot sauce. Return to the shells and replace them on the baking tray. Dot with the rest of the butter and replace in the oven for a few minutes, until the butter has melted.

Season again lightly and serve very hot, decorated with small fresh Bay leaves.

ABOVE: *Baked Squash with Bay Leaves, Capers and Madeira*

RIGHT: *Coriander Vegetable Tian*

# Coriander Vegetable Tian

*For a quicker version in single-serving portions, make the dish in buttered individual gratin dishes as shown, but halve the cooking time.*

**preparation: 20 minutes; cooking: 1¼ hours**

*about 6 tbsp fruity olive oil*
*3 ripe aubergines, thinly sliced*
*2 courgettes, thinly sliced*
*1 sweet red pepper*
*1 sweet yellow pepper*
*1 large Spanish onion, cut into thin rings*
*1 (or more) garlic cloves, smashed*
*1 tsp ground Coriander seeds*
*6 ripe vine tomatoes, deseeded, cored and sliced*
*several sprigs of fresh Coriander*
*black olives, for garnish (optional)*
*sea salt and freshly ground black pepper*

Heat 1½ tablespoons of the oil in a large frying pan over a moderate heat and sauté the aubergine slices a few at a time, until golden. Spread the slices on a double layer of paper towels and pat dry. Continue until all are sautéed, adding more oil as necessary and reducing the heat after a while. Do the same with the courgettes. Char the peppers under the grill or over a flame until blistered. Allow to cool, peel off the skin, halve, deseed, core and cut the flesh into thin strips.

In the frying pan (in a little more oil if necessary), sauté the onion rings with the garlic and ground Coriander (reserving a pinch) over a moderate heat for a few minutes. Season.

Preheat the oven to 190°C/375°F/gas 5 and lightly oil a gratin dish. Spread a layer of sautéed aubergine slices in it. Season lightly and snip over a few leaves of Coriander. Spread over half the courgettes, tomato slices, onion mixture and pepper strips. Snip over some more Coriander. Season, then repeat the layers. Sprinkle the final layer with the rest of the ground Coriander and a little more oil.

Bake for about 45 minutes. Take out of the oven and scoop out any excess liquid. Turn the heat up to 200°C/400°F/gas 6 and cook for another 15–20 minutes. Leave to cool and serve warm, garnished with black olives if you like.

Variation: to turn this dish into a vegetarian main course, add 100 g / 3½ oz grated Gruyère cheese mixed with ¼ tsp Cumin, ¼ tsp ground Coriander seeds and 12 finely chopped black olives. Spread half the mixture over the first layer of charred peppers. Scatter the rest over the top of the dish (with a little extra oil) when you take the dish out of the oven three-quarters of the way through cooking.

# Fennel, Parsnip and Carrot Gratin

*preparation: 15 minutes; cooking: 20 minutes*

*225 g / 8 oz carrots, thickly sliced at an angle*
*2 medium parsnips, cut into rough batons*
*2 fennel bulbs, trimmed and quartered lengthwise,*
*    fronds finely snipped to finish off the dish*
*oil for the dish(es)*
*45 g / 1½ oz butter*
*1 heaped tbsp cornflour*
*250 ml / 9 fl oz milk*
*4 tbsp freshly squeezed orange juice*
*2 tsp Fennel seeds*
*2 tsp finely snipped Parsley*
*1 tsp snipped Oregano or Marjoram leaves*
*85 g / 3 oz goats' cheese, crumbled or slivered*
*sea salt and freshly ground black pepper*

Cook the carrots in lightly salted boiling water for 5 minutes. Add the parsnips, bring back to the boil, then add the fennel. Cook for about 5 minutes or until just tender. Drain.

Preheat the oven to 200°C/400°F/gas 6 and lightly oil a gratin dish or 4 individual dishes. Spread the mixed vegetables in the dish(es).

Melt the butter in a little heavy-based pan. Stir in the cornflour and cook for a few seconds. Gradually whisk in the milk and half the orange juice. Bring to a simmer, still stirring, and cook for 2 minutes. Stir in the Fennel seeds, Parsley, Oregano or Marjoram, then three-quarters of the cheese.

Cook the sauce for a minute or two until the cheese melts and the sauce is smooth, stirring over a moderate heat. Adjust the seasoning and stir in the rest of the orange juice.

Spoon the sauce over the vegetables. Scatter over the rest of the cheese and season with a little pepper. Bake until golden, 12–15 minutes, then sprinkle over the Fennel leaves and serve hot.

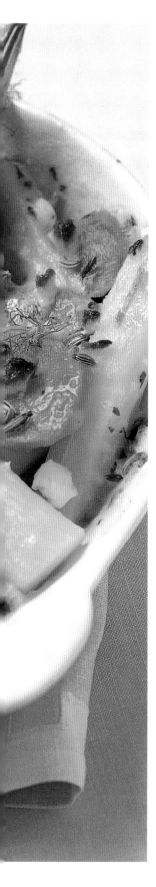

## Green Fricassée with Bergamot Salsa

*This is a good midsummer accompaniment for poultry, fish and white meat, but it is also nice as a light starter.*

**preparation: 10 minutes; marinating: 1 hour; cooking: 15 minutes**

225 ml / 8 fl oz chicken or vegetable stock
350 g / 12 oz shelled fresh or frozen baby broad
    beans
225 g / 8 oz shelled fresh or frozen peas
3 thin spring onions
small bunch of thin asparagus tips (optional)
200 g / 7 oz trimmed mange-tout peas
about 6 large soft lettuce leaves
30g / 1 oz unsalted butter
Bergamot flowers, if available, for decoration

for the Bergamot Salsa:
12–16 ripe cherry tomatoes
3–4 Bergamot leaves, finely chopped
1 tsp sugar
grated zest of ½ unwaxed lemon
3 tbsp fruity olive oil
1 garlic clove, smashed
white parts of 2 spring onions, chopped
sea salt and freshly ground black pepper

Several hours ahead, prepare the salsa: pierce the tomatoes with a fork, put in a bowl, add the chopped Bergamot leaves (reserving a few to finish), a pinch of salt, the sugar, lemon zest, the olive oil (reserving 2 teaspoons to finish), crushed garlic and chopped spring onions. Toss well to coat and set aside at room temperature for about 1 hour. Toss the mixture from time to time.

Blend the mixture very briefly in the food processor. Adjust the seasoning, stir in the reserved Bergamot leaves and olive oil. Chill until needed.

Cook the fricassée: put the stock in a large sauté pan and top up with water to a depth of at least 6 cm / 2½ in. Bring to the boil and season with salt. Throw in the broad beans, return to a simmer, then add the peas, the whole spring onions and asparagus, if using. Simmer for about 3 minutes, add the mange-tout and simmer for a few minutes more until just tender. Drain well and, when cool enough to handle, squeeze some of the broad beans to remove the skin (for taste and appearance). While the vegetables are simmering, roll up the lettuce leaves and snip into thin ribbons.

A few minutes before serving, melt the butter in the sauté pan over a moderate heat. Spread in the lettuce ribbons and wilt for a few seconds, then tip in the drained vegetables. Stir until heated through. Adjust the seasoning. Serve as soon as possible, with the Salsa and Bergamot flowers, if available.

Salsa variations: instead of Bergamot you can use Salad Burnet, Mint, Basil, mixed Parsley, Rosemary and Coriander (use 2 tablespoons chopped leaves).

## Basil-mashed Potatoes

**preparation: 15 minutes; cooking 30 minutes**

1 kg / 2¼ lb waxy potatoes, boiled whole in their
    jackets and then peeled
150 ml / ¼ pint hot milk
60 g /2 oz soft butter, plus more if you like
several Basil leaves
sea salt and freshly ground black pepper

Push the potatoes through a ricer, pass them through a vegetable mill or mash them lightly.

In a large heavy-based pan, melt the butter, add the potatoes and stir for a minute over a low heat. Pour in the hot milk, a little at a time, whisking well. Season lightly with salt and more generously with pepper. Snip in the Basil and cook for a minute or two. Check the seasoning and add a little knob of extra butter at the last minute, if you like.

LEFT: *Fennel, Parsnip and Carrot Gratin*

CHAPTER FOUR

# *Pleasure &*
# *Leisure*

*To welcome and entertain friends, aromatics offer the perfect palette for creating a cheerful and inviting atmosphere.*

From the garden gate, borders of refreshing Thyme and Clove Pinks spilling underfoot bring a smile to the face; spicy clipped Bays make jovial porch sentinels; a colourful door garland of lively herbs and bright flowers signals friendliness; and indoors, an exotic, zesty vaporizing mix of Vanilla and Lime creates a convivial welcome. Armfuls of fresh flowers and herbs, with a trail of petals from the entrance to the guest room, build an atmosphere of warm-hearted fun even before the first cork has been popped and the first joke told.

As friends mingle, the next aromatic magnet is a fanfare of enticing cooking aromas. The sharp, sweet scent of Basil blending with Garlic and olive oil, Rosemary on sizzling lamb, Tarragon butter melting over steamed fresh vegetables and Cardamom in baking bread all heighten the anticipation of pleasures to come.

Adding decorative fragrance to the dining arena has an historical pedigree which includes strewing herbs, sweet-scented table swags and wooden platters scrubbed with Mint leaves. Adventurous hosts may wish to take inspiration from Emperor Nero's extravagant banquets which featured perfume-laced water fountains, mountains of fragrant fruits, pools of aromatic wines, fingerbowls of scented flowers, and for each guest a coronet of spicy leaves and Parsley, which the Romans believed could reduce the inebriating effect of wine.

Today, we might draw the line at small jets of rosewater under each place setting to 'refresh' the guest as his or her plate was lifted between courses.

Outdoor entertaining brings further aromatic opportunities: a carpet of fragrant herb prunings under the seats, Thyme sprinkled on barbecue coals, Rosemary stems as satay skewers, and colourful beds of garnish and salad herbs ready to pick. Gardens can be lit with herbal torches for subtle fragrance and to act as insect repellents.

Whatever the style of entertaining, a concord of enticing aromas will encourage each guest to revel in the good food, conversation and laughter of friends.

CREATING AN AROMATIC WELCOME • CULINARY HERBS • PROPAGATION • SEASONAL HERB GARDENS • POTAGER DESIGN • ROOM FRAGRANCE • SWAGS & WREATHS • SCENTED CANDLES • AROMATIC TABLE SETTINGS • ENTERTAINING

*Our flavouring repertoire continues to be extended through wider travel and increased ethnic interests, while we also explore new ways of using the familiar herbs around us.*

# Flavouring Herbs

Taste buds on every continent respond to the invitation of aromatic flavourings, from the Sourdock (*Rumex arcticus*) and Bilberries (*Vaccinium myrtillus*) gathered on the Canadian tundra, to the cornucopia of exotic flavours from equatorial jungles and rain forests.

### TRADITIONAL HERBS

Traditional English cooking invokes Parsley, the universal garnish – the 'summation of all things green' – for its strong, bright flavour added to every type of savoury dish; Chives, whose slender blades belie their sharp onion bite for summer salads and soups; clean, refreshing Mint, bubbling in saucepans of new potatoes; resinous Rosemary, roasting with spring lamb; spicy Bay leaves, in autumn game dishes; and powerful 'prima donna' Sage, flavouring pork, duck and sausages while doubling as a digestive agent for these rich meats.

Well suited to their traditional roles, these classic herbs also lend themselves to newer combinations: Rosemary with oranges in wine, Chive yoghurt sauce, crisply fried Parsley sprigs, Bay in Indian curries, Mint in fruit salads, and Sage in vegetarian pâtés. Traditional combinations from superb culinary cultures such as China and France are being extended by exciting flavouring experiments with novel native herbs in the more informal societies of North America, Australia and New Zealand.

### MEDITERRANEAN FLAVOURS

For informal and outdoor parties, the Mediterranean sunshine flavours are loved by children as well as adults. Warm, spicy Basil fulfils its destiny with tomatoes; savoury Garlic, sweet-spicy Marjoram and pungent Oregano join sauces and pizzas. Thyme flavours the wine used to simmer poultry and shellfish; warm, tangy Tarragon infuses chicken and vinegars; and refreshing Lemon Balm is added to oils, vinegars and fruit salads.

### SHARP AND SPICY

From Scandinavia and Eastern Europe comes an appreciation of aromatic Dill, the flowerheads for pickles, the seeds in bread and apple pie, and the leaves to flavour the 'celebration fish', salmon; of breath-sweetening Caraway seeds, with a history reaching back to stone-age meals; and cheeky Paprika, whose colour is stronger than its bite in goulash, pickles and cheese. Fennel adds aniseed hints to salads and fish, while subtle, musky green anise-flavoured Chervil, one of the French *fines herbes*, is used to garnish and flavour delicate dishes. Sorrel gives zest

to Russian soups; Angelica stems are cooked as vegetables or have their sharp flavour tempered by crystallization; and Horseradish (*Armoracia rusticana*) has metamorphosed from a smoked fish and chicken condiment in the East to the traditional flavouring for roast beef in England.

## HISTORIC ASSOCIATIONS

Interest in unusual flavours has been kindled by historic recipes. Game and poultry marinated with Juniper berries echo Tudor banquets; the beefy celery-like leaves of medieval Lovage season broths and chicken; and Wild Celery, or Smallage, a Roman ingredient, is cooked in soups and stews. Apicius' first-century Roman cookery book includes an extraordinary range of herb flavourings including Rue and Pennyroyal (not recommended today), Alecost, Asafoetida, Catmint, Myrtle berries, Safflower (*Carthamus tinctorius*), Spikenard and Sumach (*Rhus syriacum*). Peppery Savory, mentioned in Virgil's poetry, is still used to transform bean dishes.

Grandmother's recipe book reveals milk puddings flavoured with Scented Geraniums, and acid fruits cooked with Sweet Cicely to reduce the sugar needed. High-profile chefs have shared their enthusiasms to revive the use of herbs such as Lavender, once an Elizabethan seasoning and now used to flavour vinegars and home-made ice-cream.

## EXOTIC SEASONINGS

Foreign holidays continue our flavouring education. Spanish and Arab dishes have renewed the popularity of Saffron, although its strangely rich, earthy flavour was also a medieval English luxury. Traditional paella, bouillabaisse and Cornish cakes are joined by new dishes where Saffron flavours fish, poultry, beef, breads and even ice-cream. Coconut milk, Lemon Grass, Kaffir Lime and Galangal root (*Alpinia galanga*) are popular Thai ingredients.

The wide range of popular Indian foods reflects that huge and vibrant nation. Curry flavourings include Coriander seed, Cumin, Fenugreek (*Trigonella foenum-graecum*), Chilli, Ginger, Black Pepper, Cardamom, Curry Leaf, Mustard, Nutmeg, Clove and Cinnamon. Coriander's strangely pungent leaves also make a vital contribution to Indian, Arab and South American cuisine. The elusive secret of Indian vegetarian dishes includes the intensely yellow, muskily dry Turmeric, and fetid Asafoetida, used in minute amounts for its unique oniony flavour. These are to be found in Indian grocery stores, where you might also come across Kewra water, made from the Fragrant Screwpine and used to flavour Indian sweetmeats for honoured guests.

FAR LEFT: *Aromatic feathery Dill and Rosemary.*

TOP LEFT: *Decorate tinkling ice-cubes for long summer drinks with starry-blue Borage flowers.*

LEFT: *Sprinkle perky Chive florets over stir-fries and nectar-rich Rosemary flowers on fruit salads.*

*Starting at the garden gate, any of the refreshing or sweetly scented herbs that release their fragrance on contact will create a welcoming ambience for guests.*

# An Aromatic Welcome

Along the entrance path grow Basil, Bergamot, Catmint, Hyssop, Eau-de-Cologne Mint, Lavender, Lemon Balm, Pinks, Rosemary, Sage, Savory, Southernwood, Sweet Fern, Thymes or Wall Germander.

Use pot-grown fragrant herbs to create an aromatic passageway through the front porch, hall and stairway. Choose from Bay, Lemon Verbena, Sweet Myrtle, Scented Geraniums, Incense Plant (*Calomeria amaranthoides*), Australian Mint Bush (*Prostanthera* species), Balm of Gilead, Pineapple or Tangerine Sages, Thymes, Citrus shrubs or tender Lavenders such as *Lavandula dentata*. These can be moved around to suit special occasions – a neatly shaped Lemon Verbena or Tangerine Sage as a table centre, Basil or Mint near the barbecue for flavouring and as an insect deterrent, or a collection of pots positioned to create a lush setting for an alfresco lunch.

Bunches of fresh herbs and sweetly scented flowers have instant visual and aromatic appeal. They can be arranged in generous bucketfuls, loose, informal bouquets or small, pretty posies. Indoors, float a single Peony flower in a glass goldfish bowl or a Sweet Violet in a silver eggcup.

ABOVE: *A town garden path is edged with welcoming aromatic Thymes.*

FAR RIGHT: *A generous and sweetly scented walkway of Lavender and Roses.*

RIGHT: *Entranceways and terraces lend themselves to the ancient tradition of strewing herbs – here Lavender, Sage and Catmint.*

## STREWING HERBS

Consider adopting the centuries-old tradition of strewing fragrant herbs underfoot. Sprinkle leaves or small branches outdoors on an approach path, porch or verandah; carpet the deck, terrace or garden seating area; and use them indoors as a welcoming mat or under the corner of a carpet. According to your personal preferences, or perhaps a particular mood you wish to invoke, make your choice from Alecost, Lavender, Lemon Balm, Lemon Verbena, Meadowsweet, Melilot, Mints, Mugwort, Rosemary, Sage, Southernwood, Sweet Cicely, Sweet Fern, Sweet Flag (*Acorus calamus*), Sweet Grass, Sweet Marjoram, Sweet Myrtle, Sweet Woodruff, Lemon Thyme, *Thymus* 'Fragrantissimus' or *T. odoratus*, and Pine, Eucalyptus, Thuja or Cedar branches. Even clearing away the herbs is a pleasant aromatic task.

*A garden approach with eye-catching shapes, cheerful colours and sweet scents creates a welcoming atmosphere while the aromatic garden makes a pleasant setting for entertaining.*

# Herbal Topiary

As a welcoming device, a clipped evergreen shape of Bay, Box, Lavender, Rosemary, Santolina, Savory, Sweet Myrtle, shrubby Thyme or upright Wall Germander creates a distinct and positive effect – consider the traditional ball-shaped Bays placed outside restaurants. The presence of a topiary plant says 'creative endeavour' and indicates cherished care, its completed features signal reliability, and any novelty aspect hints at mischievous fun. Both indoors and out, topiary is a conversational focal point and highlights the contrasting soft, natural shapes of other herbs. To these qualities, add aromatic leaves to brush by, pat, stroke, sniff, smile at or otherwise engage with, and you have a winning combination, especially by the front door.

## Creating Shapes

Topiary plants can be worked into formal, eccentric or romantic shapes, either in pots or growing in the ground. Choose from geometric balls, cones, columns, pyramids and spirals, symbolic shapes with personal meaning, and jovial animals or objects. Before starting to create your own topiary, it is worth studying other examples: the proportions of stem length, bulk of greenery and pot size are very important to the overall effect.

Clipping is itself a therapeutic and aromatic task. With small plants like dwarf Box, shaping begins when the plant has reached its desired height. A wire net of the required shape is placed over the plant and anything growing outside the shape is removed. Box is the most popular for intricate forms, herb garden borders and knots, because it responds well to clipping and its condensed root system does not spread out and interfere with neighbouring plants. Box hedging is expensive

because it is slow growing, but it is possible to buy a few starter plants to grow on for cuttings until you have enough plants to start a hedge.

To maintain a topiary shape or hedge, clip twice a year: once in late spring or early summer, after new shoots have formed, and again in late summer, allowing time for subsequent new shoots to ripen before the first frosts. This system means that the plant will be clothed in new shoots for most of the year and will maintain a fresh, lively appearance sometimes lacking in evergreens.

### MAKING A BALL-SHAPED BAY

Begin the training process by cultivating just one central stem, removing lower side branches as the shrub grows. Clipping the ball to shape begins when the plant is 15 cm (6 in) taller than the required height, so that the central growing tip can be cut back to encourage the side branches to produce a denser sphere. Trim the side shoots in the sphere to 2–3 leaves. When they have formed 4–5 leaves, clip back again to 2–3 leaves and repeat until the ball shape is achieved. Thereafter, prune with secateurs in early and late summer to maintain the shape, and remove suckers as they appear.

In cold areas, Bay must be grown in pots and taken in under protection for winter, especially in the early years. In borderline climates, use agricultural fleece to protect young plants from frosts, but do not give up on brown-leaved specimens which appear to have been killed – wait for warm weather, and if there was a good root system below the frost level, new shoots will sprout. On the second attempt, leave 7–9 stems up to the ball shape, as this helps to protect against frost damage.

### QUICK SCENTED SHAPES

Other shaped specimens can be created more quickly, using wire frames or hazel wigwams to support plants of Honeysuckle, Akebia, Jasmine, Wisteria or Roses. To train an umbrella-shaped standard, encourage a strong single stem to the desired height, then train stems over an upturned hanging basket for 2 years to give a good shape, and enjoy the aromatic strands wafting in the breeze.

ABOVE: *Topiary Bay and Rosemary globes with a spiral of Box. Secure your works of art firmly to prevent light-fingered admirers from whisking them away.*

Creative topiary in the famous Villandry garden highlights bright Cosmos flowers (above)
and illustrates contrasting textures of Box and Lavender (below)

# Propagating Herbs

## Seed

Seed can be sown directly into the ground if the soil has been prepared to a fine tilth. Sowing *in situ* is best for the annual umbellifers (Aniseed, Chervil, Dill, Coriander and Cumin, and biennial Parsley), as transplanting may cause them to run to seed before they have produced a useful crop of leaves. Suitable for:

ANNUALS Aniseed, Basil, Borage, Calendula, Chamomile (annual), Chervil, Coriander, Cumin, Dill, Mustard, Nasturtium, Opium poppy, Orach, Purslane, Salad Rocket, Summer Savory, Sweet Marjoram.

BIENNIALS Angelica, Caraway, Parsley (curled and broad-leaf), Smallage (Wild Celery), Woad.

PERENNIALS Chamomile (perennial, flowering), Chives, Fennel (green and bronze), Feverfew, Good King Henry, Lovage, Marjoram (French), Oregano, Rue, Sage, Salad Burnet, Sorrel, Sweet Cicely, Thyme (common), Welsh onion, Wormwood.

## Cuttings

A healthy parent plant is important for good-quality cuttings. The younger the parent plant, the more easily the cuttings will root. Suitable for:

Bay (with heat), Box, Curry Plant, Hyssop, Lavender, Lemon Verbena, Marjoram, Pelargonium, Rosemary, Rue (*Ruta graveolens* 'Jackman's Blue'), Sage, Santolina, Tarragon (French), Thyme, Winter Savory, Wormwood (cultivars).

## Root Sections

This is the easiest form of propagation. Take 5–10cm (2–4in) pieces of root, each with growing buds, and plant approximately 2.5cm (1in) deep in a pot of compost. Longer pieces are better if you are planting straight into the ground. Suitable for: Bergamot, Mint, Soapwort, Sweet Woodruff.

## Root Cuttings

A few herbs, such as Horseradish, Comfrey and Skirret, can be propagated from thick pieces of root 5–7.5cm (2–3in) long. Make a neat cutting, with the top flat and the bottom sloping so that you will remember which way is up, and insert vertically into potting compost topped with a 6mm ($^1/_4$ in) layer of sand.

## Division

Many herbs can be divided by digging up the plant, preferably in autumn or spring, and carefully separating the sections, each with a growing point and some roots. Replant or pot up, and water until the roots have re-established themselves. Some plants, such as Lovage, can be sliced vertically through the thick root, ensuring that each piece has a growing top.

Bulbous plants such as Chives and Everlasting Onion can be pulled apart in the same manner and replanted.

Aloe Vera produces offshoots (mini plants around the base) which can be removed carefully in summer, left to dry for a day and then replanted in sandy compost.
Suitable for:
Alecost, Bistort, Camphor Plant, Chamomile (lawn), Cowslip, Elecampane, Good King Henry, Lemon Balm, Lungwort, Marjoram, Meadowsweet, Primrose, Skirret, Sorrel, Sweet Joe Pye, Sweet Violet, Tansy, Tarragon (French), Wall Germander, Wormwood (Roman).

# A Potager of Seasonal Herbs

Growing herbs in attractive and convenient beds is not only useful to the entertaining cook, who can pick that vital extra sprig as needed, but also provides an enjoyable background setting for outdoor dining. Here, guests can stroll among the beds and select an unusual garnish, try a new edible flower or experiment with a novel salad ingredient.

This activity also realigns us with seasonal crops. Cooks and gourmets worldwide would agree with the Italian garden proverb 'Everything is good in its season', and value highly the intense flavour of home-grown strawberries in early summer, the first new potatoes with fresh Mint or Dill, garden-fresh courgettes, baby carrots and peas with melted butter and Chives or Tarragon, and thin-skinned, sweet tomatoes ripening alongside lush Basil leaves. Each is enjoyed as it reaches its flavour peak.

BELOW & RIGHT: *These potagers at West Green, Hampshire, and Sudborough, Northamptonshire, show that productive gardening can also be attractive; standard plants add structural impact, and scented varieties will diffuse their perfume at head height.*

# Creating a Potager

A potager is a garden planted with a decorative and useful mix of herbs, vegetables and fruit. To create one in a small town garden, raised beds offer a controllable, tidy, easy-to-maintain-and-harvest solution that is remarkably productive in a small space.

Decide on a few special vegetables such as dwarf beans, courgettes and ruby chard that taste infinitely better straight from the garden. Choose a fruit such as fig, grape, apple, pear, cherry or peach that can be espaliered or grown horizontally along a fence or on an arch over the path. Then select your favourite herbs and edible flowers, concentrating on variegated, purple and gold forms for extra visual interest. Consider which you need in bulk, such as Chives and Parsley, and those for which a single plant would be sufficient, like Sage.

Possible edging herbs include evergreen dwarf Box, Lavender 'Hidcote', Curry Plant, upright Wall Germander, Alpine Strawberry and golden Feverfew; herbaceous Chives and Winter Marjoram; biennial Parsley; and colourful annual Calendula, Tagetes and Nasturtium. Give Basil a sunny, protected site where you can keep an eye open for the myriad small insects, snails, birds and larger creatures that share our delight in its flavour.

Remember to keep the centre of each bed a reachable distance, which is about 75 cm (2ft 6in) creating a bed 150 cm (5 ft) across, and paths wide enough for a wheelbarrow. In small areas hard paths are preferred to grass as it can be difficult to get a mower into the space. Before planting ensure the soil is absolutely weed-free and enriched with compost. This will allow crops to be planted closer than in a normal garden. By raising the beds a few inches and enclosing them, you will improve the drainage and the plants will be easier to crop.

# Small Potager Plan

The design on the opposite page is for a small potager for town or country. It displays the patterns of a potager both as a decorative setting for outdoor entertaining and as the freshest possible source of gourmet vegetables and fruit. Guests can enjoy a garden stroll and select their favourite edible flower or try a new unusual herb garnish.

Formal edgings of Lavender, Dwarf box and Curry Plant provide a year round design element while the standard-grown ball-Bay and wigwams of climbing Beans and Sweet Peas add height to the visual interest.

## Salad garden

The mini salad potager of 'cut-and-come-again' crops is grown in a movable sink or trough for convenient use and to catch the sun. For 'cut-and-come-again' crops, sow a carpet of seeds in fertile soil. Grow to around 15 cm (6 in) tall, removing any dead leaves and then crop with scissors or sharp knife to 5 cm (2 in). Use the tasty tender leaves in salads, soups, sandwiches, casseroles and as garnish. If kept well watered and fertilized, crops can be harvested three to five times. Experiment with seedling crops of other salad herbs such as Fennel, Orach and Lemon Balm.

LEFT: *A potager in Spring. Neatly clipped edging creates strong visual interest throughout winter months and provides both contrast and restraint to vigorous summer growth.*

# List of Plants in Plan

### Terrace
1. Mini Salad Potager containing surround edging of clipped chives; 'V' shape dividers of Oak Leaf Lettuce, one purple; one green; 'Cut-and-Come-Again' pattern in-fills: Mustard (*Brassica* spp), Cress (*Lepidium sativum*), Salad Rocket, Fenugreek (*Trigonella foenum-graecum*); Chop Suey Greens (Edible Chrysanthemum), Summer Purslane (*Portulacae oleracea*); Winter Purslane (*Montia perfoliata*)
2. Lemon Verbena
3. Mints (Moroccan Spearmint, Black Peppermint)

4. Climbing Speckled French (Snap) Bean 'Tongue of Fire' (red streaked pods)

5. Claret-leaved Grape ('Teinturier' or 'Miller's Burgundy')

6. Sage

7. Prostrate Rosemary

8. Golden Lemon Thyme

## Potager Garden

9. Espaliered Apple (scented flowers also edible)

10. Espaliered Pear

11. Akebia

12. Lavender 'Hidcote'

13. Chives

14. Tarragon

15. Dwarf French Beans 'Purple Tepee'

16. Dwarf Box

17. Calendula

18. Carrot 'Early Nantes'

19. Parsley Curled

20. Purple Basil

21. Madonna Lily

22. Bergamot

23. Rose 'Evelyn'

24. Nasturtium 'Alaska'

25. Ruby Chard

26. Borage

27. Curry Plant

28. Marjoram

29. Bay

30. Sugar Snap Pea

31. Coriander

32. Fan-trained Cherry 'Morello'

33. Dill

34. Runner Bean 'Polestar' (to attract hummingbirds)

35. Sweet Corn 'Little Jewels' (purple husks)

36. Courgettes 'Clarella'

37. Squash 'Patti Pan'

37. Sweet Peas

38. Fan-trained Peach

A glance around the rooms of your home will reveal a number of opportunities to apply aromatics for a slow release of subtle background fragrance.

ABOVE: *Queen Anne's seventeenth-century Rosemary Room Scenter.*

# *Welcoming Fragrance Indoors*

### ROSEMARY ROOM SCENTER

Queen Anne's confectioner, Mary Eales, wrote down her favourite recipes (then called receipts) in 1682. This scenter is simple to make and smells clean and sweet. She suggests: 'Take three spoonfuls of dried and powdered rosemary and as much sugar to fill half a walnut, beaten into a powder. Scatter into a perfume pan over hot embers and soon the room will be filled with delicious perfume'. Take the same ratio of ingredients, grind them together in a pestle and mortar, and heat for 2–3 minutes in a heavy pan on a cooking ring. Stir occasionally to prevent the mix from sticking, then turn off the heat. The mixture will scent the room beautifully and can be carried through others.

## *Vaporizing Oils and Spices*

Vaporizing oils in a burner will provide a room with continuous fragrance. The oils are not actually burned – drops are placed in a pottery container of hot water, which is held above a small candle or electric heater. As the oils and water evaporate, fragrance spreads through the room to create the mood of your choice. Try a clean, refreshing scent in the entrance area; an inviting, relaxing blend to put guests at ease; an energizing, convivial mix to get the party going; or a rich, warm but bright fragrance to accompany stimulating conversation.

Fill the reservoir of the oil burner just over half full with hot water. Sprinkle in a few drops of essential oil. Light the small candle beneath and allow 5–10 minutes for the scent to diffuse. If the reservoir is kept topped up, the scent should last for 2–3 hours and change intriguingly as the various aromatic components evaporate at different rates.

## *Vaporizing Oil Mixes*

### SINGLE NOTES

A few oils are pleasant on their own: try Benzoin, Bergamot, Coriander, Grapefruit, Ho Wood, Juniper, Petitgrain, Rose Maroc, Rosewood, Rose Geranium or Silver Fir.

### GREGARIOUS BLENDS

The following mixes are light, bright and lively:
A. 2 drops each Grapefruit and Lavender.
B. 1 drop each Clove, Sweet Marjoram and Orange or Mandarin.
C. 2 drops each Peppermint and Rose Maroc.

### AN EXOTIC TOUCH

A. 3 drops Bergamot, 1 drop Ylang-Ylang.
B. 3 drops Rose Maroc, 1 drop Ginger.
C. 1/2 tsp Vanilla essence, 2 drops Lime.

### FOR STIMULATING CONVERSATION

These mixes are deep yet refreshing:
A. 1 drop each Juniper, Cypress and Bergamot.
B. 2 drops each Silver Fir and Benzoin.
C. 3 drops Frankincense, 2 drops Basil.

### RELAXING AMBIENCE

A. 1 drop each Rose Geranium and Hyssop.
B. 1 drop Vetiver, 3 drops Mandarin.

### CHRISTMAS WELCOME

2 drops each Lavender, Orange, Cinnamon, Clove.

## *Vaporizing Spices*

Place whole spices in the hot water of an oil burner and allow 30 minutes for the scent to intensify. Spices work well both singly and in combination. Choose from 1/4 Vanilla pod, 2 Star Anise, 3–4 Cardamoms, 6 Cloves or Allspice, 1/2 tsp Coriander seeds, Juniper berries or black Peppercorns, a piece of Cinnamon bark (or Cassia), Ginger root or Lemon Grass, coarsely grated Nutmeg, or thin shreds of Lemon, Orange or Lime peel. A sprinkling of sugar will enhance any of these. Powdered spices can be used but will develop a 'cooked' smell.

**TOP LEFT:** Large open containers encourage handling of potpourri to release its scent.

**TOP RIGHT:** Enjoy the elegance and sweet fragrance of 'one perfect rose'.

**BOTTOM LEFT:** Star Anise has a warm spicy scent as exotic as its appearance, and can be added whole to water in a burner.

**BOTTOM RIGHT:** The deep reservoir of this burner is ideal for parties and family gatherings as it seldom needs extra water.

## Wreaths and Swags

For subtle background fragrance, fresh and dried herbs can be fashioned into the solid shapes of wreaths or hangings for doors and walls, and the fluid sweeps of garlands and swags to surround tables, doorways, windows, mirrors, pictures or a mantelpiece, to climb pillars or posts, or to hang outdoors from branches over seats and tables. The style can range from a sumptuous Caribbean riot of colour and spices, to the epitome of elegance and refinement. Follow a seasonal theme with refreshing spring flowers, glorious summer abundance, autumn harvest or the intriguing textures and subtle fragrance of winter offerings.

ABOVE: *A sumptuous swag features Figs, Brazil nuts, Walnuts, Cinnamon quills and Nutmeg with green highlights of Rosemary, Thyme and Moss.*

RIGHT: *Delight a keen cook with a lush aromatic swag of Purple Sage, deep green Bay, Bronze Fennel and bright Applemint studded with Garlic cloves and Chillies.*

### MAKING A WREATH

Weave a base of Willow, Hazel, Lemon Verbena, Thyme or Rosemary stems into the desired shape while they are half dried and still supple. Alternatively, cover a wire base with sphagnum moss, binding it on with reel wire, or purchase a braided raffia base.

On a wreath or hanging, you are working on the front surface only. Cut small, even-lengthed branches of the main background herb, using an evergreen such as Bay, Box, Sweet Myrtle or Eucalyptus. Place them in small, overlapping groups all facing in the same direction and bind these in with wire until the base is covered. Wire in additional herbs, berries, seed pods and dried flowers, following an aromatic mood or colour theme. When all the dried elements have been attached, tuck in fresh herbs and flowers as desired.

Make an appetizing kitchen hanging with bunches of culinary herbs and spices: gorgeous red Chillies, dark Vanilla pods, Cinnamon quills and white Garlic bulbs, on a background of the contrasting leaves of Bay, Rosemary, Fennel, Ginger Mint, Golden Marjoram, Purple Sage and silver-variegated Thyme, which are then all available for emergency culinary use.

### MAKING A GARLAND OR SWAG

These can be made with fresh or dried herbs and are woven all around a central string to create a flexible 'rope' of foliage. Fresh herbs will last longer in cool rooms and are useful as an accent in dried garlands. Choose your fresh herbs from Allium, Artemisia, Bay, Basil, Box, Elder flowers and berries, Eucalyptus, Fennel, Juniper, Lavender, Lily, Pine, Rosemary, Rose, Rosehip, Scented Geranium and Sweet Myrtle; and flowering tops of Angelica, Anise Hyssop, Bergamot, Calendula, Chamomile, Dill, Feverfew, Hyssop, Lady's Mantle, Lily-of-the-Valley, Marjoram, Meadowsweet, Tansy and Yarrow. Dried herbs and spices can include Cinnamon quills, Clove buds, Eucalyptus, Lavender, Rose buds, Thyme, Vanilla pods and Yarrow.

Assemble all the ingredients before starting and mist fresh herbs periodically to keep them perky. Wire the plant material into small bunches of 3 or 5 stems. Cut the appropriate length of string, allowing for a hanging loop at each end and in the sections as needed. Bind the small bunches of herbs on to the string at intervals, varying the colours and textures. Work in a spiral to create an even, 'plump' garland. Decorate with ribbon or baubles.

ABOVE: *A circlet of warmly coloured herbs and floating aromatic candles add to the bonhomie of a small supper party.*

## Scented Candles

Most commercial candles are scented with synthetic fragrances, but there are several ways in which you can scent your own with true essential oils. Always remember that essential oils are flammable, so never apply them when a candle is lit.

Spray the outside of a candle with a perfume blend, or mix 3 drops green or floral oil with 1 drop Benzoin, Oakmoss or other fixative oil and paint this mixture over the candle.

Buy a candle-making kit and stir essential oils into the wax-paraffin blend just before pouring it into the moulds.

Buy a fat candle, light it to melt the top layer of wax, extinguish the flame, and then stir a few drops of essential oil into the melted wax to trap oil molecules within it. With a wide candle and a short wick, the fragrance can last for an hour. The process can then be repeated. Candles made from the balsamic Wax Myrtle berries burn with a mild spiciness.

127

## Fragrancing Dining Areas

Fragrance dining areas subtly to complement, not overpower, food aromas.

### TABLE CENTRES

Conjure up Edwardian refinement with an elegant wreath around silver candlesticks. Use a restricted colour scheme, with decorative greens from Lady's Mantle, Angelica leaves and green Fennel, silver Artemisia, and Sweet Peas or Roses. Celebrate a summer event in dramatic style with a rainbow river of aromatic fresh fruits such as Star Fruit, Pineapple, Strawberries, Papaya, Grapes, Mango, Peaches and Kiwi, plus herbs and flowers, all spilling across the table.

Spray decorative seed heads gold or silver and sprinkle them amid Ginger Mint leaves, double Poppies, scarlet Bergamot, golden Calendula and blue Geranium or Borage flowers. Add a sprig of Lemon Balm to water jugs and make ice cubes with Rose petals, Violet or Borage flowers, or a Peppermint leaf embedded.

### PLACE SETTINGS

Make invitations or place-name cards with a favourite herb recipe and sprig of the appropriate herb, or with Rosemary for remembrance, Southernwood or Lavender. Set a small posy vase with sprigs of culinary herbs with which guests can flavour and garnish their food individually. Choose from Parsley, Chervil, Mint, Salad Rocket, Sorrel, Borage, Calendula, Purple Orach, Lemon Thyme and Salad Burnet. Make individual celebration crackers containing a package of cook's aromatics: a Vanilla pod, crystallized Angelica stems, Star Anise and Cinnamon quills.

## OUTDOOR DINING

Try straight stems of Thyme, Bay, Savory or Rosemary as kebab skewers; lay Thyme, Hyssop or Savory sprigs over barbecue embers to flavour food; or rub a tiny piece of Asafoetida on the grill for an exotic earthy, smoked flavour. Throw Lavender stems over the embers when you have finished, to banish cooking smells and insects, and infuse Lemon Verbena in water for refreshing fingerbowls.

In hot weather, give guests paper fans scented with a cooling, insect-repelling essential oil such as Mint or Lavender – sprinkle 3 drops on a fan and seal in a plastic bag for a few days. Alternatively, make a fan by threading together large, fresh aromatic leaves like Alecost, Bay or Lettuce-leaf Basil, or bind together leafy stems of Mint or Lemon Verbena, or a mixture.

## *Fragrancing Living Areas*

An imaginative eye will discover potential areas where welcoming fragrance can be introduced.

## AROMATIC SCATTER CUSHIONS

These offer an unexpected delight as fragrance is released when guests lean against them. They can be adjusted easily to the seasons; try a single herb such as Angelica, Alecost or Sweet Gale or cheerful combinations like the Welcoming Potpourri below. Loosely woven fabric is fine for large leaves and chunky spices, but close weave or an inner muslin envelope is needed if you want to add dried leaves and spice powders. The following mixtures can also be used in curtain hems, in pockets of room dividers or anywhere else where contact or movement will release the scent.

## WELCOMING POTPOURRI

This fresh and spicy potpourri is made using the dry method (see page 64).

Fill a brass display bowl two-thirds full with Lemon Verbena leaves. Add a small handful each Bay and Eau-de-Cologne or Basil Mint, and 2 tbsp mixed Orange, Lemon and Lime peel. Lightly crush

2 tsp each Juniper berries and Angelica seeds and add with 4 Star Anise.

For party colour, add a mixture of red Tulip or Poppy petals, whole Calendula flowers, whole orange Roses, red and orange Nasturtiums, orange Day Lilies, Rowan berries or Rosehips, blue Larkspurs or Delphiniums, and Sage flowers. 'Garnish' with fresh scarlet Bergamot flowers and Dill flowerheads.

## COOK'S POTPOURRI

This treat for the cook and kitchen visitors is made by the dry method (see page 64). Crush half of each of the following ingredients for aroma, leaving the remainder whole for texture and to crush for refreshing the mix: 2 cups Sweet Marjoram; 1 cup Lemon Verbena; $1/2$ cup each Basil leaves, Basil flowering tops, Thyme and Bay; $1/4$ cup each Hyssop and Tarragon; $1/8$ cup each Lovage, Golden Sage and mixed Orange, Lemon and Lime peels; 20 each Allspice, Cardamom pods, Star Anise, Juniper berries and Cloves; 3 Nutmegs; 2 Cinnamon sticks; 1 Vanilla pod.

## SUNSHINE MIX

Choose from summer's bounty with dried Lemon Verbena, Pineapple Sage, pine- or fruit-scented Thymes, Eau-de-Cologne Mint and Scented Geranium leaves – perhaps *Pelargonium quercifolium*, with its incense fragrance. Grate in some Nutmeg for a warmer hint.

## WINTER COMFORT

To dried Rose petals, Basil and Bay, add a broken Cinnamon stick.

## AROMATIC GAMES

The Japanese incense game is a refined pursuit packaged in beautiful lacquered boxes with small, delicately carved implements and trays on which incense materials are presented to blindfolded guests to identify. Rewards are given for correct identification and, more importantly, for a stylish recital of the seasonal memory associations which each aromatic substance evokes.

ABOVE: *An individual garnish posy with Parsley, Coriander, Basil, Lemon Balm, Chervil and Mint.*

ABOVE: *A napkin sprig of Lemon Verbena and Scented Geranium.*

# Culinary Herbs

## Salad & Garnish Herbs

An ever-growing range of aromatic leaves and flower petals is turning today's salads and garnishes into a nutritional adventure. Fern-like Salad Burnet framing a salad dish, Calendula petals glistening in salad oil, Nasturtium flowers decorating shellfish – each adds visual and textural pleasure for the delighted taste buds.

AROMATIC Alecost, Anise Hyssop, Basil, Borage, Caraway, Chervil, Chives, Coriander, Dill, Fennel, Lemon Balm, Lemon Thyme, Lovage, Marjoram, Mint, Nasturtium, Parsley, Salad Burnet, Salad Rocket.

NON-AROMATIC Chicory, Cress, Lettuce, Mustard, Orach, Sorrel, Summer Purslane, Winter Purslane, Watercress.

BELOW: *A dashing salad with Red Poppies, Purple Orach and Salad Rocket.*

## Edible Flowers

Choose clean, undamaged petals and remove bitter green parts and the white base of Rose petals.

SCENTED Anise Hyssop, Bergamot, Chive, Dill, Honeysuckle, Jasmine, Nasturtium, Pea, Bean, Pink, Radish pods, Rose, Rosemary, Salad Rocket, Sweet Myrtle, Sweet Pea, Sweet Rocket, Sweet Violet and Sweet Woodruff.

UNSCENTED Borage, Calendula, Chicory, Cornflower, Heartsease, Marsh Mallow, Mullein, Musk Mallow, Poppy, Primrose, Safflower.

## Fish

COOKED Basil, Bay, Caraway, Chervil, Chives, Dill, Fennel, Lemon Balm, Lemon Thyme, Lovage, Marjoram, Mint, Parsley.

RAW The following kill parasites: Shiso (*Perilla frutescens*), Wasabi (*W. japonica*).

## Game and Poultry

Bay, Juniper, Lovage seed, Rosemary, Sage, Savory, Sweet Marjoram.

## Meat

BEEF Basil, Bay, Caraway seed, Chervil, Lovage, Mint, Oregano, Parsley, Rosemary, Sage, Savory, Tarragon, Thyme.

POT ROASTS Bay, Marjoram, Thyme.

LAMB Basil, Chervil, Cumin, Dill, Lemon Balm, Marjoram, Mint, Parsley, Rosemary, Savory, Thyme.

PORK Chervil, Coriander, Fennel, Lovage seed, Marjoram, Rosemary, Sage, Savory, Thyme.

HAM Juniper berries, Lovage, Marjoram, Mint, Mustard, Oregano, Parsley, Rosemary, Savory.

## Eggs and Cheese

Basil, Chervil, Chives, Dill, Parsley, Tarragon.

## Vegetables

ARTICHOKES Bay, Savory, Tarragon.

AVOCADO Dill, Marjoram, Tarragon.

CABBAGE Caraway, Dill seed, Marjoram, Parsley, Sage, Savory, Sweet Cicely, Thyme.

CARROTS Chervil, Parsley.

GREEN BEANS Dill, Marjoram, Mint, Oregano, Rosemary, Sage, Savory, Tarragon.

MARROW Basil, Dill, Marjoram, Tarragon.

POTATOES Basil, Bay, Chives, Dill, Lovage, Marjoram, Mint, Oregano, Parsley, Rosemary, Savory, Thyme.

PULSES Asafoetida, Coriander, Cumin, Garlic.

SPINACH Borage, Chervil, Marjoram, Mint, Nutmeg, Rosemary (soup), Sage, Sorrel, Tarragon.

TOMATOES Basil, Bay, Chervil, Chives, Dill, Fennel, Garlic, Marjoram, Mint, Oregano, Parsley, Sage, Savory, Tarragon.

## Oils

SAVOURY Basil, Garlic, Fennel, Marjoram, Mint, Rosemary, Savory, Tarragon, Thyme.

SWEET Lavender, Lemon Balm, Lemon Verbena, Pink, Rose.

## Vinegars

HERBS Basil, Bay, Chervil, Chives, Dill, Fennel, Garlic, Horseradish, Lemon Balm, Lemon Verbena, Mint, Nasturtium, Pot Marjoram, Rosemary, Salad Burnet, Savory, Sweet Marjoram, Tarragon, Thyme.
FLOWERS Elder, Lavender, Nasturtium, Primrose, Rose, Rosemary, Thyme, Sweet Violet.

## Wine Cups

LEAVES Angelica, Clary Sage, Lemon Balm, Lemon Verbena, Mint, Rosemary, Salad Burnet.
LEAVES AND FLOWERS Bergamot, Borage, Sweet Woodruff.

## Digestive Seeds

Several culinary traditions offer a final dish which includes aromatic seeds with digestive properties. The Romans served small aniseed cakes at the end of a banquet, the forerunner of spicy Christmas and wedding cakes. Caraway seeds are traditionally served with apples and cheese. Try the Elizabethan tradition of Fennel, Dill or Caraway seeds dipped in egg-white, sprinkled with white sugar and dried in a slow oven.

The traditional 'four warming seeds' consist of an equal mix of Aniseed, Caraway, Coriander and Fennel to create a tasty blend that relieves indigestion and flatulence. Indian restaurants offer a small bowl of roasted seeds to nibble after a rich meal, which double as a breath freshener.

## Desserts

Angelica, Aniseed, Bergamot, Elderflower, Fragrant Screwpine, Lemon Balm, Lemon Verbena, Pineapple and Tangerine Sage, Rose petals, Rosemary, Saffron, Scented Geranium leaves, Sweet Cicely leaves and green seed, Violet flowers.

## Bread

Aniseed, Basil, Caraway, Chives, Dill, Fennel, Lovage seed, Poppy seed, Rosemary, Sesame seed, Thyme.

# Easter Lunch

As well as the traditional eggs and chocolate, Easter is a good time to celebrate the arrival of lovely new spring vegetables and the first stirrings of meadow flowers.

## Chicken in the Nest

*None of the flavours are allowed to escape from the pot during cooking, so this dish is as deliciously fragrant as it is healthy. It is also a great way to spring-clean your stock of last year's home-dried herbs before they lose their aroma. If time is short, use a double layer of foil under the lid instead of a flour paste 'sausage' to seal the pot.*

**preparation: 15 minutes; cooking: 1 hour**

*1 tbsp olive oil*
*1 large free-range chicken*
*2 handfuls or a large bunch of mixed dried herb sprigs*
*2 tsp balsamic vinegar*
*300 g / 10½ oz flour*
*1 tsp peppercorns, crushed*
*30 g / 1 oz butter*
*3 sprigs of curly-leaved Parsley, finely snipped*
*coarse sea salt and cracked black pepper*

Preheat the oven to 220°C/425°F/gas 7. Lightly oil a deep ovenproof casserole just a little larger than the chicken and which has a tight-fitting lid. Arrange the dried herbs in the casserole, put the chicken on top so that it nestles in the herbs and season lightly. Sprinkle with the balsamic vinegar.

Mix the flour with about 150 ml / ¼ pint of water to make a paste dough. Roll this into a long sausage shape. Place along the top edge of the casserole. Put the lid in place so that the dough seals the lid to the dish. Put in the oven and cook for about 1 hour.

Leave to settle in the switched-off oven for 10 minutes. Crack the paste seal open with a heavy knife and lift off the lid. Season the chicken with coarse sea salt and bruised pepper. Dress with a good knob of butter and, if you like, a sprinkling of fresh Parsley.

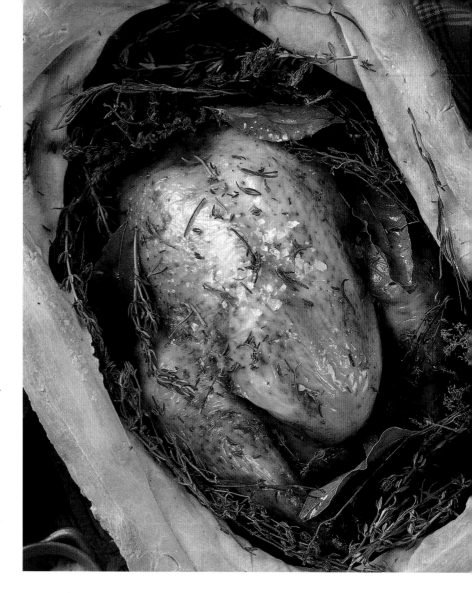

ABOVE: *Chicken in the Nest*

## Glazed Carrots and Turnips with Thyme and Parsley

**preparation : 15 minutes; cooking: about 35 minutes**

*about 400g / 14 oz unblemished baby turnips*
*about 400 g / 14 oz neat small carrots*
*2 tsp sugar*
*½ tsp ground Ginger*
*spriglets from several sprigs of fresh Thyme*
*1 scant tbsp light soy sauce*
*60 g / 2 oz chilled butter, diced*
*few sprigs of curly-leaved Parsley, snipped*
*sea salt and freshly ground black pepper*

Spread the vegetables in a large sauté pan. Season and sprinkle with the sugar and Ginger. Snip over the Thyme spriglets, reserving a few to finish, then drizzle over the soy sauce. Pour in just enough boiling water to cover. Distribute half the butter over the dish, place over a low heat and bring back to a simmer. Loosely cover the pan with foil, then cook over a moderate heat until just tender — the water will gradually evaporate and this will take about 20 minutes, depending on the age and quality of the vegetables. Shake the pan from time to time.

Turn up the heat, remove the foil and scatter over half the remaining butter. Sprinkle with a little of the Parsley, reserving the rest. Leave the vegetables to cook for about 10 minutes until golden and shiny, adding the rest of the butter a little at a time, shaking the pan frequently and turning over the vegetables from time to time. Keep an eye on the pan and reduce the heat if necessary.

Just before serving, adjust the seasoning, then sprinkle over the rest of the herbs and stir them in.

BELOW: *Chocolate Truffle Eggs with Crystallized Flowers, decorated with strips of candied Angelica.*

**Decorating ideas: chopped candied Angelica makes a nice backdrop for the Easter eggs. Try decorating the eggs with tiny Basil sprigs or experiment with a dusting of sugar and tiny curly-leaved Parsley sprigs sautéed in vegetable oil until crisp, then drained on paper towels — especially good with dark bitter chocolate.**

# Chocolate Truffle Eggs with Crystallized Flowers

*preparation: 10 minutes; cooking: 10 minutes, plus chilling*
*makes about 24 eggs*

*200 g / 7 oz top-quality dark chocolate, chopped into small pieces*
*3 tbsp crème fraîche, sour cream or whipping cream*
*1 tbsp caster sugar, or more if preferred*
*few drops of crème de menthe, Cointreau, Calvados, brandy, whisky or ginger wine*
*100 g / 3¹/₂ oz good-quality dark, milk or white chocolate, grated or melted, to finish*

*for the crystallized flowers:*
*Violet flowers, Primroses or Cherry blossoms, as available*
*1 egg white, lightly beaten*
*caster sugar*

Melt the chopped chocolate in a double boiler.

In a small pan, bring to the boil the crème fraîche and sugar. Stir into the melted chocolate, then stir in the chosen flavouring. Leave to cool, then chill until workable.

Shape the mixture into quail egg shapes and then chill until hardened.

To finish: coat the chocolate eggs with grated chocolate or dip into melted chocolate. Chill again until ready to use.

Prepare the crystallized flowers: using an artist's paint brush, paint the flowers with lightly beaten egg white, covering the whole surface lightly — this is fiddly but fun. Dust with caster sugar and leave to dry. Dust again with caster sugar and let dry completely. Shake off any excess sugar. The crystallized flowers will keep for 2 days only.

To serve: heap the eggs attractively and decorate with the crystallized flowers.

133

# Summer Barbecue

Mouthwatering smells wafting through the warm summer air... barbecues are an ideal opportunity to be extravagant with the season's crop of fresh herbs.

## Coriander Sardines with Montpellier Butter

*Shiny fresh sardines have a unique texture that is brought out to the full by simple grilling or barbecuing. Coriander complements the delicate taste, while robust sprigs of flat-leaf Parsley protect the fish and add to the flavours. Use the rich gutsy Montpellier Butter sparingly.*

**preparation: 20 minutes; barbecuing: 10 minutes**

4 medium-sized fresh sardines, cleaned, gutted and
    rinsed
½ tsp Coriander seeds
2 tbsp fruity olive oil
½ unwaxed lemon, thinly sliced
several sprigs each of fresh Coriander and flat-leaf
    Parsley
Montpellier Butter (see page 72)
sea salt and freshly ground black pepper

Prepare the barbecue in the usual way, throwing half the Coriander seeds over the coals. Crush some of the remaining seeds and set aside.

Lightly season the insides of the sardines, scatter in the reserved crushed Coriander seeds and sprinkle with olive oil. Cut each slice of lemon into quarters and put these in the sardines. Rub the outside with salt and pepper, then brush with more olive oil.

When the barbecue is hot enough, cook the sardines on the sprigs of fresh Coriander and flat-leaf Parsley, turning them over halfway through cooking, after about 5 minutes.

Serve with a little of the Montpellier Butter smeared on top.

## New Season's Potatoes Baked in Foil

*Barbecue cooks should have plenty of good-quality foil at the ready. Foil parcels make visually attractive cocoons for ingredients – they look inviting and insulate the food from excessive heat.*

*If your potatoes are too large, parboil them first for 5 minutes, then drain well, season and cook in foil. Chive butter ideally suits baby potatoes; with more mature potatoes, try Dill and Tarragon or Mint and Parsley.*

**preparation: 10 minutes; barbecuing: 20 minutes minimum**

½ recipe quantity Chive Butter (see page 72)
350 g / 12 oz small new potatoes, scrubbed
sea salt and freshly ground black pepper

Well ahead of time, make the Chive Butter as described on page 72 and put to chill.

Cut the foil into 4 double layers each large enough to enclose a helping of potatoes. Season the potatoes and wrap loosely in foil parcels. Cook on the hot barbecue grill (not immediately over the flames) until done, turning once after 10–15 minutes.

To serve, open the foil parcels and put a knob of the Chive butter on each parcel.

Variation: sweet potatoes can be cooked in the same way (1 per parcel): first pierce the flesh through a few times with a metal skewer, or parboil for 10 minutes to speed up barbecuing. Finish with a Lovage-flavoured mayonnaise: blanch a few Lovage leaves, pat dry, roll up and snip into a bowl of mayonnaise.

RIGHT: *Coriander Sardines with Montpellier Butter and New Season's Potatoes Baked in Foil*

**HERBS ON THE BARBECUE**

**Cooking and eating outside is not the time to be subtle: flavours have to be gutsy to make an impact in the open air. Experiment boldly with generous amounts of sprigs, stalks and leaves to give barbecued food richly aromatic flavours that will give an extra dimension to the already delicious combination of charred and smoky scents. Snip herbs into marinades, sprinkle them over burning coals, use strong twigs of Rosemary as skewers for kebabs, or wrap Mint, Sorrel or Lovage leaves around ingredients to protect them as they cook on the grill.**

## Charred Marinated Aubergines

*Lightly smoky and charred aubergines are here flavoured with scented Marjoram oil. For a colourful antipasto platter, serve with Sweet Peppers and Rosemary (see variation below), sliced ripe vine tomatoes and slivers of spring onion or red onion, all sprinkled with chopped Basil or flat-leaf Parsley.*

**preparation: 20 minutes; infusing oil: 24 hours; cooking: 20 minutes**

*2 ripe aubergines, cut across at an angle into thick slices, or 8 baby aubergines*
*125 ml / 4 fl oz Garlic and Marjoram Oil (page 73)*
*30 g / 1 oz feta cheese, crumbled*
*several sprigs of fresh Marjoram*
*sea salt and freshly ground black pepper*

At least a day ahead, prepare the flavoured oil as described on page 73.

Brush the aubergine slices with the flavoured oil. Season and leave to marinate while you prepare the barbecue. If you like, throw a few sprigs of Marjoram on the coals.

Cook the aubergines on (not in) a double layer of foil set on the side of the barbecue for 6–8 minutes, until tender.

Once tender, lift them away, then char directly on the grill over the flame for a minute on each side for best smoky flavour and nice charred finish.

Scatter the feta over the grilled aubergine slices before serving.

Variations: halved deseeded sweet peppers, brushed with Rosemary and Garlic Flavoured Oil (see page 73) can be cooked in the same way. Omit the feta and, if you like, add 2 finely chopped drained anchovy fillets. Take care not to char the peppers until the skin comes off – the softened cooked skin is fine to eat.

## Corn with Oregano Butter

**preparation: 15 minutes; barbecuing: 30 minutes**

*4 ears of very fresh young corn*
*Oregano Butter (page 72)*
*sea salt and freshly ground black pepper*

Remove the silks from the corns, replace the husks and secure with string.

Dip into cold water, then cook on the barbecue grill until done, turning over to cook evenly. Remove the string and serve with sea salt, black pepper and the Oregano Butter smeared on top.

## Minty Fruit Parcels

*If time allows and Lavender or Rosemary are available, make herb skewers. Strip some leaves off the herb stalks and reserve. Pierce the fruit with a metal skewer and thread them on the herb stalks as described below.*

**preparation: 15 minutes; cooking: 10 minutes**

8 chunks of fresh pineapple
handful of seedless grapes
1 clementine or satsuma, peeled and segmented
2 apricots, halved
small bunch of fresh Mint leaves
45 g / 1 1/2 oz unsalted butter
4 tbsp demerara sugar
4 tbsp rum
tiny sprigs of fresh Mint
vanilla ice-cream, to serve (optional)

Prepare 8 foil rectangles large enough to enclose the kebabs with a little space to spare. Thread the fruit pieces and Mint leaves alternately on 4 skewers (or herb stalks as above). Place each in the centre of a double layer of foil. Scatter over half the butter and sprinkle with sugar, followed by the rum. Bring together the edges of the foil and fold together to enclose the fruit kebabs loosely but securely.

Barbecue on a hot grill, but away from the flames, for 5–8 minutes. Remove from the barbecue and check that the fruit is soft and the sugar and butter is bubbling and beginning to caramelize.

Open up the parcels, sprinkle the remaining rum and butter over the contents. Decorate with the tiny Mint spriglets and serve immediately, with a scoop of vanilla ice-cream if you like.

## Jacket Bananas with Cinnamon Basil Cream

*Barbecuing intensifies the flavour of bananas, and this faintly sharp cream with a touch of spice provides a pleasant contrast. For a still more subtle flavour, use Cinnamon Basil if it is available.*

**preparation: 10 minutes; barbecuing: 10 minutes**

4 just-ripe firm bananas
few Basil sprigs, to decorate (optional)

for the Cinnamon Basil Cream:
4 tbsp crème fraîche
4 tbsp fromage frais
4–6 Basil leaves
1/3 tsp ground Cinnamon
icing sugar to taste (optional)

Make the Cinnamon Basil Cream: whisk the crème fraîche and fromage frais until blended. Snip in the Basil and add the Cinnamon. Whisk again. If you like, sweeten to taste with icing sugar, but remember barbecuing brings out the sweetness of the bananas. Chill until needed.

Put the unpeeled bananas on the hot barbecue grill, well away from the flames. After about 5 minutes, turn them over. Continue barbecuing for a few minutes until the skin blackens.

Serve with the chilled Cinnamon Basil cream and garnished with a few sprigs of Basil, if you like.

# Midsummer Night's Feast

There's no better way to evoke a little mid-summer magic than with a herbal banquet, packed with powerful flavours evocative of the garden in riot.

## Green Asparagus with Parma Ham and Parsley and Walnut Salsa

*Thin green asparagus needs very little trimming, cooks in minutes and makes a great foil for a gutsy dressing.*

**preparation: 15 minutes; cooking 10 minutes; finishing 5 minutes**

350 g / 12 oz thin green asparagus sprue
4 large thin slices of Parma ham
2 tsp olive oil
Parsley and Walnut Salsa (page 75)
45 g / 1¹/₂ oz Parmesan cheese
sea salt and freshly ground black pepper

Place the asparagus in a sauté pan, pour over boiling water to cover and season with a little salt. Simmer for 3–5 minutes until al dente. Drain well.

Put a slice of Parma ham on each plate. Distribute the asparagus between the plates, arranging them over the ham so that the tips stick out attractively. Brush the asparagus with olive oil and season. Fold over the overlapping Parma ham to half cover the asparagus. Spoon the salsa on top. Using a vegetable peeler or cheese parer, shave the Parmesan into slivers. Scatter these over the dish.

## Wok-smoked Trout

*Home-smoking is fun and the results more subtle than the ubiquitous strong smoky flavour you often get with commercially smoked products. In this recipe, the traditional partnership of Fennel and fish is revived in a foil-lined wok. The same method can be used to prepare salmon, sea bass and other fish. Use an old wok as it may get very discoloured in the process. It also needs to have a good tight-fitting lid.*

**preparation: 15 minutes; cooking sauce: 15 minutes; smoking fish: 20 minutes**

4 large skinned trout fillets
olive oil for brushing
2 tsp soy sauce
1 tsp finely grated zest from an unwaxed lemon
3 tbsp Fennel tea (or a mixture of dried Fennel
    seeds, leaves, flowers and stalks)
2 tbsp raw white rice
1 tbsp sugar
2 tsp salt

for the Fennel Sauce:
1 tbsp oil
30 g / 1 oz butter
1 Fennel bulb, finely chopped, some fronds reserved
3 spring onions, snipped
2 garlic cloves, crushed
few stalks of Parsley, snipped
200 ml / 7 fl oz fish, vegetable or chicken stock
1 tbsp drained capers
1 tsp finely grated or pared zest from an unwaxed
    lemon
3 tbsp single cream or fromage frais
sea salt and freshly ground black pepper

Prepare the fennel sauce: heat the oil in a heavy pan and add the butter. Add the prepared fennel, spring onions, garlic and Parsley stalks. Sauté for about 10 minutes, stirring frequently, over a low heat. Add the stock, season and simmer for 5–8 minutes, until thickened. Adjust the seasoning and reserve.

To smoke the fish: lightly brush the fillets with olive oil, sprinkle with soy sauce and scatter over the lemon zest. Line a large wok (with a tight-fitting lid)

ABOVE: *Wok-smoked Trout in preparation;* LEFT: *Wok-smoked Trout served with Fennel Sauce and Early Summer Salad.*

with a double layer of thick foil. Scatter in the dried Fennel mixture, rice, sugar and salt. Brush a metal steamer or flat sieve with oil. Place the fillets on the prepared steamer, rack or sieve and set in the wok. Cover tightly with foil, then with the lid.

Put over a high heat for about 5 minutes. Reduce the heat and cook for a further 4 minutes. Turn off heat and leave the fish in the closed wok for 6–8 minutes. Open and check for doneness. If necessary, return to a high heat for 40 seconds more, then leave to settle for 1–2 minutes.

Just before serving, pass the sauce through a sieve and discard the seasonings. Return to the heat and stir in the capers, lemon zest and the cream or fromage frais. Adjust the seasoning.

Serve the trout with the reserved fennel fronds, a dribbling of sauce on top and the rest under the fish or in a sauce boat. Serve with steamed new potatoes and Early Summer Salad (page 80).

## Melon and Fruit Cups with Ginger Mint

*The spicy peppery flavour of Ginger Mint nicely spikes this fruit salad. If it is not available, use your local Mint and a touch of dried Ginger.*

**preparation: 20 minutes; cooking syrup: 10 minutes**

4 small or 2 large ripe Charentais melons
about 350 g / 12 oz ripe mixed fruit, such as
    honeydew or cantaloupe melon flesh, raspberries,
    fraises des bois or small strawberries, cherries,
    redcurrants or white currants, small chunks of
    peeled mango, peach or nectarine, etc.
several small sprigs of fresh Mint
$\frac{1}{4}$ tsp ground Ginger
few drops of lime juice
crushed ice, Rose petals and more Mint leaves, to
    serve (optional)

for the syrup:
115 g / 4 oz caster sugar
1 tbsp lime juice
1 tbsp Orange flower water
6-8 fresh Mint leaves
$\frac{1}{4}$ tsp ground Ginger

First make the syrup: in a small heavy saucepan, combine the sugar with about 150 ml / $\frac{1}{4}$ pint water, bring to the boil and simmer until slightly thickened and syrupy. Take off the heat. Stir in the lime juice and Orange flower water, then snip in the Mint and add the Ginger. Leave to cool.

If using larger melons, cut each in half. Cut off a thin slice from the base to ensure the melon cups stand upright. If using small melons, cut a lid from the top of each and reserve these until ready to serve. Scoop out and discard the seeds. Scoop out most of the flesh. Put this in a bowl with any juices and the Ginger. Snip in a few Mint leaves. Add the mixed fruit to the bowl. Moisten with the syrup and toss gently. Taste and sharpen the flavour with a little lime juice. Divide the mixture between the melon cups and chill until ready to serve.

Just before serving, top each melon cup with a sprig of the remaining Mint and replace the lids at an angle, if using. If you wish, serve the whole thing on crushed ice strewn with Rose petals and more Mint leaves.

ABOVE: *Melon and Fruit Cups with Ginger Mint*

# *Teatime Treats*

Herbs are also very useful in giving extra punch to classic cakes, pastries and biscuits.

## *Rosemary Cheesecake*

preparation: 15 minutes, plus chilling; baking: 30 minutes, plus cooling and chilling
serves 8

for the base:
115 g / 4 oz melted butter, plus more for the pan
about 15 digestive biscuits, crushed
60 g / 2 oz caster sugar
1 tbsp dried Rosemary

for the filling:
450 g / 1 lb light Philadelphia cream cheese
100 g / 3½ oz caster sugar
2 sprigs of fresh Rosemary, snipped
2½ tsp genuine liquid Vanilla extract
3 large fresh eggs, separated
250 ml / 9 fl oz chilled crème fraîche
icing sugar to taste

First make the base: butter the insides of a 20-cm / 8-inch diameter loose-bottomed cake tin. Put the crushed biscuits in a bowl and mix in the Rosemary, sugar and melted butter, then spread the mixture in the prepared tin. Chill until hardened.

Make the filling: preheat the oven to 190°C/375°F/ gas 5. Mix two-thirds of the cheese, the caster sugar, Rosemary, half the Vanilla, and the egg yolks until blended. Beat the egg whites to soft peaks and then whisk into the mixture. Tip into the tin, smooth level and bake for 20 minutes. Allow to cool and then chill for at least 2 hours.

Preheat the oven to 230°C/450°F/gas 8. Whisk the crème fraîche with icing sugar to taste, the remaining cream cheese and Vanilla extract. Spread this over the cake and bake for 10–12 minutes, until slightly coloured. Leave to get cold and then chill for at least 4 hours.

## *Orange Cake with Lemon Verbena*

*The subtle lemony fragrance of Lemon Verbena goes well with the equally light orange flavour of this cake.*

preparation: 15 minutes; baking: 45 minutes, plus cooling
serves 6–8

115 g / 4 oz caster sugar
100 g / 3½ oz soft unsalted butter, plus more for the pan
2 large eggs
125 g / 5 oz self-raising flour
1 tsp baking powder
juice and zest of 1 large unwaxed orange
10-12 Lemon Verbena leaves, finely snipped, plus more leaves to decorate the cake

for the glaze:
4 tbsp lemon juice
8 tbsp icing sugar, plus more for sifting (optional)

Preheat the oven to 190°C/375°F/gas 5 and generously butter a 1.25-litre / 2-pint non-stick loaf tin.

In a large bowl, beat the sugar and butter until creamy. Beat in the eggs one at a time. Sift the flour and baking powder over the mixture and fold in. Stir in the orange juice (reserving 1 tablespoon for the glaze) and zest, and the Lemon Verbena.

Spoon the mixture into the tin and knock the base against a work surface to get rid of any air bubbles. Bake for about 45 minutes, until firm but still bouncy to the touch. Leave to cool in the tin for a few minutes, then take out and leave to cool on a rack.

Glaze the cake while it is still quite warm: gently heat the lemon juice with the reserved orange juice. Stir in the sugar to make a thick syrup. Brush over the cake.

Serve cold, decorated with extra leaves of Lemon Verbena. If you like, sift a little extra icing sugar over the cake at the last minute.

# *Autumn Harvest Lunch*

*As the days shorten, food starts to suit more mellow flavours like Sage and Thyme. Now is also the time to start using home-dried herbs, like Lavender.*

## *French Roast Pork Stuffed with Sage, Parma Ham and Boursin*

**preparation: 15 minutes, plus chilling; marinating: several hours; cooking: 1¾ hours**

1.35 kg / 3 lb loin of pork, taken from the middle, boned, trimmed and tied
350 ml / 12 fl oz dry white wine, plus more if needed
3 tbsp thick Greek-style yoghurt
1 sprig of Thyme
1 large sprig of Parsley
2 Sage leaves
1 Bay leaf
4 mini Savoy cabbages, each cut into 4 wedges
½ Spanish onion, chopped
25 g / ¾ oz butter, to finish the sauce (optional)
sea salt and freshly ground black pepper

for the stuffing:
1 garlic clove, crushed
6 Sage leaves, finely chopped
85 g / 3 oz pepper Boursin, crumbled, or good cream cheese seasoned with black pepper
1½ tbsp milk
1½ tbsp olive oil
2 thin slices of Parma ham, rolled tightly, snipped into thin shreds, then into slivers

First prepare the stuffing: in a bowl, mash together the garlic, Sage, cheese, milk, olive oil and Parma ham. Season. Using a sharp knife, working between the pieces of string, cut into the pork as if to make medium-thick slices, but taking great care to stop two-thirds of the way down. Using a palette knife, insert the stuffing between the 'slices'.

Mix the wine with the same amount of water and 2 tablespoons yoghurt. Add the herbs. Put the pork in a freezer bag, add the wine marinade and tie securely. Chill for several hours or overnight, shaking the bag from time to time.

Preheat the oven to 180°C/350°F/gas 4 and grease a large deep pan. Place the pork in the middle of the pan or dish, with the marinade, and roast for about 2 hours, until cooked through. Turn it over a few times during cooking. If the dish looks too dry, add a little extra water and wine and cover loosely.

After about 1 hour, blanch the cabbage wedges for 3 minutes in lightly salted boiling water. Drain well, allow to cool a little and gently squeeze out excess moisture. Put the cabbage wedges in the pot around the pork, sprinkle over the onion and season lightly. At the end of cooking, leave to settle for 5–10 minutes in the switched-off oven. Remove the strings. Arrange the pork and cabbage in a warmed dish.

Finish the sauce: strain the cooking liquid into a saucepan over a moderate heat, stir well and adjust the seasoning. Whisk in the rest of the yoghurt and butter, if using. Spoon over the pork and cabbage.

## *Pommes Lyonnaise*

**preparation: 25 minutes; cooking: 15 minutes**

about 575 g / 1¼ lb new potatoes
2 tbsp olive oil
30 g / 1 oz butter
1 large pale mild or Spanish onion, thinly sliced
few sprigs of Thyme, picked from the stalks
1 scant tsp Caraway seeds
sea salt and freshly ground black pepper

Put the potatoes in a pan of lightly salted boiling water and cook for 15 minutes, until three-quarters cooked. Drain well, patting dry, if necessary.

Return the pan to a moderate heat, tip in the oil and

ABOVE: *French Roast Pork Stuffed with Sage, Parma Ham and Boursin, served with Pommes Lyonnaise.*

# Mushroom Surprise

*You can also try fresh Thyme, Marjoram or even Tarragon in place of the Basil.*

**preparation: 15 minutes, plus chilling; cooking: about 20 minutes**

2 courgettes
4 large flattish brown mushrooms
3 ripe vine tomatoes
4–5 tbsp fruity olive oil
small handful of Basil leaves
60 g / 2 oz Gorgonzola, chopped, crumbled or
    slivered (according to texture)
sea salt and freshly ground black pepper

Thinly slice the courgettes and sprinkle lightly with coarse sea salt. Place on a large plate lined with a double layer of paper towels, cover with more paper, put a weight on top and chill for 30 minutes.

Cut off the mushroom stalks, scrape the gills on the underside to give more room for the filling. Put the mushrooms on a large plate, underside down, cover and microwave on high for 5 minutes.

Thinly slice the tomatoes. Using a sharp knife, cut out the central pulp and extract the seeds. Put on paper towels to drain.

Preheat the oven to 220°C/ 425°F/gas 7 and lightly oil a baking tray. Press the mushrooms gently to drain. Pat dry. Arrange on the baking tray and brush the cup sides with oil. Season lightly with salt and more generously with pepper.

Rinse and drain the courgettes, then press dry with paper towels. Arrange a circle of courgette slices on each mushroom, leaving the mushroom rim well clear. Snip over a few Basil leaves and drizzle with a little oil. Arrange a circle of tomato slices on top, again staying well away from the edge. Season lightly, drizzle with a very little oil and snip over more Basil. Put a little mound of Gorgonzola in the centre and season with a little pepper.

Bake for 15 minutes until bubbly. Decorate with small Basil leaves (snip if too large) to serve.

butter and add the onion, Thyme and Caraway. Stir to coat and cook over a moderate heat for a few minutes until softened but not coloured. Stir in the potatoes and season. Cover and cook over gentle heat for 15–20 minutes, shaking occasionally, until tinged with gold.

## *Apple, Pear and Lavender Tart Tatin*

*This classic French upside-down tart can also be flavoured with Rosemary (fresh or dried), Thyme (fresh or dried, use sparingly), or a mixture of Coriander seeds and fresh leaves (use sparingly).*

**preparation: 15 minutes, plus chilling; cooking: about 50 minutes**

*125 g / 4¹/₂ oz chilled unsalted butter, cut into slivers*
*125 g / 5 oz caster sugar, plus a little extra for the pastry*
*about 700 g / 1¹/₂ lb crisp eating apples, peeled, cored and cut into quarters*
*about 700 g / 1¹/₂ lb ripe but firm small rounded pears (i.e. not Conference), peeled, cored and cut into quarters*

*for the pastry:*
*225 g / 8 oz flour*
*1 tbsp caster sugar*
*pinch of fine sea salt*
*about 35 g / 1¹/₄ oz dried Lavender flowers, plus more for decoration*
*125 g / 5 oz unsalted butter*
*1 tbsp chilled single cream*

Make the pastry: sift the flour into a bowl, add the sugar and salt. Whiz the dried Lavender flowers for a few seconds in the food processor. Stir one-third into the flour mixture. Work in the butter, then mix in the cream. Roll into a ball and chill for at least 20 minutes.

Melt half the butter in a flameproof 25-cm / 10-inch diameter round cake tin over a moderate heat. Sprinkle in half the sugar and mix in.

Away from the heat, arrange the prepared apples and pears tightly in the tin, in alternating concentric circles. Sprinkle with half the rest of the sugar and half the remaining ground Lavender. Dot with the rest of the butter.

Put the tin over a moderate heat for 15–20 minutes to allow the butter and sugar between the apples

and pears to caramelize. Shake the tin from time to time and reduce the heat after 10 minutes to prevent burning. Turn off the heat and leave until cool enough to handle.

Preheat the oven to 200°C/400°F/gas 6. Roll the dough out into a thin circle 3.5 cm / 1¹/₂ inches larger than the tin. Mix the rest of the Lavender with the reserved sugar, sprinkle over the pastry and press in gently.

Put the pastry circle over the apples and pears. Tuck the overlapping edge in between the fruit and tin.

Bake for about 25–30 minutes, until the pastry is cooked and golden. Leave to cool for at least 10 minutes before serving.

To turn out, cover the tin with a somewhat larger serving platter and quickly invert on to the dish, so that the caramelized apples and pears are on top of the pastry. Tap the tin a few times and lift away. Hide any problems with a little icing sugar and pop under a very hot grill for a minute. If you like, decorate with small dried Lavender flowers which have first been dampened and dipped in sugar.

# Infused Herb Custards

*Allowing herbs to steep in hot milk before you whisk in the eggs and sugar is an easy way to transform an ordinary custard into an exquisite accompaniment to desserts.*

*For subtly flavoured concoctions, try Lavender, Lemon Balm, Fennel, Aniseed, Borage, Angelica, Rosemary, Lemon Thyme, Elderflower, Spearmint or Apple Mint and Juniper Berries. Use a generous amount – say a small handful of leaves, sprigs or heads, a couple of tablespoons of berries – and bruise them first to help their flavours seep out. Strain the flavoured milk after steeping.*

*Herb-flavoured custards also make good bases for elegant ice-creams (see the Basil and Vanilla Ice-cream on page 177).*

# Angelica and Vanilla Custard

*preparation and steeping: 20 minutes; cooking: 15 minutes, plus chilling*
*makes about 700 ml / 1¹/₄ pints*

*600 ml / I pint full-fat milk*
*good handful (about ¹/₂ cup) Angelica leaves, bruised*
*2 Vanilla pods, split lengthwise, or 1 tsp genuine*
*    liquid Vanilla extract*
*1 tsp Orange flower water*
*4 very fresh large egg yolks*
*5–6 tbsp caster sugar*
*1 tsp cornflour*
*4 tbsp single or whipping cream*

Put the milk in a pan with the Angelica leaves, Vanilla and Orange flower water and bring to boiling point over a low heat. The moment it starts bubbling, turn down the heat and continue to simmer very gently for at least 10 minutes, and up to 20, keeping the heat very low, to allow the flavours to infuse. Take off the heat. Strain, cover and keep hot.

In a bowl, whisk together the egg yolks and sugar until smooth. Whisk in the cornflour.

Remove the Vanilla pods and Angelica leaves from the milk. Pour the hot milk a little at a time over the egg yolk and sugar mixture, stirring vigorously. Pour the mixture into the pan and return to a very low heat. Very slowly bring almost to boiling point but not quite, stirring constantly. The cream will thicken gradually. Do not let it boil and take it off the heat occasionally while it is cooking. If it looks at all lumpy, strain the custard through a sieve into a cold bowl. Stir from time to time as it cools. Stir in the cream once cool. Serve very well chilled with pies, tarts, fruit salads, etc., decorated with small Angelica leaves.

LEFT: *Apple, Pear and Lavender Tart Tatin*

# Slow-cooked Winter Dinner

*Long- and slow-cooked dishes, like braises and stews, are perfect winter fare and also develop the full potential of strongly flavoured herbs like Thyme, Oregano and Rosemary.*

## Scarborough Fair Pilaff

*Instead of finishing this pilaff with spring onions or pumpkin, you can stir in 2 tablespoons of the Red Onion and Bay Leaf Marmalade on page 76.*

**preparation: 15 minutes; cooking: about 20 minutes**

1 good-quality chicken or vegetable stock cube
2 shallots, finely chopped
1 tbsp oil
30 g / 1 oz butter, plus more for greasing
350 g / 12 oz long-grain rice mixed with wild rice
small bunch of Parsley, snipped
4 Sage leaves, snipped
3 Rosemary sprigs, snipped
3 Thyme sprigs, snipped
3 tbsp pine nuts

to finish:
30 g / 1 oz Parmesan cheese, cut into shavings
2 spring onions, snipped, or 3 tbsp diced cooked
    pumpkin
sea salt and freshly ground black pepper

First prepare the stock: crumble the cube and dissolve it in 700 ml / 1¼ pints of boiling water.

In a deep sauté or frying pan, sauté the shallots in the oil and a little of the butter. Tip in the rice, stir and cook for a minute or two until the grains are well coated. Stir in half the herbs, cook for a minute, season, then add the boiling stock and cook until the rice is tender (see packet for times). Stir in the pine nuts about 10 minutes into cooking.

Drain, stir in half the remaining herbs and butter. If convenient, put the pilaff in a buttered gratin dish and reheat gently in a warm oven.

To finish the dish, adjust the seasoning, then lightly stir in the Parmesan, and spring onion or pumpkin, together with the remaining herbs and butter.

## Lamb Daube with Provençal Herbs

*If serving the daube without the preceding pilaff, make it more substantial by serving it with flageolets or cannellini beans and some good bread.*

**preparation: 15 minutes; cooking: 3 hours**

1.25 kg / 2½ lb boneless lamb, shoulder or neck,
    trimmed of any excess fat
1 Spanish onion, chopped
1 shallot, chopped
2 Bay leaves
several sprigs each of Thyme and Parsley
2 sprigs of Oregano or Marjoram
few black peppercorns
2 tbsp olive oil
about 600 ml /1 pint red wine
4 thick slices of rindless smoked streaky bacon
2 garlic cloves, crushed
4 ripe tomatoes, chopped, or 1 small can of chopped
    tomatoes)
225 g / 8 oz mushrooms, thinly sliced
12 black olives, stoned and chopped
sea salt and freshly ground black pepper
Gremolada, to finish (optional, see page 74)

Cut the lamb into 5-cm /2-inch chunks. In a bowl, combine the meat, onion, shallot, Bay leaves, Thyme, Parsley, Oregano or Marjoram and peppercorns with half the oil and just enough red wine to cover. Leave in a cool place to marinate overnight.

Preheat the oven to 160°C/325°F/gas 3. Chop the bacon. In a frying pan, heat the rest of the oil, add the bacon and sauté until it is crisp. Lift the lamb

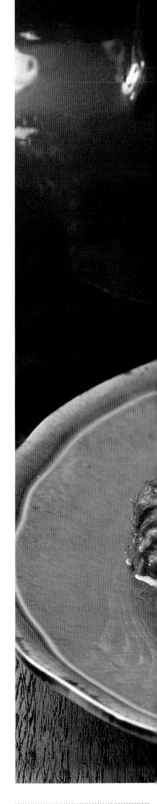

ABOVE: *Lamb Daube with Provençal Herbs, served with flageolets.*

146

out of the marinade, reserving the marinade. Drain and pat dry with a clean cloth or paper towels. Add to the bacon and brown on all sides for a few minutes over a fairly high heat.

In an ovenproof casserole, mix the meat and bacon with the marinade. Add the garlic, tomatoes, mushrooms and half the olives. Season and stir well.

Cover the dish tightly and cook in the oven for a good 2½ hours, occasionally stirring and checking to see that there is still enough liquid to keep it moist. Add a little extra wine if necessary.

When the meat is tender, stir in the remaining olives and, if you like, some gremolada. Leave to settle with the lid on for 5–10 minutes before serving.

## SALAD LEAVES AND HERBS

Sorrel, Rocket and some of the sharper-tasting young leaves and shoots, such as spinach, beetroot and ruby chard, can be wonderful in mixed salads instead of traditional herbs. Use sparingly, perhaps torn, shredded or snipped, with milder-tasting lettuce varieties. If some leaves taste too peppery or bitter, add a little honey to the dressing and be very mean with the vinegar or lemon juice.

## Spinach, Pink Grapefruit and Watercress Salad with Dill

**preparation: 10 minutes**

*about 100 g / 3¹/₂ oz baby spinach leaves, trimmed*
*about 85 g / 3 oz Watercress, trimmed*
*1 pink grapefruit, peeled and cut into segments*

*for the dressing:*
*1 tbsp white wine vinegar or cider vinegar*
*2 tsp liquid honey*
*juice of ¹/₂ lemon*
*1 tbsp creamy yoghurt*
*several fronds of fresh Dill, snipped*
*2-3 sprigs of flat-leaved Parsley, snipped*
*3¹/₂ tbsp light-flavoured olive oil*
*sea salt and freshly ground black pepper*

First prepare the dressing: mix the vinegar, honey, lemon juice, yoghurt and half the snipped Dill and Parsley with the olive oil. Season to taste.

Combine the spinach and Watercress in a large shallow bowl. Add the grapefruit segments (halved if necessary), and toss lightly. Dribble over the dressing, toss lightly, then sprinkle with the reserved Dill and Parsley.

ABOVE: *Spinach, Pink Grapefruit and Watercress Salad with Dill.*

RIGHT: *Apple and Lemon Balm with Meringues.*

## *Apricot and Lemon Balm Cream with Meringues*

*preparation: 15 minutes; macerating: 30 minutes, plus chilling; cooking meringues: 2 hours*

*350 g / 12 oz plump dried apricots (sometimes known as 'semi-dried')*
*2–3 tbsp brandy*
*3 tbsp chopped Lemon Balm (defrosted, if frozen), plus extra leaves to decorate*
*500 ml / 18 fl oz whipping cream (or a mixture of equal parts whipping cream and Greek-style yoghurt)*
*caster sugar to taste*
*3 tbsp shelled pistachios or hazelnuts*
*small knob of unsalted butter or 2 tsp vegetable oil*

*for the meringues:*
*2 egg whites*
*tiny pinch of salt*
*115 g / 4 oz vanilla-flavoured caster sugar*
*2 tsp herb-flavoured white wine or cider vinegar (see pages 72–3)*

Make the meringues: preheat the oven to 120°C/250°F/gas ½ and line a large baking tray with non-stick baking paper.

Whisk the egg whites with a pinch of salt until stiff. Add half the caster sugar and the vinegar and whisk again until stiff and shiny. Fold in the rest of the caster sugar. Using a tablespoon, dollop the mixture onto the prepared tray, keeping the heaps well apart.

Bake for 1½-2 hours until dry throughout. If not using within a few hours, keep in a tin or other airtight container until ready to serve.

To prepare the apricot cream: put the apricots in a bowl and sprinkle with the brandy. Cover with 6 tablespoons of boiling water and the chopped Lemon Balm. Stir, cover and leave to macerate for 30 minutes.

Whisk the cream until thick and sweeten to taste. Whiz the apricots and the liquid until puréed. Stir into the whipped cream. Chill for at least 1 hour in the coldest part of the refrigerator.

To serve: sprinkle the pistachios or hazelnuts with a little sugar and sauté them in a pan lightly greased with butter or oil. Spoon the chilled cream into stemmed glasses, sprinkle with the nuts and decorate with spriglets of fresh Lemon Balm. Serve the meringues on a side plate.

CHAPTER FIVE

# Love & Romance

*The poets and troubadours of every culture have celebrated the seductive powers of sweet perfumes — and whose romantic soul would not be stirred in a starlit bower of Honeysuckle, Roses and Jasmine?*

'By thy scent my soul is ravished' wrote the Persian poet Sadi in praise of a Rose. The fragrance of a flower is its alluring call to its pollinator, its instrument of procreation. It is offered freely to all who pass by and this generous outpouring can touch us all.

As ambrosial perfumes open the door to romance, so also romantic encounters heighten our awareness of scent. Love puts all our senses on high alert and attending scents become deeply imprinted. Even the elusive beginnings of a liaison are etched in our scent-memory: a fleeting flowery aroma as she sauntered by, the fresh-air scent of his crisp shirt when he stopped to ask directions. A second encounter with a fragrance can rekindle memories of the first stirred feelings.

Perfumes like Rose and Orange Blossom earn their aphrodisiac reputation by soothing the mind and reducing inhibitions; others like Jasmine and Lilies are unsettling, suggesting exotic mystery and adventure. Aphrodisiac spices such as Star Anise and Cardamom are vital ingredients in stimulating, sensuous and tonic foods. The musky scents more directly invoke human sexuality and are added as a tiny but evocative undercurrent to perfumes.

Our sense of smell is our most ancient and primeval courtship preceptor, and it is willing to be seduced by sweet fragrance. Layered with subtlety, perfumes add delicate magnetism to the body, skin, hair and breath, and contribute to a warm, sensuous environment. Then delicious aromas will intensify the pleasure of being together, swirled in aromatic baths, aphrodisiac dishes and hypnotic passion brews.

The power of fragrance can also enhance long-term relationships; a love-potion spray of favourite oils kept for special times when you are alone together, and taken on trips to personalize a holiday suite, will invoke the early romance. Love is the balm of life and fragrance can encourage, enrich and expand it.

SENSUAL HERBS & OILS • ROMANTIC ROSE GARDENS • SECRET GARDEN DESIGN • THE ART OF PERFUMERY • PERSONALIZED PERFUMES • SEDUCTIVE RECIPES FOR BATH & BODY • WEDDING BOUQUETS & FLORAL CHAPLETS • APHRODISIAC DINNER FOR TWO

*The sensuous range of fragrances associated with romance and seduction falls broadly into five response groups.*

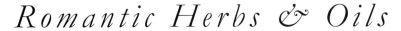

# Romantic Herbs & Oils

## Unbidden Smile

These scents are gentle and relaxing as they generate a smile of well-being and openness; they are the light-floral and sweet-green scents.

### ROSES

First is the universal fragrant symbol of love, the Rose, sacred to Venus and Bacchus and intimately connected to Cupid, who is often shown with bow, arrow and Roses. As its cultivation spread out from Persia, the delicate but deeply emotive scent of the Rose delighted and inspired artists, warriors and lovers in every land. It eventually became the world's most popular flower.

Appreciating its aphrodisiac qualities, Cleopatra seduced Antony knee-deep in Roses. Harem brides were washed in rosewater and the Romans sprinkled petals on the marriage bed, a custom echoed today in wedding confetti, which was originally Rose petals.

For today's lovers, the gift of Roses offers an eloquent choice of messages from the rainbow of Rose perfumes. So shun the long-stemmed, scentless anomalies and choose from the delicate, pure, heart-opening, angelic-pink scent of 'Celestial', the refined, pale flesh fragrance of 'Maiden's Blush' and the gentle tea-rose scent of reliable 'New Dawn'; or the blowsy pink extravagance of 'Fantin Latour', the lusty cerise perfume of 'Madame Isaac Pereire' and the dark velvet aroma of crimson 'Guinée'.

Passion tonics and aphrodisiac foods dating back to ancient Persia are flavoured with Rose using fresh or dried petals, rosewater or Rose essential oil. In a caliph's court, rosewater perfumed an exotic energizing mix of meat, fruit, nuts and spices. Crusaders returned with the sensuous Rose-flavoured Turkish Delight: *rahat lokum* – 'giving rest to the throat'. Indian sweetmeats are suffused with Rose syrup. Troubadour's Elixir is a liqueur made with Musk Roses, Jasmine and Orange blossom, spiced with Madagascar Nutmeg and Mace.

Clean, undamaged petals from strongly scented Roses, with the white base pinched off, give the best results. The scent of fresh and dried Rose petals is different, but dried petals briefly release a fresh Rose scent if they are put in a blender or crushed with a pestle and mortar. For a romantic dinner, Roses can be added to whipped cream, ice cubes, pastry, meringues and salads, with petals sprinkled on the tablecloth or as a trail leading where you wish.

The ultimate romantic use of Rose fragrance is in perfumery, where it features in the most prized blends. Its exquisite, soft but lasting odour rounds a perfume nicely; it enhances other ingredients and sits well on all skins. Rosewater was the basic liquid in the original face cream developed by the Greek Galen

2,000 years ago, and in any cosmetic recipe that requires water, rose-water can be substituted with beneficial results. Rose essence is among the safest substances known, with a tonic effect on the skin, circulation and nervous system. In aromatherapy it is used for emotional problems linked to feminine sexuality, especially the restoration of confidence in desirability – and desirability itself.

### ORANGE BLOSSOM

The light and clean but luxurious scent of Orange blossom (very different from the citrus scent of the fruits) is another world favourite. Rolling across the Mediterranean landscape on a seasonal breeze, the fragrance adds immeasurably to the romance of the area. The essential oil – as expensive as Rose – with its haunting bittersweet fragrance is called Neroli, after a Princess who loved the scent, and is widely used in both male and female perfumes. In aromatherapy, like Rose essence it stimulates healthy new skin cells and calms nervous states, particularly apprehension before a stressful event. Its aphrodisiac reputation stems from this ability to reduce anxiety before a sexual encounter and explains its value in bridal bouquets. Orange flower water flavours many ambrosial foods.

The similarly gorgeous scent of white-flowered *Philadelphus*, the Mock Orange, fills the garden with its honeyed aroma in early summer, and in cooler climes takes the place of Orange blossom in bridal wreaths. The Mexican Orange Blossom (*Choisya ternata*), with its star-shaped white flowers in late spring (sometimes repeated in autumn), offers another garden evergreen with this fragrance.

There is a similar perfume in both the tiny flowers and the leaves of Sweet Myrtle. When Paris awarded Venus a golden apple for her beauty, she wore a wreath of Sweet Myrtle leaves and bathed in Sweet Myrtle water. In the Middle Ages the leaves were rubbed over the body as a sexual stimulant, an action which would rouse the circulation as well as imparting the delicious fragrance. Sweet Myrtle, too, is included in bridal wreaths and lovers' posies.

### PEONY

The large, voluptuous blooms of the Peony, recorded growing in the Imperial Gardens of Peking since the fourth century, have a surprisingly demure perfume, offered only to those who pause close by. The Peony was a favourite of China's most notorious and beautiful royal concubine, Yang Kuei-fei, and marble terraces were built to grow many varieties for her pleasure, with attendant gardening maidens in rich attire and bells of precious metal fixed to the blooms to deter marauding birds. Peony flowers came to represent feminine loveliness and were embroidered on silk gowns and painted on scrolls.

ABOVE: *Voluptuous Peonies have a soft romantic scent.*

BELOW: *The world delights in the fragrant beauty of Roses, here seen* en masse *in a Welsh garden.*

### VANILLA AND BENZOIN

Tropical orchids shimmer 'romance' and one yields the alluring, creamy scent of Vanilla from its 'cured' seed pods. This process was developed by the Aztecs, who used Vanilla to flavour chocolate drinks reserved for nobility. It has a high aphrodisiac value in foods, room and body perfumes, and love potions. Benzoin essential oil has a similar scent and is a useful base note in room fragrances.

### HONEYSUCKLE AND HENNA

The sweet scent of Honeysuckle becomes powerfully alluring in the evening as it radiates its magnetic perfume on the night air. Its tenacious grasp as a climbing plant has made it a symbol of fidelity.

'Oh odours of Paradise: Oh flowers of Henna', sang the street vendors in Cairo. The leaves of the Henna shrub yield the red dye used to stain intricate patterns on the hands and feet of Hindu brides, but it is the tiny white flowers that provide the delectable floral sweetness. It is the camphire of the *Song of Solomon* and one of Milton's 'odorous bushy shrubs'. Henna is believed to have grown in the Hanging Gardens of Babylon, the ancient city once the centre of the Eastern perfume trade. Henna flowers produced Cleopatra's famous seductive perfume Cyprinum, with which she scented the sails of her barge as an aromatic envoy on her approach to meet Mark Antony.

ABOVE: *Elegant white Lilac entices butterflies and lovers into the garden with its warm, wafting scent.*

### OTHER SCENTS

This large group of romantic fragrances also includes the delicate perfume of Lily-of-the-Valley and Gardenias, favourite of the prom corsages; the unique fragrance of Sweet Violets beloved by both the Empress Josephine and the last Empress of China, and the soft, warm wafting scent of Lilac. The delicious plummy, spicy, floral scent of white Osmanthus flowers (*Osmanthus fragrans*) is strong enough to detect inside a motorcycle helmet as it wafts in autumn across the Chinese garden city of Hangzhou, luring all to visit, including the ancient Emperors. Other light fragrances play an important role in perfumery to highlight top notes or as nuances to round out blends.

## *Exotic*

Usually from white flowers, these have a heady, intensely sweet and slightly unsettling odour hinting at unknown excitement. Most of their powerful extracted essences need to be diluted to be recognized as the flower fragrance.

### LILY

The star of this group is the Lily with its 1930s bias-cut, white satin, film-star glamour – exotic, daring, yet slightly aloof. Best admired from afar when the perfume is heady and tantalizing; up close its effect can be giddy and overpowering.

### JASMINE AND TUBEROSE

The rich narcotic perfume of tropical Jasmine flowers radiates peak potency on

warm evenings, giving it the Indian name of 'Moonlight of the Groves'. In the East, whole streets are given over to Jasmine flower sellers, seen threading the blooms for local women to perfume their hair or to offer to the gods. The flower essence has a deep, warm, creamy, encompassing perfume with fruity-green undertones, which becomes more seductive on skin contact. Among perfumers it is the most popular floral absolute, providing a benchmark for describing other exotic 'White Flower' essences. It shares one of the highest price brackets with Rose, Neroli and Tuberose, as it requires 8 million blossoms to make 1 kg ($2^{1}/_{4}$ lb) of essence.

The white-flowered Tuberose (Night Hyacinth) exudes possibly the most intense, sweet honey-floral scent with a provocative earthy undertone and yields an incredibly expensive essential oil – literally worth its weight in gold.

### YLANG-YLANG AND MIMOSA

The inconspicuous yellow flowers of tropical Ylang-Ylang (Flower of Flowers) have a Jasmine fragrance also used by Eastern women to perfume their hair and prepare for an amorous encounter. The essential oil is much less expensive, slightly sharper and less tenacious than Jasmine, and is sometimes mixed with Allspice to intensify the clove undertones.

The yellow flower clusters of Mimosa spread their intoxicating floral-green-violet aroma along the Riviera in mid-January. The essential oil has a powerful, penetrating scent with intriguing straw-like bitter undertones and is used to enhance quality perfumes.

### HYACINTH

The strong narcotic perfume of *Hyacinthus orientalis* with its sweet-green top note is occasionally extracted for use in fine fragrances. The Greeks, who named it after Apollo's beautiful youth, believed the scent would invigorate a tired mind. Aromatherapists use it to boost self-esteem and trust. Its high price means that most Hyacinth products are fragranced with synthetics.

## *Spicy*

These scents are warm and stimulating, arouse circulation and invite playful contact. All the spice scents have been used in seductive perfumes for both men and women, in room fragrances, in love philtres and are popular in aphrodisiac foods.

TOP LEFT: *A quiet garden spot, ringed with Honeysuckle, is filled with perfume as evening approaches.*

LEFT: *Pluck individual tubular Honeysuckle flowers and suck the ambrosial nectar from their base, or scatter them over creamy desserts.*

ABOVE: *Dainty Clove Pinks surprise with their exotic spicy chocolate clove scent.*

RIGHT: *A heady bouquet features a seductive mix of Roses, Lilies and Honeysuckle.*

### CINNAMON

The highest vote goes to Cinnamon's warm, convivial fragrance with its ancient reputation for 'provoking lively desire'. It is often included in passion brews, mulled wines and desserts – including pumpkin pie, which recently topped an American list of foods that could lead males to amorous activity.

### GINGER AND STAR ANISE

Ginger has a well-deserved reputation for rousing the system, and it is one of the luxuries which inspired Rome's insatiable desire for Chinese goods traded along the Silk Road. As a gourmand's delight, the finest quality is crystallized, often dipped in dark chocolate, and sold in Chinese jars. It features in many love concoctions and magical potions, while its flowers are found in the garlands of Hawaiian dancers.

The Latin genus name for Star Anise – *Illicium,* from allurement – was inspired by its scent. All parts of the tree are fragrant, including the pretty star-shaped seed pods with their lively, sweet-spicy aroma, an asset in seductive room scents and stimulating feasts.

### OTHER SCENTS

Sweet-green-spicy Coriander seed, used to flavour drinks at Tudor weddings, was described in the *Arabian Nights* as an aphrodisiac. Warmly aromatic Cardamom, with balsamic floral undertones, was a Greek and Roman perfume, an ingredient of witches' love potions and is a favourite in Arab cuisine. Deliciously pungent and breath-sweetening Cloves, another traditional aphrodisiac, are forever linked with the exotic island of Zanzibar, but their intense scent finds a surprising echo in English cottage gardens, wafting from the dainty flowers of Clove Pinks.

The rich, warm and inviting fragrance of Bay, Nutmeg, Mace and Allspice and the zesty spiciness of Black Pepper and Basil are each used in potent and inviting foods, drinks and perfumes.

## Woody and Earthy

The various tree, moss and fern scents are rich, resonant forest smells that suggest deeper connections and ancient rituals. The deep, warm, suggestive and persistent notes of these plant parts and their essential oils have both reassuring qualities and classy sex appeal. They appear as base notes in most high-quality scents, with greater emphasis in aftershaves and sultry women's perfumes.

### SANDALWOOD AND CEDAR

With at least 4,000 years of perfume application, the warm, woody scent of Sandalwood lives up to its ancient reputation as an aphrodisiac. Its molecular structure is almost identical to that of testosterone, a human pheromone (sexual scent) emitted by both sexes. Sandalwood oil, like Rose and Neroli, is beneficial to dry and oily skins, and in massage, bath and cosmetic products it leaves an enticing, lingering fragrance on the body.

The characteristic soft, spicy scent of Cedarwood gives warmth and body to blends and creates an aura of strength and courage which is alluring to women.

### VETIVER AND PATCHOULI

Vetiver roots have a wonderful mellow, dry scent and in the tropics are made into aromatic screens to shade verandahs on languorous afternoons. The essential oil has a resinous myrrh-violet scent, used in India to flavour sweetmeats, and is popular in men's fragrances.

The delight of Patchouli-leaf essential oil is the intense sweet, forest-floor odour with hints of spicy balsam. Those who think they dislike it, from cloying 1960s memories, may be surprised at the light brightness of a good-quality oil, and to discover the wide range of perfumes, aftershaves and bath products that include it. Sachets with a sprinkling of the more softly scented leaves blended with Rose petals will perfume clothes and linen with subtle eastern promise.

### OAKMOSS, BIRCH AND ANGELICA

Oakmoss gives a rich, old-smoky, mossy spice with leather notes. Several Birch species yield Birch Tar oil, which has a woody, tarry, smoky odour with sweet, oily leather tones carefully treated for use in perfumes. This characteristic Russian Leather scent is magnetic to many women.

The root oil of Angelica is an intricate fragrance with a peppery green top note, an earthy heart mingled with dark flowing streams and a hint of musk, which it gives to specialist perfumes.

### SAFFRON

One of the oldest plants in cultivation, the Saffron crocus – 'Karcom' of the amorous Song of Solomon – produces culinary stigmas with a powerful aroma with intriguing sweet-earthy undertones. It has a long history as both a perfume and an aphrodisiac, partly because of its perceived cordial effect on the brain and heart. In Greek legend, a girl consuming Saffron for one week could not resist a lover.

## Musk

'Musk' scents have an erogenous edge that hints at animal passion. They can be unpleasant on their own but add an arousing undercurrent and excellent fixative properties to perfume blends. These feral odours whispering of pagan rites were originally taken from animal scent glands, but there are now plant sources.

### ELDER, BLACKCURRANT AND AMBRETTE

Elder exhibits a musky-foxy note but the essence is not extracted. The flowers give a muscatel flavour to wine and aphrodisiac desserts. Blackcurrant shares the foxy note and its buds yield an expensive complex essence, Cassis, that gives a special cachet to perfumes. Tropical Hibiscus, Ambrette (*Abelmoschus moschatus*) seed oil has floral musky notes with distinct Cognac hints for fine perfumes.

*The arena of love and romance offers the most fertile realm for the ambrosial power of fragrance. Create the perfumed garden of your dreams and enjoy it with the one you love.*

# Romantic Gardens

A secluded fragrant garden offers an opportunity for the soft perfumes of nature to work their magic on the human heart. It is also the perfect setting for refined pursuits, a wonderful prelude to courtship. Minds heightened with fine music, enriching prose and challenging philosophical discussion soar more readily into sublime emotions.

Medieval courtly love was often played out in a fragrant garden. The heart of an amorous knight, strumming his lute and that of his lady sitting on a Chamomile seat surrounded by Lilies and Thyme were both tenderized by the sweet herbs.

Or can we better the guidance of ancient Tibetan texts which consider sensual love to be one of the paths to radiant inner awareness. In one fragment, suggestions for creating sensuality are presented beneath the drawing of a secluded garden: 'choose desirable surroundings with the sweet sound of water and chirping birds … pleasant conversation, gentle embracing … and aphrodisiac foods'.

Begin your romantic garden with a beckoning path through a protective hedge. Keep the seat or bower hidden from view. Along the route place aromatic plants underfoot like Chamomile and Peppermint to refresh bare feet, others along the edge like Lavender to indulge trailing hands, some at nose height like Sweet Peas and Roses, inviting immediate attention, or the large tropical-like Angelica for an Alice in Wonderland feeling, and Buddleia to lure the bees and butterflies. Overhead, drifts of Wisteria with its gentle perfume will complete the picture frame. Surround the seat with a protective trellis of Roses and Honeysuckle and nearby grow succulent fruits such as Peaches, Figs and Alpine Strawberries to tempt the palate, and the velvety-leaved Marshmallow to heighten the sense of touch.

With riches to please all the senses, you might consider following the Chinese practice of placing a calligraphy plaque on the approach to a special scene to increase expectations. Poetic scholars would vie with each other to encapsulate the unique atmosphere of an approaching space in an evocative phrase. 'The Pavilion of Lapping Waves' or 'Rendezvous with a Nightingale' will heighten awareness and focus the senses.

A seat is vital – a place to pause, play, discover the meaning of quirky cloud shapes in the bright blue of the day or count shooting stars in the deep indigo of night; a time to absorb the rich tapestry of sensual experience, and translate it into the fabric of love.

ABOVE: *A happy fragrant wilderness of Lavender and Roses.*

LEFT: *A romantic trellis of Roses at Wollerton Old Hall, Shropshire provides a sense of privacy, while highlighting the beauty of the garden.*

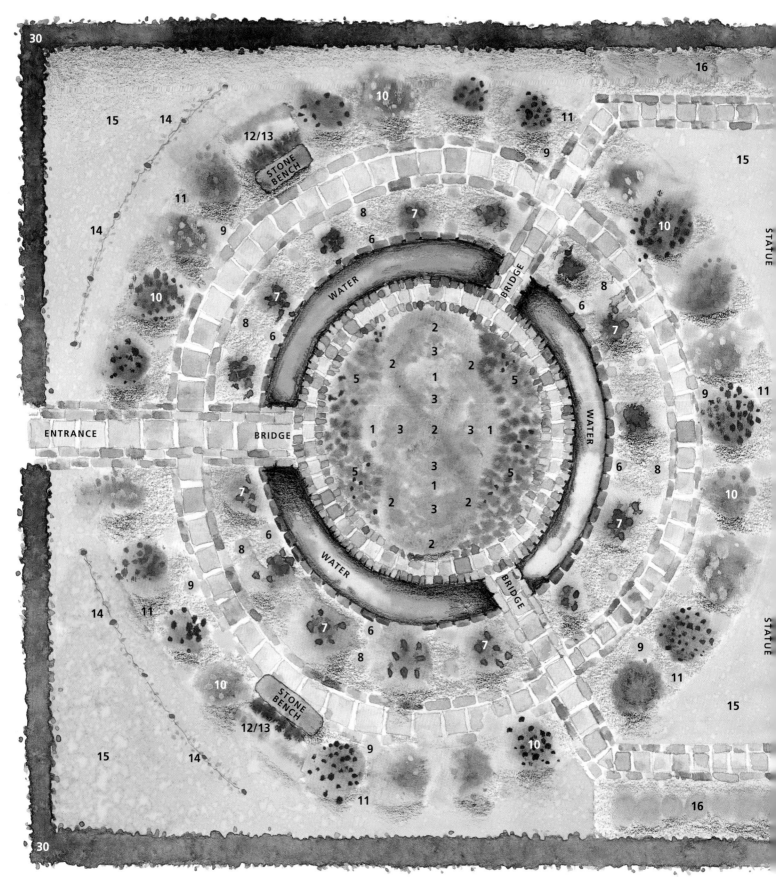

# Secret Garden

Fragrant flowers speak to us directly. The fragile petals, luminous colour and delicate scent can convey subtle emotions more eloquently than words, making them universal symbols of love. With the wealth of associations between plants and romance, the secret garden has evolved as a place for lovers to meet out of public gaze. In this garden the private fragrant space is hidden, waiting to be discovered amid the tall curved Yew hedges with mysterious areas of light and dark, and the occasional waft of sweet fragrance to enhance the sense of expectation.

ABOVE: *A narrow arch through the Yew hedge beckons to a secret garden.*

## List of Plants in Plan

### Lover's Knot (centre)
1. Silver Santolina (*Santolina chamaecyparissus* syn *S. incana*)
2. Box
3. Sweet Violet
4. Miniature Roses in scarlet, pink and white.
5. Clove Pinks

### First Ring
6. Iris, smoky blues and violets
7. Peony, scented in scarlet, pink and white.
8. Gypsophila, white.

### Second Ring
9. Geranium 'Johnson's Blue'
10. 'Old' Shrub Roses in scarlets, pinks and whites
11. Delphinium, deep blue
12. Bergamot, scarlet flowers
13. Madonna Lilies, white

### Surround
14. Climbing Roses
15. Lawn
16. Southernwood (next to path leading to secret area)

### Secret Garden
17. Sweet Cicely
18. Eau-de-Cologne Mint
19. Buddleia, scented purple flowers
20. Lilac, lilac to blue flowers
21. Osmanthus, white flowers, dark green evergreen leaves
22. Philadelphus, white flowers
23. Purple Honeysuckle (*Lonicera japonica* var. *repens*) purple-red stems and purple-pink flowers
24. Soapwort, double pink flowers
25. Sweet William (*Dianthus barbatus*)
26. White Evening Primrose
27. Sweet Rocket, lilac and white forms
28. Narcissus, white ('Cheerfulness')
29. Thyme 'Fragrantissimus'

### Hedging
30. Yew

*Step into the shoes of the alchemist's apprentice and enter the exotic world of the parfumier. Explore the delights of this ancient art and learn to create your own unique perfume.*

ABOVE: *Rose petals yield perfume's favourite essential oil.*

# Romantic Blends

Here begins a lifelong friendship with the art of blending essential oils to create aromatic elixirs, pleasurable in both the making and the using.

These concentrated blends of essential oils can be used in several ways (after safety checks, see pages 250–1). They can be added directly to the water in vaporizers (page 124) or room sprays (page 68), sprinkled on potpourris, used to scent paper, ink and candles (pages 172 and 127), mixed with vegetable oil as a skin cream or massage oil (page 98), or mixed with alcohol and water as a traditional perfume.

### TONE UP YOUR SENSE OF SMELL

Your first tool is a keen sense of smell, and practice and concentration are the keys to improving it. Become familiar with the character of each of your essential oils by sniffing them at different times and seasons, and listing all your observations in a notebook. Choose a clean, quiet room with natural humidity. To clear your nose, breathe in fresh air or sniff woollen fabric.

Avoid inhaling directly from the essential oil bottle, which can deaden your sense of smell. Prepare sniffing blotters (narrow strips of unsized paper), tip a drop of oil on to the blotter and wave it gently. Be relaxed, quiet and comfortable and, with your eyes closed, sniff the air. Note your observations straightaway, as the nose tires quickly. Ask yourself questions such as: is the scent sweet, floral, woody, mossy, smoky, resinous, green, dry, heavy, light, exotic or narcotic? Note the layers of different aromas from a single oil, and list personal memory associations. Over time, you will become aware of subtle feelings and moods engendered by different oils. Test no more than five oils in succession.

To develop your scent memory, do blind tests, first with markedly different oils like Lavender and Peppermint; then tackle similar oils like those of the Citrus group.

### INGREDIENTS

For mixing perfumes you will need: good-quality essential oils with dropper dispensers, alcohol, pure water (distilled or filtered), small lidded dark glass or ceramic bottles and labels, measuring teaspoon, small funnel and notebook.

Alcohol is a preservative and solvent for essential oils and helps their dispersal. The best scentless alcohol is ethyl alcohol, a licensed product available in some counties, usually sold 'denatured' through perfumers. Alternatively, use food-grade isopropyl alcohol or vodka.

### SIMPLE MIXTURES

Start with pairs of essential oils, mixing the drops in a tiny bottle or eggcup, or putting them directly into a vaporizer. These first experiments will provide ideas for the building blocks of more complex perfumes and you will begin to 'sense' oils that work well together. Try a drop each of Lavender and Grapefruit, Frankincense and Rose, Mandarin and Clove, Bergamot FCF and Cedarwood.

# The Art of Perfumery

The perfumer's art is to blend the notes to make a harmonious chord, to create an 'accord'. Four useful oils which provide a bridge between other scent groups are Lavender and Rosewood (especially between citrus and floral notes), and Vanilla and Sandalwood (between base and middle notes). Rose, Jasmine or Ylang-Ylang will sweeten the initial 'cough medicine' or 'paint' scent of some oil mixtures.

When you want to create your own perfume, decide on a fragrance mood; perhaps light and airy, or rich and woody, or exotic and mysterious. Visualize colour associations, links with flowers and trees, and settings in which the perfume would be used, to lead your mind towards the kind of ingredients it might include.

## CATEGORIES OF FRAGRANCE

In the perfume industry, names indicate blended strengths. The quantities given are for a 25 ml / fl oz / 5 tsp / 500 drop bottle.

### PERFUME

(15–25 per cent essential oil)
75–125 drops essential oil, tsp alcohol, approx $^1/_5$ tsp water.

### EAU-DE-PARFUM

(10–15 per cent essential oil)
50–75 drops essential oil, $^1/_2$ tsp alcohol, approx tsp water.

### EAU DE TOILETTE

(6–10 per cent essential oil)
25–50 drops essential oil, $^1/_2$ tsp alcohol, approx $^1/_4$ tsp water.

### EAU DE COLOGNE

(3–6 per cent essential oil)
10–30 drops essential oil, $^1/_2$ tsp alcohol, approx $^1/_3$ tsp water.

### SPLASH COLOGNE

(1–3 per cent essential oil)
5–15 drops essential oil, tsp alcohol, 2 tsp water.

### TOILET WATERS

are essential oils in distilled water.

## Making Perfume

First choose the strength you wish, then consider the essential oils. Several recipes are offered here to get you started. If you wish to copy a famous fragrance, a German publication, the *H&R Fragrance Guide* by Glöss & Co, lists the key ingredients of 800 perfumes. Although these are only a fraction of the odours in their secret recipes, it is fun to attempt rough 'copies'.

A perfume usually includes top, middle and base notes. These are categories based on the evaporation rates of essential oils. Top notes evaporate first and are the light, bright, stimulating aromas noticed first in a perfume. Middle notes are the heart, the dominant character of a blend. Base notes are sedative, calming odours; they give the perfume a lasting quality and are fixatives which make all the ingredients evaporate in a smooth curve rather than patchily. The division between notes is inexact, because each essential oil is made up of many compounds which evaporate at different rates, so a single oil like Jasmine can spread over all the categories.

## Perfume Notes

TOP NOTES Scent vanishes within hours:
Angelica, Basil, Bergamot, Cardamom, Citrus (all), Coriander, Eucalyptus, Fennel, Hyacinth, Lemon Grass, Melissa, Peppermint, Petitgrain, Pine, Spearmint, Tarragon.

MIDDLE NOTES Scent lasts 24–60 hours:
Black Pepper, Chamomiles, Clary Sage, Cypress, Galbanum, Geranium, Ginger, Jasmine, Juniper Berry, Lavender, Marjoram, Mimosa, Myrtle, Neroli, Nutmeg, Palmarosa, Rose, Rosemary, Rosewood, Tea Tree, Thyme, Ylang-Ylang.

BASE NOTES Scent lasts from 60 hours to 6–7 days:
Balsam of Peru, Benzoin, Cedarwood, Cinnamon, Frankincense, Myrrh, Oakmoss, Patchouli, Sandalwood, Vanilla, Vetiver.

## The Process

In a small bottle, first place the base notes, then add the middle notes, and then the top notes, rolling the mixture between each addition to amalgamate the odours and smelling the result. List your ingredients accurately. Leave the mixture to mature for 48 hours; sniff and adjust the recipe if required. Add the alcohol and leave again for 48 hours, then add pure water and leave to mature for 4–8 weeks in a cool, dark place. Label and date. Store out of sunlight in a suitably beautiful, preferably dark bottle.

## Using Perfume

Use generously as all perfumes, once opened, have a limited shelf life: usually one year for high concentrates down to three months for low concentrates. Apply fragrance to pulse points, wrists, the back of the neck, behind the ears, the inside of the elbows and the back of the knees, and also to the cleavage, hollow of the throat, shoulders and hair.

## The Recipes
### True Eau-de-Cologne

This all-time favourite is a light, refreshing blend which changed the fashion in scents. Blend the following drops of essential oils in a 70ml bottle: 44 Bergamot, 15 Lemon, 4 Neroli, 2 Lavender, 1 each Rosemary and Clove. Add 50 ml alcohol. Leave for 48 hours, then add 12 ml pure water. Mature, label and store out of sunlight.

The following eau-de-Cologne recipes are given in drops of essential oils to be added to a 25 ml bottle, then add 3½ tsp alcohol and after 48 hours top up with (approx 1½ tsp) water. Mature for 6 weeks. Label and date.

1 ml = 20 drops
1 tsp = 5 ml = 100 drops
1 fluid oz = 5 tsp = 25 ml

## Refreshing Colognes

**RONDELETIA** Popular since the sixteenth century.
8 Lavender, 4 Bergamot, 3 Clove, 2 Rose.

**ZEST** 10 Palmarosa, 8 Orange, 3 each Petitgrain and Lime, 1 Black Pepper.

**ENGLISH LAVENDER** 12 Lavender, 3 Bergamot, 1 each Rosemary, Clary Sage, Geranium, Cedarwood and Oakmoss.

## For Romance

**INTRIGUE** 4 each Mandarin and Juniper, 2 each Clary Sage, Ylang-Ylang and Black Pepper.

**FASCINATION** 4 Jasmine, 2 each Patchouli and Lemon, 1 Lavender in Lemon vodka.

**MAGNETISM** 5 Frankincense, 3 each Bergamot, Orange and Lemon, 1 Ginger.

**DANCING TILL DAWN** 10 Vanilla extract, 4 Lemon, 3 Grapefruit, 1 each Bergamot and Mint.

**CASTAWAY** 5 Mandarin, 4 Sandalwood, 2 each Ylang-Ylang and Petitgrain.

**SMOOTH AND CREAMY** 4 Bergamot, 2 Ylang-Ylang, 1 Clove, 1 tsp Vanilla extract.

**SUN DRENCHED** 5 Orange, 3 Jasmine, 2 each Sandalwood and Patchouli.

**SECRET GARDEN** 3 Sandalwood, 2 each Rose, Jasmine and Bergamot.

**AFFINITY** 3 each Neroli, Bergamot and Lavender, 2 Vetiver.

**MELTING MOMENTS** 10 Vanilla extract, 6 Sandalwood, 3 Rosewood, 2 Orange.

**CONSUMED** 6 Sandalwood, 5 Orange, 1 tsp Vanilla extract.

**HONEYMOON** 3 Rose, 2 each Jasmine and Lime, 1 Cinnamon.

## Just for Women

**HARMONY** 5 Coriander, 3 each Rose and Frankincense, 2 Lime.

**CASCADE** 5 Rose, 3 Bergamot, 2 Lemon, 1 Cinnamon in Lemon vodka.

**CONSTANTINOPLE** 4 each Ylang-Ylang and Black Pepper, 3 Rose, 2 Rosewood, 1/2 tsp Vanilla extract.

**CONCUBINE** 3 each Jasmine and Rosewood, 1 each Sandalwood, Ginger and Mint.

**ARABESQUE** 6 Bergamot, 4 Rosewood, 3 Sandalwood, 2 each Cedarwood and Patchouli.

**FREE SPIRIT** 4 Jasmine, 3 Bergamot, 2 Lemon, 1 Orange.

**VENUS NOIR** 4 each Rose and Sweet Myrtle, 3 Sandalwood, 2 Patchouli and Oakmoss.

**PERFECT LOVE** 10 Rose, 6 each Bergamot and Jasmine, 4 Coriander, 2 Sandalwood.

## Especially for Men

**VITALITY** 3 Juniper, 2 Bergamot, 1 Coriander.

**MOUNTAIN AIR** 6 Cedarwood, 2 each Cypress, Lemon, Rosemary and Sandalwood.

**ANDALUSIA** 3 each Rosewood and Lime, 2 Vetiver in Lemon vodka.

**PEACOCK** 6 each Orange and Bergamot, 2 Basil, 1 Coriander.

**ALFRESCO** 3 Lime, 2 each Cardamom and Cedarwood.

**ADVENTURE** 5 Bergamot, 2 each Jasmine and Sandalwood, 1 each Cedarwood and Grapefruit.

**HIDDEN FIRE** 3 each Frankincense, Black Pepper and Lavender.

**MOONSHINE** In Lemon vodka: (top note) 3 each Mandarin and Bergamot, 2 each Lavender and Lemon; (middle note) 4 Jasmine, 2 each Pine needle, Geranium, Petitgrain and Juniper Berry, 1 Rose; (base note) 2 Cedarwood, 1 each Oakmoss, Angelica root and Vetiver.

ABOVE: *Dried Roses have a special beauty; for their longlasting scent and rich colour they were the original ingredient of potpourri.*

## Other Aromatic Products

A phenomenon recorded in history in a rare few people, including Alexander the Great and Walt Whitman, is the constant radiation of a natural sweet perfume. The rest of us may indulge with delight in applied aromatic potions and lotions. Use the essential oil blends given on page 167 for a whole range of other scented ideas.

### AFTERSHAVE

Mix any of the essential oil blends with Witchhazel instead of ethyl alcohol and water, to create a delicious aftershave.

### OIL-BASED PERFUME

You can use a carrier oil instead of the alcohol-water mix. Jojoba (actually a liquid wax) is best because it has excellent keeping qualities; next best is fractionated coconut oil, usually labelled 'light coconut oil'. Blend 7–10 drops essential oils per 1 tsp carrier oil. Label and date. Mature for 2 weeks in a cool, dark place, swilling daily. Use as perfume; it will keep for up to 6 months. This blend is 2–3 times more concentrated than a massage blend because only a little is applied, but it means a skin test is advisable before use.

### FLORAL WATERS

For a splash cologne, mix 8 drops Lavender, Rose or Neroli essential oil in 250 ml (10 fl oz) distilled water in a screw-topped bottle and shake vigorously. For a scent, mix 15 drops essential oil with 25 ml (1 fl oz) alcohol.

### BATH OIL

Add 4–6 drops essential oil to 1 tbsp almond oil (for dry skin) or to creamy milk (for better dispersal). For a bubble bath, add the oils with 1 tbsp mild liquid soap or baby shampoo.

### SOAP

Soak cottonwool balls or muslin in your chosen essential oils mixture and wrap them around a bar of unscented soap. Seal in cling film and leave to mature for 6 weeks.

## *Romantic Body Recipes*

Establish your fragrant trademark to create a sub-liminal but potent aromatic trigger in the memory of someone you love.

### SATIN BODY TREATMENT

Fruit acids remove dull, dead skin cells, revealing silky skin beneath. Mash 3 large Peaches, Apricots, Strawberries, Love Apples (Tomatoes) or slices of Pineapple. Stir in 1 tbsp runny honey, and 1 tsp yoghurt if desired. Smooth over the body and leave for 5–10 minutes before rinsing off with warm water. Apply moisturizer. Newly revealed skin will be more vulnerable, so avoid direct exposure to sunlight immediately afterwards, and use with caution on the face.

### EXOTIC BODY POWDER

Put a thin layer of arrowroot or cornstarch powder in a small, deepish cardboard box (such as a jewellery gift box) with a snug-fitting lid. Add a layer of one type of freshly picked flower, such as winter or summer Honeysuckle, Violet, Rose, Jasmine, Lilac, Sweet Pea or Mock Orange (*Philadelphus*). Cover with a layer of powder and repeat the process with 2–3 layers of flowers. Fit the lid and leave for 3–4 days, shaking occasionally. Sift out the flowers and repeat the process with fresh ones, then remove. The powder will take on a delicate fragrance, which increases if left for a few weeks. For a spicy alternative, mix some very finely powdered spice, such as Allspice or Clove, into the plain powder and leave for 1 week to 10 days. Dust over the body as talc.

### FRAGRANT TRESSES

Sprinkle Rose, Orange flower or other aromatic water on damp hair after washing and leave to dry naturally. Alternatively, spray flower water on to dry hair, or touch a little neat essential oil to the strands of your hair, avoiding skin, scalp and clothes.

### KISSABLE LIP BALM

To 1 tsp runny honey, add 1/4 tsp rosewater concentrate (ask your pharmacist for 31x strength, which the pharmacist dilutes to prepare triple-strength rosewater) or alternatively 1/4 tsp rosewater and 1 drop Rose essential oil.

### SCENTED LINGERIE

Add a sensuous touch to your lingerie by storing it in fragrant drawers. Put 5–10 drops of essential oils on a cotton wool ball and rub the backs of paper drawer liners (you can use decorative wall paper). An alternative is to amplify the scent of a handful of dried flower petals: sprinkle on 5 drops essential oil, put in a small glass jar and leave for 2–3 days to absorb the scent. Then scatter the petals in the drawer, place in a muslin, silk or velvet sachet, and tuck a few into your partner's pocket as a fragrant reminder of the night before.

## *The Aromatic Setting*

For the playful game of seduction, spice the air with fragrance, spread sensuous silks and velvet and sprinkle an inviting trail of fresh petals.

### 'LOVE IS IN THE AIR' POTPOURRI

2 cups Rose petals, 1 cup each small whole Roses and Rose buds, Honeysuckle and Mock Orange, 1/2 cup Sweet Myrtle leaves and flowers, 2 Cinnamon sticks, 2 Vanilla pods, 30 g (1 oz ) Oakmoss. Add essential oils: 2 drops each Rose, Neroli and Bergamot, 1 drop Jasmine.

### OIL VAPORIZERS

Add drops of essential oils for a seductive atmosphere as follows: 6 Sandalwood and 2 Orange; 5 Sandalwood and 2 Rose; 6 Jasmine and 4 Orange; 5 Rose, 2 each Jasmine and Bergamot; 2 each Vanilla or Benzoin and Lime.

ABOVE: *Exotic Body Powder scented with Violets.*

## SPICY ROOM FRAGRANCING

Many of the spicy burning mixtures given on page 124 will add romance to the air.

## Sensual Sachets

Tuck sachets of the following mixes behind *chaise longue* cushions or use them to scent bedlinen.

FRESH MIX   Rose, Mock Orange, Honeysuckle, Sweet Marjoram, Sweet Myrtle, Violet, Blackcurrant leaves.

DRIED MIXES   Rose petals and Cardamom; Rose petals, Patchouli leaves and Vanilla pod; Sweet Myrtle and Star Anise; Rose petals, Sweet Myrtle and Sandalwood chips.

## Intimate Treats

Prepare a scented candle, room spray or massage oil with your aromatic 'trademark' (see page 169) and intensify sensual sharing by adding aphrodisiac fragrance to romantic activities.

HOT TUB OR BATH   Use up to 6 drops of sensuous oils and disperse well.

JACUZZI   Use 3 drops of essential oil per person and add when you enter the jacuzzi, as the jets circulate and disperse the fragrance quickly.

## SAUNA BLEND

For a seductive blend: blend 5 drops Sandalwood, 3 drops Bergamot FCF and 2 drops Lavender. Add 2 drops to each 600ml (1 pint) water and sprinkle a little on the heat source at intervals. For relaxing and detoxifying, use oils which can be inhaled and expelled via perspiration such as Pine, Eucalyptus (common, Lemon or Peppermint) or Tea Tree.

## ROSE TOES

To 3 tsp Almond oil, or 2 tsp Almond oil with $^{1}/_{2}$ tsp Avocado oil and $^{1}/_{2}$ tsp Calendula oil, add 2 drops Rose Maroc essential oil and 1 drop natural Vanilla extract. Massage sensuously into the feet.

## ENERGIZER BATH

Into a muslin bag place 1 walnut-sized piece fresh Ginger root, crushed or chopped, 1 handful Nasturtium leaves, 1 small piece Cinnamon stick or 2 Star Anise, and 1 tbsp honey. Hang under running hot water.

## ORIGINAL SIN BATH

Chop and simmer 5 Apples with sugar and $^{1}/_{2}$ tsp Cinnamon. Strain the excess juice into a jug. Place the Apple pulp with a handful of skin-soothing oatmeal into a muslin bag and suspend it from the hot tap. Add the excess juice, with 1 tsp Vanilla extract, to the bath. Scatter crimson Peony petals across the water.

## PEACHES AND CREAM BATH

Slice 2 Peaches, crack their stones and put both in a muslin bag under running hot water. To the drawn bath, add 1 tbsp cream mixed with 1 tsp Vanilla extract. Scatter the surface of the bath with fresh, fragrant Rose petals.

## PASSION WINE

To 200ml ($^{1}/_{3}$ pint) of red wine add a handful of fresh Basil leaves, $^{1}/_{4}$ tsp Cinnamon, $^{1}/_{4}$ tsp powdered Ginger. Infuse in a dark, cool place for 1–2 weeks, then sieve out the Basil, and strain through muslin cloth to remove the spices. Drink neat from liqueur glasses, or $^{1}/_{3}$ fill crystal wineglasses and top up with champagne.

## THE ULTIMATE SEDUCTION

Create a fragrant body map by placing different perfumes on each of your favourite zones and invite your lover to discover how many perfumes you have applied.

ABOVE: *Pillow slips absorb the scents of Lavender and Roses while drying in the sun.*

LEFT: *Scatter Roses for a truly sensual bath.*

ABOVE: *A wedding bouquet composed with the Language of Flowers: Roses speak of 'true love'; Daisy 'I share your sentiments'; Honeysuckle, 'fidelity and generous devotion'; Strawberry 'perfection'; Ivy 'marriage'.*

RIGHT: *A fragrant midsummer circlet of Lavender, Love-in-the-Mist, Elderflower, white Sweet William, scented Geranium leaves and Alpine Strawberries.*

# Aromatic Wedding Preparations

### INVITATIONS

Scented paper and ink would provide both a pleasurable surprise to the recipient and an instant envoy of goodwill. Choose a scent that echoes what you wear or keep a distinctive fragrance for special correspondence. For instant fragrance, add a few Lavender flowers inside the envelope of any communication that aims for a harmonious result.

### SCENTED PAPER

Place 1 tbsp dried herbs in a closed box of writing paper with a Tonka Bean or other fixative (choose from Cardamom, Cinnamon sticks, Lemon Verbena leaves, Patchouli leaves, Rose petals, Star Anise, Sweet Myrtle leaves, *Thymus* 'Fragrantissimus', Vanilla pod and Vetiver roots). Alternatively, place 5–10 drops of your favourite essential oil(s) such as Rose, Jasmine, Bergamot or Sandalwood on a piece of cottonwool and place it in the box. Leave for at least 2 weeks, then remove a scented sheet of paper as required.

### SCENTED INK

Scent your writing ink with a matching or complementary fragrance by adding 5 drops of essential oil to a bottle of ink, remembering to shake the bottle each time before refilling your pen.

### PETAL CONFETTI

Flowers have always been part of a wedding day, and throwing lightly fragrant petal confetti is a joyful celebration, when earlier butterfly nerves are forgotten and sentimental tears have been dried and replaced with bubbling laughter. Gather blossoms from your garden in advance and dry them as outlined on pages 64–5. Dark Rose petals make the best confetti, and can be highlighted with blue Love-in-the-Mist, orange Calendula petals or purple Lavender flowers.

# Romantic Dinner for Two

*Flavours for intimate meals à deux need to be intriguing but piquant, exemplified by the combination of Lovage with the kick of Tabasco on the oysters.*

## Lovers' Coupe

*If you don't have any Angostura bitters, add 2 or 3 thin curls of pared orange zest, squeezing them over the glass to encourage the essential oils into the drink.*

**preparation: 10 minutes; chilling: 30 minutes**

**makes 4 glasses**

4 sugar cubes
2 tbsp brandy
few drops of Angostura bitters
few sprigs of Borage with flowers
150 ml / ¼ pint chilled peach juice or peach and
    orange juice
½ bottle chilled dry Champagne
few sprigs of Lemon Balm with flowers, or other
    suitable flowers, to decorate

In a small bowl or deep saucer, soak the sugar cubes in the brandy and sprinkle over a few drops of Angostura bitters. Put 1 cube in each of 2 chilled champagne flutes, reserving the remaining cubes for seconds.

Add the Borage to the peach juice or peach and orange juice, reserving a few sprigs and flowers to decorate. Stir in and chill for 30 minutes.

Remove the Borage from the juice and pour two-thirds of it into the flutes — chill the rest for refills.

Top up the glasses with Champagne and chill the rest. Decorate with Borage and Lemon Balm or other suitable flowers. Sip as soon as possible.

## Oysters with Lovage and Tabasco Cream

**preparation: about 20 minutes**

1 dozen oysters
2 shallots, chopped
crushed ice
juice of 1 lemon
3–4 small ripe sweet tomatoes
few Watercress leaves
few Lovage leaves
175 ml / 6 fl oz crème fraîche
few drops of Tabasco sauce
freshly ground black pepper

Scrub the oysters well and then open them carefully, with the curved shells downwards to retain as much of the juices as possible. Using the flat of the knife, loosen the oysters from their shells but leaving them in place.

Lifting each oyster just slightly, put a little of the chopped shallot under each. Set the oysters on 2 plates lined with crushed ice. Squeeze over a little lemon juice and season with pepper.

Put the tomatoes in a bowl, pour boiling water over them and leave them for a minute. Drain and remove their skins. Halve, deseed and cut the flesh into dice. Shred the Watercress and Lovage leaves.

Flavour the crème fraîche to taste with a few drops of Tabasco. Spoon this over the oysters and scatter over the shredded herbs and tomato dice. Serve immediately.

LEFT: *Oysters with Lovage and Tabasco Cream served with Lovers' Coupe.*

## Pan-fried Prawns with Chives and Ginger

*preparation: 10 minutes; chilling: 30 minutes,*
*cooking: 5 minutes*

6 raw jumbo or other large prawns
1 garlic clove, smashed
2.5-cm /1-inch piece of peeled fresh root Ginger,
    frozen and grated
1 stalk of Lemon Grass, tender central core only,
    snipped
¼ tsp five-spice powder
3 sprigs of Coriander, snipped
1 tbsp Kikkoman or other good soy sauce
juice of ½ lime
2 tbsp groundnut oil
1 tbsp dark Oriental sesame oil
1 tbsp dry sherry
small bunch of Chives
Chinese noodles tossed with butter and Rocket, to
    serve
freshly ground black pepper

Peel and devein the prawns, but leave the tails on.

Put the garlic and Ginger in a bowl with the Lemon Grass, five-spice powder and half the Coriander. With a fork or small spoon whisk, stir in half the soy sauce, lime juice and groundnut oil and mix well. Season lightly with pepper.

Sprinkle the prawns generously with sesame oil, then coat them with the spice mixture. Chill for about 30 minutes, or longer if convenient.

To finish, heat half the remaining groundnut oil in a wok, sauté or deep frying pan and stir-fry the prawns for 5–6 minutes. Remove the prawns from the wok or pan and keep them warm on serving plates.

Add the dry sherry and the rest of the groundnut oil to the wok or pan together with the rest of the soy sauce and the lime juice. Stir in 3 tablespoons of water and snip over half the bunch of Chives. Heat through, then spoon or pour the mixture over the cooked prawns. Sprinkle over the remaining Coriander sprigs and snip over the rest of the bunch of Chives.

Serve the prawns at once, with Chinese noodles that have been boiled and tossed with butter, and lots of snipped Rocket leaves.

ABOVE: *Pan-fried Prawns with Chives and Ginger served with Chinese noodles and Rocket.*

RIGHT: *Basil and Vanilla Ice-cream.*

176

# *Basil and Vanilla Ice-cream*

*preparation: 20 minutes; freezing: 2–3 hours*

*300 ml / ½ pint full-fat milk*
*3 split Vanilla pods*
*4 egg yolks*
*115 g / 4 oz caster sugar*
*150 ml / ¼ pint chilled double cream or crème fraîche*
*1 tbsp very finely snipped Basil, plus more whole*
*    leaves for decoration*
*black pepper (optional)*
*fraises des bois or small strawberries, to serve*

Put the milk in a pan with the Vanilla pods and bring to boiling point over a low heat. The moment it bubbles, turn down the heat and simmer for several minutes. Take the pan off the heat and keep it warm.

In a large bowl, whisk together the egg yolks and sugar until light and frothy.

Remove the Vanilla pods from the milk and pour the hot milk, a little at a time, over the egg yolk and sugar mixture, stirring vigorously.

Pour the mixture into the saucepan and return to a very low heat. Bring almost to boiling point but not quite, stirring all the time with a large wooden spoon. The cream will thicken gradually until it can coat the back of the wooden spoon. Do not allow to boil and lift off the heat a few times during cooking. Strain through a fine sieve and stir frequently while it cools.

Whisk the double cream until standing in firm peaks, then fold it into the cold custard. Stir in the Basil and, if you like, a modest grinding of black pepper.

Pour the mixture into an ice-cream maker and churn, or pour into a suitable container and freeze for 2–3 hours. If not using an ice-cream maker, after about 45 minutes, remove the container from the freezer, blend in the food processor for a few seconds and return to the freezer. After about 45 minutes, repeat the process again, then leave the ice-cream in the freezer until completely frozen.

Remove the container from the freezer about 10 minutes before you want to serve – the timing will depend on room temperature. Spoon into individual coupes or glasses. Decorate the ice-cream with very small sprigs of Basil, and serve with fraises des bois or small strawberries.

Quick tip: if you haven't got the time or inclination to make the custard, buy the best available vanilla ice-cream, allow it to soften very slightly, blend it with the snipped Basil (and pepper, if liked) in a food processor and freeze; there is no need to take this out and blend again.

CHAPTER SIX

# *Rest, Meditation & Sleep*

*At the end of the day, when we have quiet, reflective time, rich resinous aromas will slow and deepen our breathing and return us to a state of peaceful contemplation. From this rested state we can choose to lift our thoughts to higher realms, or to release them into gentle sleep.*

The sense of warmth and security induced by the sight of a log fire crackling with Cedar and Pine is a shared experience reaching back to the earliest cave fires. When the burning wood was resinous branches of Frankincense or Juniper, ancient tribes noticed that the rich balsamic fragrance spread well-being through the group with a profound uplifting effect. This early communal experience of fragrance is acknowledged in the word 'perfume', from *par fume*, meaning 'by smoke'. To regulate this experience, the balsamic resins were made into incense for prayer and meditation, and it is still used by the major religions. The thirteenth-century mystic Ramon Llull 'found in trees and herbs a type of the divine potency by which the natural world might serve as a ladder to the spiritual'.

On warm summer nights, a similar deep serenity accompanies a starlit stroll in the garden, when night reveals a different dimension. Under the moon, silver leaves shimmer; white Peonies and Lilies, and the froth of Sweet Cicely and Meadowsweet flowers, seem to be lit from within; and we can almost see the ultraviolet markings on the lip of the Foxglove flower luring bees far inside. Deep indigo and purple skies magnify night-scented flowers 'seen' with the nose, as drowsy Lilac, Honeysuckle and Mignonette drift across the night air.

When we are ready for the renewal and regeneration of sleep, there are aromatics to coax the conscious mind into letting go and drifting into sweet dreams: soothing herb teas of Lime blossom or Chamomile, deeply relaxing baths with Clary Sage or Neroli, a soporific herb pillow, and sheets that smell of Lavender.

HERBS & OILS
FOR REST & SLEEP •
NIGHT-SCENTED
GARDEN DESIGNS •
FIRESIDE AROMATICS
& SOOTHING HERBAL
PREPARATIONS •
EVENING TISANES

*The fragrances of several familiar herbs encountered on a garden stroll in the gloaming are calming and prepare one for satisfying sleep.*

# Evening Scents

## Tranquil Lavender

The cool sweet scent of Lavender is relaxing and harmonizing. It helps the mind to let go of the day's events: the perfume and its deep violet colour, associated with compassion, work together on a subtle level to make forgiveness seem a sensible solution. In a sleep pillow, Lavender counters insomnia and eases the passage to deep, refreshing sleep – an effect recently demonstrated in hospital wards.

A further trio of fragrant violet-coloured flowers to smooth the passage to sleep includes Sweet Violet, whose soothing tea reduces nervous headaches and insomnia. This charming flower, revered by writers from Homer to Shakespeare, was the favourite perfume of the last Empress Dowager of China. She imported bottles of 'Violette Regia' from Europe and, swathed in violet silks, repeatedly played the role of the Goddess of Compassion, Kwan Yin, in her Summer Palace theatre.

Another is Lilac, with flower clusters of small, beautiful florets and a scent so powerful it verges on the narcotic. It is particularily soothing to children lying in bed on early summer evenings, when the diluted perfume drifts in through an open window.

The third is the purple or white Sweet Rocket, also known as Vesper Flower for its gentle perfume on the evening breeze. This is an easy-to-grow, old-fashioned, cottagey biennial that evokes childhood memories, real or imagined, of happy country gardens.

## Moonlight Flowers

Clary Sage, a herb 'under the dominion of the moon', radiates a mysterious relaxing, insomnia-reducing muscatel fragrance from its spires of dusty rose, pink and lilac flowers. Clary wine was famous for its narcotic properties, although the combination with alcohol can cause nightmares. Clary's essential oil has a clean, warm, slightly nutty green aroma that counters stress and tension from physical and emotional sources and shifts inhibitions, to create a feel-good factor ranging from relaxing, mildly inebriating or aphrodisiac to uplifting and almost spiritual, as it enhances the direction the mind wishes to go. Added to an evening bath it is relaxing and uplifting, and may induce vivid dreams plus the beneficial ability to recall them with an understanding of the lessons they may have to offer.

White flowers have a dreamy, otherworldly appearance in the evening, reminding us that this part of the day belongs to the 'Night with her train of

LEFT: *Rich purple Lavender evokes the peace of Night.*

BELOW: *Held in great affection by the old herbalists, the unique scent of Sweet Violets charms both men and women.*

stars. And her great gift of sleep' (W. E. Henley). The sumptuous white Peony has a sweet fragrance to lure the mind straight into soft, downy dreamland. Peony seeds were once strung into necklaces as an antidote to witchcraft.

Lily-of-the-Valley exerts its charm in the evening. Legend tells of the love between a nightingale and the flower, and how the bird would not return to the wood until the Lily-of-the-Valley bloomed each spring. Another legend records that the small white bell flowers were formed from the tears of the Virgin Mary, making the floral infusions so valuable in the Middle Ages that they were kept in gold and silver vessels. Through this, the plant acquired another name, 'Ladder to Heaven', hinting at the sleep of divine dreams.

The scent of the elegant white, blue or pink Roman Hyacinth (*Hyacinthus orientalis*) is strong but tranquillizing. In aromatherapy, its strength is helpful for soothing stress and grief. Its fragrance can create a calm and forgiving state, restore equalibrium, protect against bizarre dreams and bring peaceful sleep.

The light-reflecting daisy flowers of Chamomile are infused as a digestive tea, especially after overeating, which is drunk to calm nerves, relieve insomnia and prevent nightmares. The tea is soothing and mildly sedative for restless children.

ABOVE: *Drowsy Clary Sage can induce vivid dreams.*

## Ghostly Twilight

Evening Primrose has soft yellow or white flowers that unfurl at twilight, releasing a soothing sweet scent on the night air and a slight luminescence. The seed oil offers numerous remarkable health benefits, including the easing of withdrawal from alcohol which may help attain restful sleep.

Graceful swags of Hops produce ghostly strobiles (female flowers) which contain a soporific compound that is sedative and tranquillizing. Used as tea bags or in herb pillows, the scent is reminiscent of beer and does not suit everyone.

## Ethereal Blue

Perhaps most ethereal in the evening light are the blue-flowered herbs: the faintly scented Forget-me-Not, whose flowers appear to hover in the air, the Madonna-blue Borage with its cucumber scent, and the sweet, fruity *Thymus* 'Fragrantissimus', whose blue leaves shimmer in starlight and which, of all the many Thymes, would most aptly fit Kipling's 'wind-bit thyme that smells of dawn in Paradise'.

*The most important aromas for creating a deeply tranquil state come from balsamic tree resins, substances valued in every culture for their long-lasting soothing and healing fragrance.*

# Aromatic Woods & Resins

ABOVE: *Wood from drowsy Lilac releases its sweet aroma on log fires.*

Resins are a tree's first-aid device, with their own internal circulation system enabling them to travel quickly to any point in the tree that is attacked or wounded. To fulfil this protective role resins are antiseptic, antiviral and antifungal, which gives them legendary healing properties in addition to their relaxing, calming and uplifting qualities.

## Uplifting Resins and Oils

Several applications evolved for using aromatic resins, including solid incense sticks and liquid recipes, such as the famous *kyphi* of Egypt, an intoxicating concoction whose fragrance, wrote Plutarch, 'allayed anxieties and brightened dreams and was made of those things which delight most in the night'. This was a warm, comforting, complex mixture which apothecaries of many countries tried unsuccessfully to reproduce.

Resinous branches are used in smoke bath purifying rituals by African desert tribes and in sweat lodge healing and purification ceremonies by the natives of North America. Branches of Juniper, Cedars and herbaceous Sagebrush are used in sweat lodges to create purifying smoke, and laid on open woven beds over warm coals to provide healing smoke for invalids. Juniper and Sagebrush are used in smudge-sticks for purification and protection, and Sagebrush offers herbal apprentices a route to understanding illnesses by learning to 'tap the spirit' of the plant.

Frankincense and Myrrh were the two most precious Biblical resins. Frankincense resin burns slowly to give off a rich balsamic smoke that deepens breathing and is warming, calming and inspiring. An essential oil from the resin eases tension and opens the mind to elevated thoughts, making it popular for meditation. In Patricia Davis' enlightened book *Subtle Aromatherapy*, she notes that it will help the mind to break negative ties with the past. Frankincense will also help to clear the mind for profoundly relaxing sleep. The essential oil of Myrrh has a rich balsamic odour similar to Frankincense but with a slightly sweeter, sharper edge. It is considered both grounding and uplifting, providing a firm base for those who want to move forward in their spiritual development. Aromatherapists use the essential oil of India's most popular aromatic tree, Sandalwood, to reduce depression and stress in patients, and to quiet mental chatter and create a deeper meditative state in themselves before healing work. Cedar wood is used as a meditation aid by Tibetan Buddhists to enhance a nobility of spirit. Juniper oil is considered emotionally cleansing and is used to detoxify body systems and to reduce nervous tension.

BELOW: *Hidden at the back of borders, tender biennial Incense Plant (*Calomeria amaranthoides*) wafts its church-incense scent across the garden to the surprise and delight of early evening strollers.*

Rosewood is made into rosaries and worry beads to release the soothing balm of its sweet, woody-rose fragrance in the hand. The wood yields a beautifully calming essential oil that can be used to enhance physical or spiritual love.

Glistening dark Aloeswood from species of the *Aquilaria* tree is the most highly prized resinous wood. Its rich warm exotic fragrance was first used in China for the Emperor's scrolls, but its source remained a mystery until this century. In vain, adventurous traders bribed or spied their way into the jungle. Even when the tree was shown to a few, the soft, white, faintly-scented wood was unconvincing. Its secret is that only small internal sections that are pathologically diseased, causing a dense growth of fibres saturated with resin, are transformed into this valuable aromatic substance.

Benzoin is the aromatic vanilla-scented resin of the wild Styrax tree used in Russian church incense. It eases anxiety, calms and pacifies emotional states. Copal resin, from the *Hynenaea courbaril* tree, has a light sweet balsamic fragrance with hints of pine and lemon. It is the main incense of Central America and often mixed with pine needles and wood chips to make a purifying, cleansing and protective mixture for domestic use.

ABOVE: *The magnificent cedar, famed for its aromatic wood, yields an essential oil considered strengthening and confidence-building.*

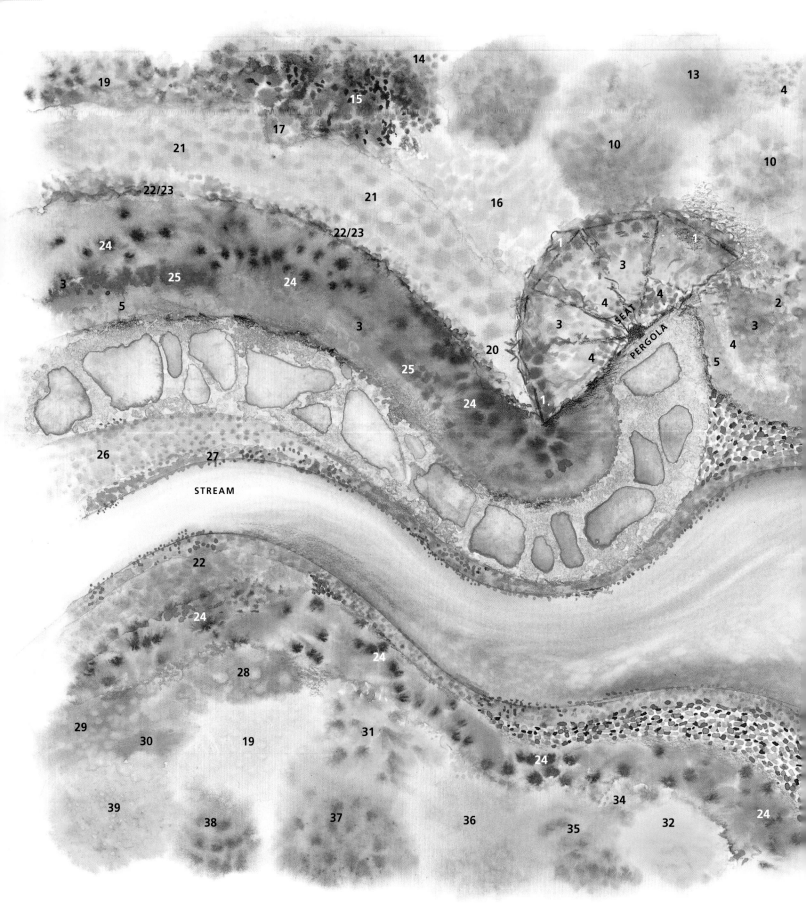

STREAM

PERGOLA

SEAT

## List of Plants in Plan

### Pergola Area

1. Wisteria, white & purple
2. Night-Scented Stocks (*Mathiola longipetala* subsp. *bicornis*)
3. Sweet Violet.
4. Lily-of-the-Valley
5. Silver Artemisia (*A. schmidtiana* 'Nana')
6. Purple Honeysuckle
7. Camassia
8. Sweet Woodruff

### Main Area

9. Linden Tree
10. Silver Birch
11. White Bramble (*Rubus biflorus* var. *quinqueflorus*)
12. Bluebells
13. Cut-leaf Elder
14. Winter-flowering Honeysuckle (*Lonicera* x *purpusii*)
15. Delphinium, deep blue
16. Peony, white
17. Purple Sage
18. Southernwood
19. White Evening Primrose
20. Borage
21. Silver Santolina
22. Catmint
23. Chamomile
24. Lavender 'Hidcote'
25. Purple Petunia
26. Thyme 'Fragrantissimus'
27. Moss
28. Madonna Lily
29. Clary Sage
30. Anise Hyssop
31. Sweet Rocket
32. Meadowsweet
33. Sweet Cicely
34. Monkshood (*Aconitum napellus*)
35. Buddleia, blue
36. Tree Peony (*Romneya coulteri*)
37. Lilac, purple
38. Angelica
39. Philadelphus
40. White Water Lily (*Nymphaea* 'Gonnère')

# Night-scented Nightingale Garden

As light fades into evening, sounds, textures and fragrance are heightened. Among the crickets and cicadas, frogs and owls, the most hauntingly beautiful sound must be that of the nightingale. Legend tells of the love between a nightingale and a Lily-of-the-Valley, and how the bird would not return to the wood until the flower bloomed each Spring. In this garden Lily-of-the-Valley and Bluebells are planted in the woods amidst the undergrowth of Nettles and Bramble to entice the nightingale to nest there. The white trunks of the Birch trees and the sensuous curves of silver, white and blue plants all shimmer in the starlight. The timber frame provides an arbour for fragrant Wisteria. The perfume of Honeysuckle, Sweet Rocket and Night-Scented Stock are strongest in the evening and twilight triggers the opening of Evening Primrose to release its honey scent and faint luminescence. The fragrance of Lilac, Philadelphus and Buddleia waft on the evening breeze and, with the rich purple, blues and iridescent whites, create a velvety cloak of serenity.

# *Moonlight Meditation Garden*

To be in the presence of a sacred grove of noble trees touches a memory of ancient wisdom. Within this ring of thirteen Druid calendar trees is a circle of Silver Sagebrush; the inner circles of calming white Lavender and silver Thyme complete the peaceful atmosphere and allow thoughts to soar to the starry night sky. Then a waft of fragrant herbs gently reconnects us to the earth.

A fragrant grove could also be created with a surround of the Incense Cedar (*Calocedrus decurrens*) which has powerfully scented wood and foliage, or the Juniper tree with its protective aromatic needles. Below the trees grow Sweet Grass for its new-mown hay scent and to burn in purification ceremonies following the natives of North America. Lawn Chamomile underfoot means every movement will release sweet fragrance.

In the centre of this reflective space, make a moon dial to trace the path of the moon or place a shallow bowl of water to reflect it. Float perfumed flowers or scented candles in the bowl for a magical evening. And after a time in the peaceful serenity of this meditation garden, retire to tranquil slumber.

ABOVE: *The play of evening light and water creates a magical atmosphere in a formal garden of clipped herbs.*

## List of Plants in Plan

### Trees
1. Birch
2. Rowan
3. Ash

4. Alder
5. Willow
6. Hawthorn
7. Oak
8. Holly
9. Hazel

10. Vine (on post)
11. Ivy (on post)
12. Dwarf Elder
13. Elder

### Underplanting
14. White Bluebells (*Hyacinthoides hispanica* 'La Grandesse')
15. Sweetgrass

### Inner Circle
16. Sagebrush
17. White Evening Primrose
18. Madonna Lily
19. Moonflower (*Ipomoea alba*)
20. Lavender, white
21. Narcissus, white
22. Pinks, white 'Mrs Simkins'
23. Chamomile
24. Silver Thyme

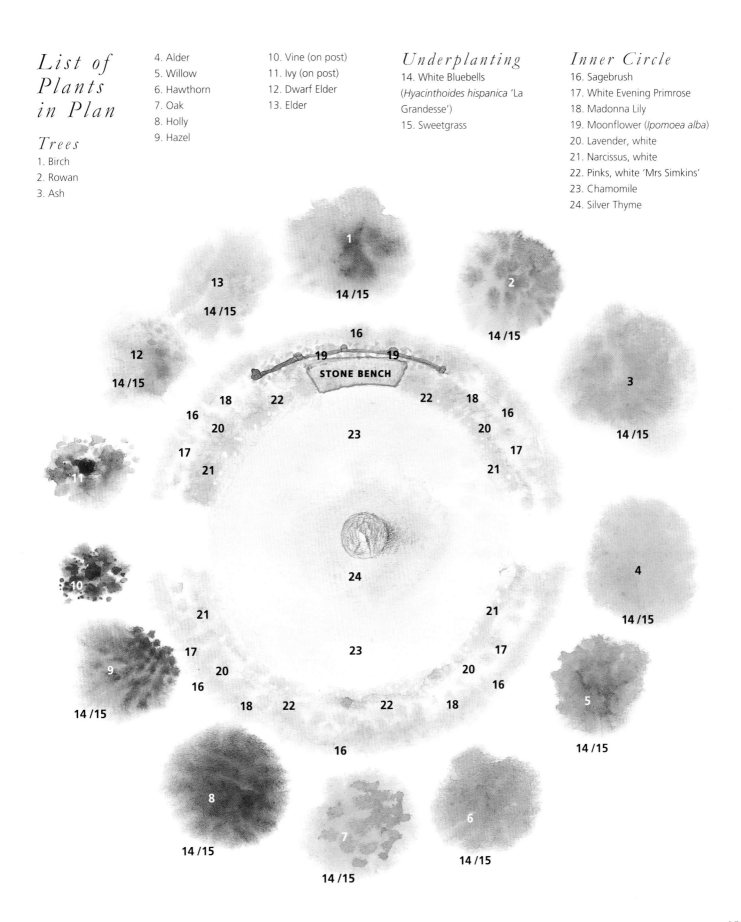

ABOVE: *Fireside aromatics – fragrant woods and scented Pine cones for a relaxing and nurturing evening.*

RIGHT: *Scented candles and incense for a contemplative atmosphere.*

# Incense Mixes & other Aromatics

Making your own incense opens up the range of aromas and offers the pleasure of handling the raw ingredients. Indoors, this type of incense produces much aromatic smoke for several minutes (switch off the smoke alarm!), which then disperses throughout the house, gradually ebbing away to leave a subtle fragrance for 30 minutes to 1 hour. Outdoors in a sheltered place in the garden, you will need to waft some of the smoke gently towards you. The most important ingredient in each mix is the resin, which should make up 50 per cent or more of the volume.

Purchase small self-igniting charcoal discs, which are specially created for burning incense. Place a disc on a heat-resistant dish and hold a match (or 2 or 3) to it until it begins to catch. It will 'sparkle' before starting to burn. When the whole disc is grey/red, lay $1/2$ tsp of incense mixture at a time on the disc to fragrance several rooms. Store the remaining discs in an airtight container to maintain their self-igniting property.

## Ingredients

All the ingredients below are dried. Add a little sugar to any mix for extra sweetness of scent.

RESINS AND GUMS   Copal, Dragon's Blood (*Dracaena* species), Gum Benzoin, Frankincense, Myrrh, Pine.

WOODS AND ROOTS   Aloeswood (*Aquilaria agallocha*), Sweet Flag (*Acorus calamus*) root, Cedarwood shavings, Cinnamon quills, Ginger pieces, Liquorice root (*Glycyrrhiza glabra*), Orris root, Sandalwood shavings, Tamarac branchlets (*Larix laricina*), Vetiver root.

HERBS AND SPICES   Allspice, Cardamom, Citrus peel, Cloves, Coconut, Fennel seed, Mace, Mint, Rosemary, Star Anise, Thyme, Vanilla pod.

OTHER PLANT PARTS Eucalyptus seed pods or dried leaves, Juniper needles and berries, Lavender flowers and stems, Patchouli leaves, Pine needles, dried Rose petals, Tonka bean.

## The Mixes

Legendary Frankincense is most fully enjoyed by burning small pieces of resin either on their own to create a reflective atmosphere and scent clothes or bedding, or added to other incense mixtures – 3 parts Frankincense to 1 part Myrrh is an ancient religious mix.

EVENING MEDITATION ¹/₄ tsp each Myrrh and Sweet Flag root, ¹/₈ tsp Frankincense, 3 Juniper berries.

WINTER MIX ¹/₄ tsp Frankincense, ¹/₄ tsp total Pine needles, Citrus peel and Cinnamon stick.

EASTERN MEDITATION ¹/₈ tsp each Gum Benzoin, Myrrh and Sandalwood, 3–4 Rose petals.

ISLAND BLEND ¹/₄ tsp Gum Benzoin, ¹/₈–¹/₄ tsp total Coconut and Lavender, 2 whole Cloves.

PURIFYING SMUDGE-STICK
Traditionally used by North American natives for purification and protection. Pick 3 pieces of Juniper and 21 of White Sage (*Salvia blanca*), each 25cm (12in) long. Lay them so that the leaves run in the same direction and strip the leaves from the bottom 8cm (3in). Dry for 3–6 days, until almost dry but not brittle. Use the Juniper as the centre of the smudge-stick and enclose it with Sagebrush, keeping the bare stem ends together. Take decorative string or strong embroidery thread, roughly 2 arm-lengths long, and tie it tightly around the bare stems. Spiral the rest of the thread around the bunch and back again, binding the stems into a bundle which will be plumper in the middle. Leave it to dry for a further 3–7 days.

To use: hold the bundle by the bare stem end, light the tip and then blow out the flame so that it smoulders. Circle yourself or the room with the strongly aromatic smoke, or stand the smudge-stick upright in a bowl of sand. To extinguish it, push the smoking end into sand or earth for several seconds – this will allow one smudge-stick to be used several times.

VAPORIZING OILS
Essential oils for meditation include Frankincense, Myrrh, Sandalwood, Neroli, Cedar, Juniper, all Chamomiles, Lavender, Rose, and Clary Sage. Use them in a burner or vaporizer, candles or in a pot-pourri mix.

## Fireside Aromatics

WOODS
Pleasantly aromatic firewoods include: Apple, Balsam Poplar, Bay, Cedar, Cherry, Eucalyptus, Hazel, Juniper, Lilac, Linden/Lime, Pear, Pine and Thuja.

HERBS
Keep large herbal sprigs and prunings in a jar by the fire. Towards the end of the evening, when the fire has died down to glowing embers, dried sprigs of herbs can be added: their essential oils create a brief bright flame and release tantalizing puffs of fragrance. Suitable herbs include Angelica root, Artemisia, Bay, Juniper, Lavender, Lemon Verbena, Rosemary, Sage, Southernwood, Sweet Myrtle, Thyme, old kitchen herbs and spent potpourri.

AROMATIC PINE CONES
On autumn walks, encourage your children to collect decorative Pine cones, then dry and store them. As spring approaches, take the cones and paint the 'leaves' of each one very thinly with vegetable oil scented with essential oil. Leave them to dry, then store in an airtight container until the weather is warmer and fires are no longer needed. When the grate has been cleaned and blacked, fill it with the aromatic Pine cone focal point, repainting the cones when their aroma fades. At the end of summer, they can be used as tinder for the first autumn fires.

191

# *Sweet Dreams*

## *Drowsy Potpourris*

Fill a bowl by the bedside with potpourri to finger before drifting to sleep, or put it into sachets to slip beneath pillows for a soothing waft if you wake or turn in the night. All the ingredients in the following mixes are dried.

### INNER JOURNEY

Create a tranquil mix of incense wood shavings and resins from as many sources as possible. Filter your fingers through this spiritual history of distant cultures and ancient trees.

### HERBAL SOOTHER

Dried Rosemary has a soft, clean scent, not the sharp pungency of the fresh herb or essential oil, and is traditionally associated with preventing nightmares. Mix 2 tbsp Lavender, 1½ tsp Rosemary, 1 tsp Chamomile flowers and 2 tsp Orris powder.

### SWEET SLUMBER

Mix 2 tbsp Rose petals, 2 tsp Woodruff, Melilot or Sweet Grass, 1–2 pinches Vetiver root and 1 tsp Orris powder.

### ARABIAN DREAM

Mix 2 tbsp Rose petals, 2 drops Moroccan Rose oil and 2 tsp Atlas Cedar shavings.

### THUNDER BALM

Citrus and Cinnamon scents are head-clearing during tense, oppressive weather, cheerful Verbena eases aggravation and the Vanilla scent is both relaxing and comforting. Mix 2 tbsp Lemon Verbena, 1 tbsp Lavender (optional), 2 tsp powdered Orange peel, 1 pinch Cinnamon and ½ Vanilla pod.

## *Moonlight Garland*

Create a dried circlet of 'ghostly' greys and whites with delicate blue or white flower sprays to catch the moonlight on a bedroom wall. Into a base of woven pale young twigs, tuck sprigs of Southernwood and other Artemisias, Oakmoss, Honesty (*Lunaria annua*), Lavender, and Gypsophila, and dot it with blue Cornflowers (*Centauria cyanus*), Larkspur (*Consolida ambigua*) or Delphiniums.

## *Relaxing Evening Baths*

The following milky baths are relaxing and soothing to the skin.

### ELDERFLOWER MILK

Infuse 5 fresh Elderflower heads or 3 Elderflower teabags in 300–600 ml (½–1 pint) creamy milk for a few hours then add the milk to a drawn bath. The flowerheads can be floated in the water.

### SOOTHING SODA BATH

Put 3 heaped tbsp bicarbonate of soda (very soothing for itchy skin) in a glass jar. Place 3–4 drops of Chamomile, Lavender or Neroli essential oil on a paper wand, add to the soda and seal. Leave for 1–7 days, shaking occasionally. Remove the wand and add the soda to a drawn bath.

### INSPIRATIONAL SLEEP

Put 4 tbsp powdered milk in a jar. Add 3–4 drops Clary Sage, Frankincense or Vetiver essential oil, seal and leave for 1–7 days, shaking occasionally. (Liquify Vetiver oil by placing its bottle in hot water for a few minutes.) Add to a drawn bath. Scatter the surface with fresh purple Violets or crimson Honeysuckle, or place a white Peony flower in a vase and enjoy its elegant beauty while you relax in the sleepily scented water.

## Oils and Herbs for Fanciful Dreams

Essential oils to enhance dreams include Clary Sage, Sandalwood, Jasmine, Cedarwood and Vetiver. Put 1 drop on a hanky near your pillow and inhale the aroma as you drift off to sleep. Keep a dream notebook by your bed to record your adventures.

### AROMATIC DREAM CATCHER

In a tightly lidded box, add several drops of protective Juniper, Lavender or Frankincense to a cottonwool ball and store with your dream catcher or teddy bear for 3 weeks to infuse the fabric.

### FANTASY DREAM HERBS

Hang posies or garlands of protective Juniper. Add a flowerhead of Dill 'to hinder witches of their will' and a Nutmeg to lure and intoxicate the Bird of Paradise! Place a sprig of Rosemary under the bed to prevent nightmares and Mugwort as protection against evil. Lay a sprig of Southernwood under the pillow to reduce sleeplessness or Lavender to enable you to see ghosts. Add Clary Sage for vivid dreams, and sprinkle Thyme outside your bedroom window so that you can see the fairies at dawn.

### PSYCHIC DREAM TEA

Mix 1 tbsp Rose petals, 1 tsp Jasmine, a small piece of Cinnamon, 1 small Clary Sage floret and 1 Mugwort leaf, $1/2$ tsp lecithin in 2 cups boiling water; brew 5 minutes; drink 1 cup just before sleep.

### ASTRAL PILLOW

Place 1 tbsp each Frankincense, Sandalwood, Mugwort and Rose petals with 1 Vanilla pod in a sachet and slip inside the pillow cover.

RIGHT: *Lavender and dried Woodruff leaves have relaxing, reassuring aromas. Mix them in a small sachet to tuck inside hot waterbottle covers or soft toys for your children to snuggle up with while you read them their bedtime story.*

# *Puddings & Desserts*

*For sweet dishes, pungent flavours, like the obvious Mint or the less obvious Hyssop, can set off fruit and cream beautifully. Some bold cooks even use Basil and Thyme in their fruit desserts.*

## *Poached Nectarines with Ginger Mint and Lemon Balm*

*Herb-scented syrups are good for dressing fresh summer fruit. The mixture of Ginger Mint and Lemon Balm can be replaced by Lemon Mint – or whichever Mint is available – and Lemon Grass or strips of lemon or lime zest.*

**preparation: 10 minutes; cooking: 15 minutes, plus cooling and chilling**

*8 ripe but still firm nectarines and/or peaches*
*several sprigs each of Ginger Mint and Lemon Balm, plus more spriglets for decoration*
*2 tbsp brandy*
*100 g / 3¹/₂ oz caster sugar*

*to finish (optional):*
*115 g / 4 oz fresh raspberries*
*icing sugar to taste*

Put the fruit in a saucepan, pour in water to cover generously and remove the fruit. Bring the water to the boil, add most of the Ginger Mint and Lemon Balm, and simmer for 10 minutes. Add the fruit back to the pan and poach it for 5 minutes in the gently bubbling water. Drain, reserving the liquid.

Leave the fruit to cool a little, then peel off skins. Cut into attractive pieces, collecting the juices and adding them to the liquid. Moisten the fruit with the brandy and chill.

Bring the liquid back to a vigorous boil, stir in the sugar and reduce by two-thirds. Leave to get cold.

Spoon some of the syrup over the fruit and chill if not using within an hour or so. The rest of the syrup will keep for several days in the refrigerator and can be used to prepare appetising fresh fruit platters for breakfast and dessert.

Serve at room temperature, with a scattering of fresh raspberries dusted with icing sugar, if you wish, and with spriglets of Mint and Lemon Balm.

Winter variation: poach semi-dried plump fruit of your choice (apricot, mango, pear, apple, prunes) in weak tea flavoured as described above. Add shelled pistachios to the syrup halfway through boiling.

## *Rhubarb Fool with Tansy & Orange*

*If Tansy is difficult to obtain, replace it with fresh young Angelica leaves.*

**preparation: 5 minutes; cooking: about 25 minutes, plus cooling and chilling**

*1 kg / 2¹/₄ lb rhubarb, strings removed and chopped into chunks*
*2 Bramley apples, peeled, cored and chopped*
*juice and grated zest of 1 large unwaxed orange, with a few strips of zest set aside for decoration*
*about 10 Tansy leaves*
*85 g / 3 oz golden unrefined caster sugar, plus more to taste*
*300 ml / ¹/₂ pt herb-infused Custard (see page 145)*
*150 ml / ¹/₄ pt half-fat crème fraîche, whipped lightly*

Put the rhubarb in a pan with the apples, orange juice and zest and most of the Tansy leaves (reserving a few for decoration). Add the sugar and just enough water to cover. Bring to the boil, reduce the heat and simmer until the rhubarb is tender. Drain and leave to cool.

Blend everything in the food processor until smooth. Whisk in the custard and whipped crème fraîche and add a little more sugar, if you wish.

Chill until ice-cold and serve in glasses, decorated with snipped Tansy leaves and strips of orange zest.

## *Apricot, Mint and Hyssop Cobbler*

*Yoghurt, Hyssop and Mint give this easy down-home pudding a pleasing sharp tang. This dish can also be made more quickly in individual portions as shown. Just set 2 or 3 apricot halves on buttered individual gratin dishes and proceed as directed, reducing the cooking time to 20–25 minutes.*

**preparation: 15 minutes; baking: 40 minutes**

butter for the dish
1 kg / 2¼ lb ripe apricots, halved and stoned
1 tsp snipped Hyssop leaves
1 tbsp snipped Mint leaves
2 tbsp lime juice and a little grated zest
3 tbsp orange juice and a little grated zest
60 g / 2 oz demarara sugar, plus a little more to
    sprinkle over the apricots, to serve
    cream, custard, yoghurt or vanilla ice-cream

for the cobbler topping:
225 g / ½ lb self-raising flour
pinch of salt
1 scant tbsp baking powder
2 tbsp ground hazelnuts
about 85 g / 3 oz butter
30 g / 1 oz demerara sugar
200 ml / 7 fl oz bio yoghurt

Generously butter a 1.5-litre / 2¾-pint pie dish, soufflé dish or deep baking dish. Put in the halved apricots, snip in the Hyssop and Mint, drizzle over the lime and orange juice and sprinkle over the zest. Sprinkle lightly with a little sugar.

Preheat the oven to 200°C /400°F/gas 6. Prepare the topping: put the flour, salt, baking powder and ground hazelnuts in a large mixing bowl and rub in the butter until the texture is like coarse breadcrumbs. Stir in the sugar, reserving 2 tablespoons. Make a well in the middle, add the yoghurt and mix to a very soft dough.

Cover the fruit with thick dollops of dough. Sprinkle over the reserved sugar and bake for 35–45 minutes until well browned.

Serve warm, with cream, custard, yoghurt or vanilla ice-cream.

## Flower and Herb Ice Bowl

*Use any attractive herbs and flowers available at the time for this bowl, going for a good mixture of colours. As the bowl is purely decorative, the flowers don't even need to be edible. It is best to use the bowl for a simple, plainish dessert, although a good mélange of summer fruit as shown looks spectacular.*

Half fill a large bowl with water and scatter in the mixed herbs and flowers. Place a smaller bowl in the centre and weight it down with ice cubes. Cover tightly with a cloth secured with a string around the under-rim of the bigger bowl and freeze overnight.

Next day, take out of the freezer and leave to soften slightly. Lift off the cloth and the smaller bowl. Wait until you can loosen the bottom bowl. Return ice bowl to the freezer until ready to use.

Fill with your chosen chilled dessert at the last minute. Place a folded tea towel or napkin under the ice bowl to absorb any drips.

## Apple and Thyme Granita

*Golden Marjoram also works well in this recipe in place of the Thyme.*

**preparation: 10 minutes; cooking: 15 minutes;
chilling: 1 hour; freezing: 3 hours**

*275 g / 10 oz (3 medium-large) sharp eating apples,
    such as Cox's, peeled, cored and chopped
60 g / 2 oz sugar
few sprigs of fresh Thyme, preferably lemon-scented
    and with tiny flowers
4 tbsp Calvados*

Put the prepared apples in a heavy-based pan with 6 tablespoons of water, bring to a simmer and cook until the apples are fairly soft. Mash to purée and leave this to get quite cold.

Meanwhile, bring 200 ml / 7 fl oz of water to the boil and stir in the sugar. Once the sugar has dissolved, drop in most of the Thyme and simmer for a few minutes. Stir in the Calvados and leave to get cold. Remove the Thyme sprigs and chill. Also chill the cooked apple.

Mix the chilled apple and the herb-flavoured syrup. Pour into a shallow metal container and freeze. Take out and stir 3 or 4 times over the next 3 hours.

Just before serving, spoon the grainy slushy granita into glasses and decorate with spriglets of Thyme, preferably with flowers.

LEFT: *Flower and Herb Ice Bowl filled with mixed summer fruit.*

RIGHT: *Apple and Thyme Granita*

# Night-time Drinks

*As well as being soothing and comforting in bed-time nightcaps, herbs like Chamomile and Fennel also have proven powers to relax you, help aid the digestion and promote good healthy sleep.*

## After-dinner Tisanes

*Preferably use herb leaves whole, rather than ground or snipped, when available. If you find that you miss the kick of full-bodied teas, add a little Earl Grey, lapsang or green tea (say a scant teaspoon) to your herb infusion. On average, a well-packed tablespoon of leaves infused for 3–5 minutes will yield 2 cups.*

*Both fresh and dried herbs are enjoyable, but dried herbs and flowers usually have a gentler taste which makes the tisane more soothingly suitable for the last drink of the day before retiring.*

Drink your tisane straight or try sweetening it with a little honey rather than sugar. Nice after-dinner mixtures include:

Lemon Verbena and Chamomile (equal parts)
Elderflowers and Chamomile (equal parts)
Lime Flowers and Lemon Verbena (equal parts)
Chamomile and Sage (3 parts to 1)
Chamomile and Fennel (3 parts to 1)
Rosehip and Mint (3 parts to 1)
Rosehip and Raspberry leaves (3 parts to 1)

ABOVE: *Various After-dinner Tisanes*

## Old-fashioned Foaming Minted Chocolate

*Mint and chocolate is a marriage made in heaven – a new species of Mint actually has a delicate but marked chocolatey taste. In its absence, try Black Peppermint, which has a vibrant pervasive flavour.*

**preparation and infusing: 15 minutes; cooking: 10 minutes**

**makes 600 ml / 1 pint**

*600 ml / 1 pint semi-skimmed milk*
*1 tbsp finely snipped Mint, plus more leaves for decoration (optional)*
*1 or more tbsp caster sugar (optional)*
*100 g / 3½ oz best dark chocolate*

Put the milk in a saucepan with the finely snipped Mint and the sugar, if you wish. Bring the milk to scalding point, remove from the heat, cover and

198

RIGHT: *Aniseed Biscuits with Old-fashioned Foaming Minted Chocolate*

keep hot for at least 15 minutes to allow the flavour to develop.

Chop, blend, grate or break the chocolate into very small pieces (the smaller, the easier to melt) and melt in a small heavy saucepan over a very low heat.

Once the chocolate has softened, whisk in a small ladleful of very hot milk. Still over a low heat, whisk until combined, then gradually whisk in the rest of the milk.

Serve at once in china cups, decorated with Mint leaves, if you like.

## Aniseed Biscuits

*Made with half the sugar, these biscuits are also excellent with the cheese course.*

**preparation: 15 minutes, plus chilling; baking: 15 minutes, plus cooling**

***makes about 18***

*100 g / 3¹/₂ oz unsalted butter, cut into small pieces, plus more for the baking tray*
*45 g / 1¹/₂ oz golden caster sugar*
*150 g / 5 oz flour, sifted, plus extra for dusting*
*1 tbsp cornflour*
*1 scant tbsp ground almonds*
*1 tsp orange flower water or a pinch of ground cinnamon*
*2 tsp dried ground Aniseed or Poppy seeds*
*1 small egg, plus 1 extra yolk for glazing*

Put the butter and sugar in the bowl of a food processor fitted with the metal blade. Blend until pale and fluffy. Scrape down the sides of the bowl with a spatula.

Add the other ingredients (reserving the egg yolk for glazing). In short bursts, blend until the dough comes together in a ball. Dust the dough with flour, wrap in cling film and chill for at least 20 minutes.

Preheat the oven to 190°C/375°F/gas 5 and lightly grease a baking tray.

Dredge a cold working surface and a rolling pin with flour. Put the dough on the floured surface and roll it out thinly. Stamp out circles of dough with a 6-cm / 2¹/₂-inch diameter round biscuit cutter. Put these on the baking tray.

In a cup, mix the egg yolk with 2 teaspoons water and brush this glaze lightly on the biscuits

Bake for 12–15 minutes, until the biscuits are lightly cooked and coloured. Leave in the oven to cool and harden a little, then slide the biscuits on to a cooling rack and leave until cold.

*A-Z of*
*Aromatic Herbs*
*& Essential Oils*

## How to Use the A–Z

The A–Z lists the aromatic herbs featured in the book alphabetically under their botanic Latin names for clear identification, and also gives the common names. Each entry includes a plant and scent description, with noteworthy varieties and related species where appropriate; anecdotes about the use of the herb; description of the essential oil scent and uses; cautions for the herb and essential oil; and information on cultivation and propagation.

The zoning system (Z1–11) included in the growing information, which states average annual minimum temperature, has become an accepted and useful guide. It must, however, be regarded only as a rough indication, as many other factors affect whether or not a plant will thrive: these include humidity, summer temperature, wind factor, soil type, annual rainfall, drainage, genetic plant characteristics and so on.

Similar factors also affect the height and spread that a particular specimen will reach at maturity, but a guide is given for each plant (H = height, S = spread).

### AVERAGE ANNUAL MINIMUM TEMPERATURE ZONES

| Zone | °F | °C |
| --- | --- | --- |
| 1 | < -50 | < -45.5 |
| 2 | -50 to -40 | -45.5 to -40.1 |
| 3 | -40 to -30 | -40.0 to -34.5 |
| 4 | -30 to -20 | -34.4 to -28.9 |
| 5 | -20 to -10 | -28.8 to -23.4 |
| 6 | -10 to 0 | -23.3 to -17.8 |
| 7 | 0 to 10 | -17.7 to -12.3 |
| 8 | 10 to 20 | -12.2 to -6.7 |
| 9 | 20 to 30 | -6.6 to -1.2 |
| 10 | 30 to 40 | -1.1 to 4.4 |
| 11 | > 40 | > 4.4 |

# Index of Herbs

Herbs in the A-Z are listed by
Latin name. The following index of
page numbers lists them by common
name for easy reference.

YARROW

*Achillea millefolium*

## YARROW

This upright perennial has downy stems of feathery, pleasantly pungent leaves and flat heads of white or pink-tinged, summer to autumn flowers with an herbaceous-fruity scent when crushed.

USES The dried stems were used by the Druids to foretell weather and by the Chinese with the I Ching oracle. The slightly bitter, peppery young leaves are chopped into soft cheeses and salads, or can be pressed fresh against shaving and other small cuts to arrest bleeding. In the garden, yarrow deepens the fragrance and flavour of nearby plants and helps them to resist disease and strengthen their medicinal properties. A leaf infusion provides a copper fertilizer, and a finely chopped single leaf acti-vates decomposition of a whole wheelbarrow of compost.

ESSENTIAL OIL This has a fresh, green-fruity scent with a medicinal edge, used in perfumery and by aromatherapists to treat skin problems, rheumatism and flu stress.

CAUTION HERB: Avoid in pregnancy. Take in small doses. Might make the skin sensitive to sunlight. OIL: Not yet formally tested, possible skin irritation and phototoxic reaction.

GROWTH & PROPAGATION Z 2; H 1m (3ft); S 20cm (8in). Grow in a sunny position, although it tolerates light shade, in moderately rich, moist soil. Sow seed or divide roots in spring or autumn. Thin or transplant to 30cm (12in) apart. Deadhead for a second blooming. Harvest leaf, flower and stem in late summer.

*Acorus calamus*

## SWEET FLAG

This perennial has sword-like leaves, tangerine-scented when crushed, a yellow-green summer flowering spike and a spicy-cinnamon-scented rhizome. *A.c.* 'Variegatus' and *A. gramineus* 'Ogon', both with cream-striped leaves, are fine ornamental forms.

USES The leaves and rhizomes were a popular Tudor strewing herb often used in Church festivals and carried the favourite scent of the last Czarina of Russia. Use the powdered rhizome in potpourri, to scent clothing and as a white ant repellent. The leaf buds and inner stems were once used in salads and the rhizome flavoured spirits. It is used in Chinese and Indian medicine, by Native Americans and by some Europeans in candied form.

ESSENTIAL OIL The woody-spice-scented oil is used as a fixative fragrance in perfumes, face creams (0.02 per cent max) and hair and tooth powders.

CAUTION HERB: Banned from commercial use in foods in many countries, but danger may be restricted to certain forms. OIL: Contains asarone which may be an internal toxin and carcinogen, although North American and Siberian plants are asarone free. Unless labelled safe, AVOID.

GROWTH & PROPAGATION Z 3; H 1.5m (5ft); S indefinite. Grow in a sunny position in wet soil or shallow water. Propagate by division of rhizomes in autumn or early spring. Lift rhizomes at any time except during flowering, dry and store to allow their scent to develop fully.

*Agastache foeniculum*

## ANISE HYSSOP

This upright perennial or biennial has soft, serrated leaves with pale undersides and stalks topped by long-lasting, nectar-rich, pale purple flower spikes with protruding bracts, in late summer. Leaf and flower share a sweet green aniseed scent.

USES The leaves make a refreshing, fragrant tea, unusual salad green and a seasoning. The flowers add a sweet anise taste when chopped into salads and desserts, or a minty-anise flavour and pale blue colour if infused as a tisane. Adored by bees, it was intro-duced to Europe by beekeepers for the light, fragrant honey it produces. Use stems, leaves and flowers in potpourri. North American tribes used this plant as a cough medicine to relieve congestion and increase sweating. Korean Mint (*A.rugosa*) is a short-lived perennial with mint-scented leaves and purple flowers, used in salads, teas, as seasoning and in Chinese medicine. Rose-flowered *A. mexicana* has eucalyptus-scented leaves.

GROWTH & PROPAGATION Z 8; H 80cm (32in); S 45cm (18in). Plant in sun in rich, moist, well-drained soil. Anise Hyssop and Korean Mint cross-pollinate, making identification difficult – use leaf scent as a guide. Sow seed in spring; divide creeping roots in summer. Treat *A. mexicana* as an annual. Cut and dry leaves and stems in spring and summer, and flowers when open.

ANISE HYSSOP

AGRIMONY

*Agrimonia eupatoria*

## AGRIMONY

This pretty perennial with serrated leaves is known as Church Steeples for its tall, elegant spikes of small, yellow, honey-scented flowers from early summer. The dried herb and roots have a long-lasting, subtle apricot scent.

USES The dried herb and roots are ideal for sweet bags. The aerial parts give a scented astringent tea which is digestive and a gentle remedy for diarrhoea. It soothes sore gums, yields a gargle for coughs and throats and restores sparkle to eyes. An important medieval wound herb, recent tests show that Agrimony inhibits tuberculosis, deserving further research with the re-emergence of this disease. Aerial parts yield a pale yellow dye in summer and a richer yellow in autumn. Fragrant Agrimony (*A. procera*) is a woodland plant of moist, heavy soils, with strongly scented flowers.
*A. pilosa* is a powerful blood coagulant with a high Vitamin K content and tested extracts inhibit all cancers except leukaemia.

**CAUTION** Avoid medicinal use with constipation.

GROWTH & PROPAGATION
Z 6; H 45cm (18in); S 30cm (12in). Tolerant, but prefers sun and well-drained soil. Sow seed in spring or divide roots in early autumn. Harvest leaves in early summer or the whole flowering plant in late summer before burrs develop. Air-dry slowly in warm shade. Store away from damp.

*Akebia quinata*

## AKEBIA

This elegant semi-evergreen or deciduous climber has circles of 5 leaves and bears pendulous groups of small, pale claret male flowers and larger purple female flowers in spring. These waft a rich honey-vanilla scent, and in warm climates are followed by unusual sausage-shaped edible purple fruits.

USES An attractive, fast-growing plant for the aromatic arbour or pergola, the long flexible stems are used to make baskets and wreathes. Five-leaf and Three-leaf Akebia (*A. trifoliata*) are used interchangeably in Chinese medicine. The woody stem and fruits stimulate circulation and lactation. Due to its potassium salt content the stem is diuretic, helping to reduce fluid retention while strengthening digestive tract muscles. Roots are given to treat fever. Tests have shown Akebia fruits and seed to inhibit cancer cells, and they are included in several Chinese formulas for treating cancer.

AKEBIA

GROWTH & PROPAGATION
Z 5; H 12m (40ft); S 6m (20ft). Plant in sun or semi-shade in moisture-retentive, well-drained soil. Sow seed in spring, take semi-ripe cuttings in summer with bottom heat or layer in winter. Protect young plants in winter. Akebia dislikes being disturbed. Pick and dry fruits in summer, stems in autumn.

ALLIUMS (CHIVES)

*Allium* species

## ALLIUMS

Alliums are bulbous perennials or biennials with long, thin leaves and attractive clusters of tiny summer flowers. They have a range of sharp, savoury aromas which makes them the world's most popular flavouring agents.

USES The Onion family all contain iron and vitamins and are mildly antibiotic. Chive leaves (*A. schoenoprasum*), with their lively, green taste and mildly onion-scented mauve flower-heads, are available fresh for many months of the year as a garnish or to flavour salads, potatoes, eggs, vegetables, cheese – in fact, most savoury dishes. Dried leaves can be re-moistened with lemon juice to add zest to winter salads. Chive plants or Chive tea spray will deter aphids, apple scab and mildew. Chinese or Garlic Chives (*A. tuberosum*) have starry white flowers and flat leaves, both with a subtle garlic flavour; sheathed flowerheads and blanched stems are important Chinese seasonings. Welsh Onions (*A. fistulosum*) have larger, strong-flavoured leaves that are coarser than Chives but are available in winter. Onions (*A. cepa*) and Garlic (*A. sativum*) are universal cooking ingredients and have extra benefits, as a diet rich in these will guard against infection and heart disease. Garlic is effective in lowering blood pressure, blood cholesterol and blood clotting, and can be taken by all for general fitness and to help prevent repeat heart attacks. It also clears catarrh in colds and respiratory conditions and has been used to treat tuber-

culosis. Both Garlic and Onions regulate blood sugar levels, which helps diabetics. Cooking Garlic with fresh Ginger reduces the slight nausea some experience from Garlic, and chewing Parsley or Cardamom seeds after a meal will sweeten the breath. For regular or larger doses, odourless capsules are available. Planted under Peach trees, Garlic reduces leaf curl; near Roses it will enhance their scent. Wild Garlic (*A. ursinum*) scents whole woodlands and has an edible bulb used medicinally and in weight-loss diets. Tree Onions (*A. cepa* var. *proliferum*) grow small pickling Onions on stem tips which sprout further new tips. Everlasting Onions (*A. cepa* var. *aggregatum*) are small bunching Onions rich in vitamins A, B1, B2, B5, C and E.

### GROWTH & PROPAGATION

Z 4–9; H to 1m (3ft); S to 30cm (1ft). Most are frost hardy. Grow in sun or part shade in rich, moist, well-drained soil. Take offsets or divide bulbs in autumn or spring; plant Garlic cloves 4cm (1½in) deep in autumn; sow seed in spring (not available for Everlasting and Tree Onion). Thin to 23cm (9in); Garlic to 15cm (6in). Water in dry spells and enrich the soil annually (or monthly, when cutting Chives). Divide and replant clumps every 3–4 years. Pot up in autumn for an indoor supply.

### HARVEST & STORAGE

Chives: cut leaves, leaving 5cm (2in) for regrowth. Pick flowers as they open. Leaves will stay fresh for a week in sealed bags in the refrigerator, or can be frozen in ice cubes or dried. Remove flowers for improved leaf production. Garlic: dig bulbs in late summer after 5 leaves have turned yellow, handling them *very*

ALLIUMS (WILD GARLIC)

gently to avoid bruising. Store bulbs away from light in a damp-free, aerated environment or use them to make oil or vinegar. Onion: cut and air dry ornamental flowerheads. Lift bulbs and store as for Garlic, make into chutney or pickle in vinegar.

## *Aloysia triphylla* (syn. *Lippia citriodora*)

### LEMON VERBENA

This shrub has long, lax stems covered in whorls of 3 or 4 long, light green, fibrous leaves with a strong, fresh lemony scent reminiscent of boiled sweets, and tiny white or pale purple summer flowers.

USES Cleanly and persistently fragrant, dried leaves retain their scent for several years: wonderful in potpourri and sachets, or used to scent ink and paper. Fresh leaves are added to summer drinks, fruit puddings, ice-creams, and barbecue finger bowls, or are infused in oil or vinegar. Leaf tea is both refreshing and mildly sedative, soothing bronchial and nasal congestion, indigestion, flatulence and nausea, and is a soothing bath for puffy eyes. Lemon Verbena vinegar softens skin and eases heat-induced headaches. The closely related

Lemon Bush (*Lippia javanica*) is used locally in Africa as a tea to reduce malarial fever. *L. dulcis* contains a sweet compound 1,000 times sweeter than sucrose.

ESSENTIAL OIL The lemony-fruity-floral oil is used in perfumes and bath lotions, and previously in aromatherapy for insomnia and stress, but its high price and phototoxicity means it should not be used at home.

**CAUTION** HERB: Prolonged use of large quantities of the leaf may cause stomach irritations. OIL: Phototoxic. Do not use – beware of substitutes unless labelled *Litsea cubeba* oil. This is from the pepper-shaped fruit of the Litsea tree with a similar intense, sweet-fruity lemon odour

ALLIUMS (WELSH ONION)

LEMON VERBENA

and is non-toxic, although possibly sensitizing in some people.

GROWTH & PROPAGATION
Z 8; H&S 3m (10ft). Half hardy. Only plant outdoors in a well-drained, sunny, sheltered spot if winter temperature does not drop below -10°C (14°F). New growth can appear very late so never discard a plant until late summer. A conservatory, greenhouse or pot plant enjoys being outdoors in summer, indoors in winter. Winter leaves may drop. Prune lax stems for shape and gently in autumn. Take softwood cuttings in late spring or sow seed in spring. Pick leaves as needed and dry for winter use.

*Anethum graveolens*

DILL

All the aerial parts of this annual – thread-like foliage, umbels of tiny yellow summer flowers and oval seeds – share its unique sweet, green-spicy aroma and flavour.

USES The freshest and sweetest flavour is in the flower-heads and immature green seeds; add to gherkins, salmon and potato salad. The leaves have a fainter aroma and the ripe seeds a harsher flavour. Immature umbels and young leaves flavour cream cheese, sour cream, cabbage and grilled meats and can be frozen. The mineral-rich seeds are useful in salt-reduced diets, and flavour seafood, sauerkraut, pickles and breads. Chewed at the end of a meal they sweeten the breath, aid digestion and treat flatulence, hiccups and insomnia.

ESSENTIAL OIL There are two essential oils of the same colour:

DILL

one from the seeds, and one from the other aerial parts. Both have a spicy aroma – lighter in the seed oil, which is included in many pharmaceutical digestives, such as baby's gripe water. Both oils are used commercially in drinks and foods and the aerial oil also in perfumery, detergents and soaps.

GROWTH & PROPAGATION
Z 8; H 60cm (24in); S 30cm (12in). Frost hardy. Grow in full sun in a sheltered position in rich, well-drained soil. Dill prefers the long days of cooler climates. Do not plant near Fennel, as the two cross-pollinate and flavours become muddled. Sow *in situ* from spring until midsummer. Seeds are viable for 3–10 years. Self-seeds. Thin to 23–30cm (9–12in) apart. Can be grown indoors. Gather the leaves when young. Pick flowering tops just as fruits begin to form and infuse them in vinegar. To collect seed after the flowering heads turn brown, hang the whole plant over a cloth.

*Angelica archangelica*

ANGELICA

This tall, handsome 3-year 'biennial' has a tropical appearance with its large divided leaves and clean, cucumber-peel and gin scent. It produces spherical heads of tiny green-white flowers in the summer of its third year, and has an aromatic root.

USES Leaves picked before flowering are cooked with gooseberries and rhubarb to reduce tartness. They are chopped into sauces and salads and brewed as a tonic tea for colds and flatulence. Pencil-thick stems are crystallized before midsummer and the late-summer seeds flavour pastry. Crushed leaves freshen car interiors and reduce travel sickness, and the root latex is a potpourri fixative. A plant compound, xanthotoxol, is anti-nicotinic.

ESSENTIAL OIL Extracted from root and seed, sometimes combined, this flavours gin and vermouth. The root oil first exudes an earthy, chamomile oil scent, then becomes a rich green frankincense fragrance with a tobacco undertone. It is employed in perfumery and used in massage to reduce toxin accumulation in joints, scars and bruises, as well as to reduce stress fatigue and nervous tension.

CAUTION HERB & OIL: Avoid in pregnancy or with diabetes. ROOT OIL: Phototoxic, skin sensitizer.

GROWTH & PROPAGATION
Z 4; H 3m (10ft); S 1.3m (4½ft). Grow in a light-shaded position in deep, moist soil. Allow the plants to self-seed or sow in early autumn with fresh seed.

*Aniba rosaeodora*

ROSEWOOD

This yellow-flowered tropical Amazonian tree has red-barked timber which yields a sweet, woody-rose-scented oil.

USES Once used almost exclusively by fine craftsmen to make intricately carved furniture, short-sighted logging companies now fell and export Rosewood on a massive scale for more mundane items such as chopsticks. Third World debts and other social priorities create both a reluctance to curb hardwood exports and insufficient funding for regulating the trade.

ESSENTIAL OIL The steam-distilled oil, also called Bois de Rose, is taken from wood chips of 10–15-year-old trees and is clear to pale yellow with a sweet-woody-rose odour. It was used

ANGELICA

CHERVIL

extensively in perfumery (now largely replaced by cheaper synthetics), in skin care products for its healing and rejuvenating effects, and by aromatherapists for calm and spirituality. It is difficult to obtain from renewable sources, though skilled aromatherapists can offer alternatives.

GROWTH & PROPAGATION
Z 10; H 25m (80ft); S 15m (50ft).
Tropical rainforests.

*Anthriscus cerefolium*

CHERVIL

This hollow-stemmed annual has fern-like, bright green, finely divided leaves, often tinged purple in late summer, when its umbels of tiny white flowers normally appear. Chervil has a fresh, delicate, parsley-like flavour with myrrh-aniseed overtones.

USES This frost-hardy culinary herb can be available year round with monthly sowings until autumn. Then plants over 15cm (6in) tall will 'mark time' through winter to give a welcome fresh ingredient, and flower the following spring. The leaves contain vitamin C, carotene, iron and magnesium and in small amounts enhance the flavour of other herbs – one reason for its inclusion in the French *fines herbes* mix. The best-flavoured foliage is grown in light shade, gathered before flowering and added fresh to salads, fish, butter sauces, soups, vegetables, chicken and egg dishes, and often used as a garnish. Add at the end of cooking to prevent flavour loss. In face masks, the leaves are cleansing and skin softening; infused as tea, they are digestive and help in toxin elimination.

GROWTH & PROPAGATION
Z 6; H 60cm (24in); S 30cm (12in). Grow in fertile, light soil, in partial shade in summer as it quickly runs to seed in hot, sunny conditions. Autumn seedlings enjoy full winter sun. Ripe seed germinates quickly and can be used 6 – 8 weeks after gathering. Scatter on the soil and press in lightly. Thin seedlings to 15–23cm (6–9in) apart; do not transplant. In winter, give cloche protection against hungry creatures. Pick when above 10cm (4in) tall. Left to self-seed Chervil will give a spring and autumn crop.

*Artemisia dracunculus*

TARRAGON

French Tarragon is a perennial with many branches carrying narrow, aromatic leaves and insignificant greenish summer flowers. Also known as Little Dragon, the leaves have a sweet, peppery taste with anise undertones.

USES A staple of classic French cooking, part of the *fines herbes* mix, and added sparingly to sauces, salad dressings, egg, fish and chicken dishes, the leaves are rich in vitamins and minerals and aid digestion. Chewing a leaf will numb the taste buds before taking unpleasant medicine, and weak leaf tea will stimulate the appetite after illness. Russian Tarragon (*A. dracunculoides*) is a hardier, taller plant with narrower leaves that more readily sets seed, but it has a coarser, less aromatic flavour which improves marginally as the plant ages.

ESSENTIAL OIL Oil from Russian Tarragon has a sweet-spicy, anise-green scent used in perfumes and cosmetics as well as industrial fragrances. It is added in tiny amounts to foods, drinks and alcohols, and is sometimes used in massage oils for menstrual problems.

CAUTION OIL: Avoid during pregnancy.

GROWTH & PROPAGATION
Z 3; H 1m (3ft); S 40cm (16in). Half hardy. Grow in a sunny, sheltered position in light, dryish, humus-rich soil. Divide roots in

TARRAGON

spring; take stem cuttings in summer; sow seeds of Russian Tarragon in spring. Thin or transplant to 30–45cm (12–18in). Cut back in autumn. Give winter protection of straw or a similar mulch. Can be grown indoors. Harvest any healthy leaves and freeze or dry them quickly at 27°C (80°F), or infuse in oil or vinegar.

*Artemisia* species

ARTEMISIAS

This attractive group of herbs is valued for its silver foliage and leaf scent, which ranges from pungent to fruity-sweet. Most produce tiny summer flowers, from yellow to rust in colour.

SPECIES & USES
MUGWORT *A. vulgaris* Z 3;
H 1.5m (5ft). An ancient, green-scented magical herb featured in many spells. The leaf down is rolled into cones for Chinese moxibustion (heat treatment). Leaves are finely chopped to add sparingly to pork stuffings and rice cakes. It is a stimulant digestive tonic, but avoid when pregnant. The Chinese put a leaf in the nose to stop a nosebleed. The plant deters insect pests.
WORMWOOD *A. absinthium* Z 4;
H 1m (3ft). A bitter, pungent herb used to flavour the banned liqueur absinthe. The Russian name is Chernobyl, and a Nostradamus prophecy spoke of a great disaster at the site of Wormwood. The plant is a garden asset with its silver leaves, fast growth, and ability to deter fruit moth, cabbage butterfly, lice from the hen house, and carrot and onion fly if laid between rows. It is long lasting in bouquets, wreaths, posies and linen bags.
SAGEBRUSH *A. tridentata* Z 8;

ARTEMISIAS

H 2m (6ft). A pungent shrub used in sacred and purifying ceremonies.
SOUTHERNWOOD *A. abrotanum* Z 4; H 1m (3ft). A semi-evergreen subshrub of filigree leaves with a sweet, green-lemon scent ideal for moth-repelling sachets and herb sleep pillows. *A. campestris* subsp. *borealis* has a similar scent and red-tinged florets.
SWEET ANNIE *A. annua* Z 8; H 1.5m (5ft). A fragrant annual and effective anti-malarial drug.
ROMAN WORMWOOD
*A. pontica* Z 4; H 40cm (16in). A creeping perennial with silver filigree foliage, used to flavour vermouth.
WHITE MUGWORT *A. lactiflora* Z 4; H 1.4m (4½ft). Has plumes of honey-scented white summer flowers and is used in Chinese medicine for liver problems.
CALIFORNIA SAGEBRUSH
*A. californica* Z 3; H 1.5m (5ft). Has produced several sports with citrus names and delightful orange or fruity aromas.
SILVER KING *A. ludoviciana* Z 5; H 1m (3ft). Intensely silver.
MAT ARTEMISIA *A. pedemontana* Z 5; H 10cm (4in). A silver carpet.
TREE ARTEMISIA *A. arborescens* Z 8; H 1m (3ft). Half hardy.

'Faith Ravens' H 1m (3ft). and frost hardy, 'Powis Castle' H 60cm (24in) and hardy with feathery, bright silver leaves, *A. alba* (syn. *A. camphorita*) Z 6; H 1m (3ft) with a camphor scent, and *A. canescens*, H 50cm (20in), hardy with beautiful curled, thread-like leaves; all have silver foliage that is stunning in a moonlit garden and in posies. The pungent leaves have insecticidal properties.
FRAGRANT WORMWOOD
*A. capillaris* H 60cm (24in). A liver tonic subshrub with sweetly aromatic, silky thread leaves and purple stems.
SWEET WORMWOOD *A. apiacea* A biennial used in Chinese medicine to reduce fevers and in medicinal and 'beautifying' meals as a detoxifier.

ESSENTIAL OIL Toxic. Wormwood oil is used in tiny amounts in perfumery.

**CAUTION** HERB: For qualified herbalists only. OIL: Toxic. Available to industry only. Avoid in pregnancy.

GROWTH & PROPAGATION Z 3–8; H 9cm–2.5m (3½in–8ft); S 30cm–1.4m (12in–4½ft). Full sun in light, dry, well-drained soil. Site carefully as rain washes growth-inhibiting toxin out of the leaves, affecting nearby plants. Sow seed when available. Take semi-hardwood cuttings in late summer. Divide every 3–4 years.

## *Borago officinalis*

### BORAGE

The rough-textured leaves of this hardy annual release a cucumber scent when crushed. Its sky blue (rarely pink or white) star flowers

BORAGE

have large black stamens. The white form is *B.o.* 'Alba'.

USES The sight of this cheerful herb lifts the spirit and can have a similar effect on the physical body. A symbol of courage and joy, the leaf and flower infusion stimulates adrenaline and helps dispel depression, grief and the after-effects of steroid therapy. The flowers garnish salads and puddings and can be crystallized or used to decorate ice cubes. The calcium, potassium and mineral-rich young leaves are finely chopped for use in salt-free diets, salads and dips. It is the classic garnish for Pimms No 1. Pressed seed oil, used in specialist massage and cosmetics, is sometimes called Star Flower oil and contains gammalinoleic acid similar to Evening Primrose oil.

**CAUTION** Eat leaves in moderation.

GROWING & PROPAGATION Z 7; H 1m (3ft); S 60cm (24in). Prefers an open, sunny position in light, dry, well-drained soil. Sow seed *in situ* or singly in pots in spring for summer flowers; autumn for spring flowers. Self-seeds freely. Set young plants 30cm (12in) apart. Can appear messy when it grows large. Plant specimens among pink Roses for support and a mutual colour intensifying effect.

## *Boswellia carteri*

### FRANKINCENSE

This small, attractive, leafy ever-green tree or shrub has white to pale pink flowers and rich, warm, woody aromatic resins.

USES All wild-collected *Boswellia* resins are called Frankincense and release their dry-sweet, rich fragrance when burned or steam distilled. Highly valued in antiquity for its spiritual effect as incense and later for its medicinal and cosmetic uses, the trade, quality and price was controlled from Southern Arabia. Different qualities of the naturally exuded 'tears' of resin are used for medicine and incense, with the pale 'white' resin chewed in Arabia for its benefit to teeth, gums, breath and mental state.

ESSENTIAL OIL The best-quality pale yellow oil is distilled from *B. carteri*, with some from

CALENDULA

*B. serrata*. Used in perfumery, including as a fixative, it has a rejuvenating reputation in face creams for dry or mature skins. Frankincense (also called Olibanum) is used for asthma and other respiratory problems, and during meditation or prayer to calm and deepen breathing and ease stress and tension.

CAUTION Avoid during the first trimester of pregnancy.

GROWTH & PROPAGATION Z 11; H 5m (15ft); S 3m (10ft). Tender. Semi-desert. Full sun in well-drained to dry soil. Min temp 10–15°C (50–60°F). Take semi-ripe cuttings in summer. Prune lightly in early spring if required.

## *Calendula officinalis*

### CALENDULA/POT MARIGOLD

This annual to perennial has hairy, fresh green leaves, succulent stems and golden-orange, daisy-like flowers throughout summer into autumn. The whole plant has a sharp, clean, herbaceous aroma.

USES This plant is called Calendula by herbalists, Pot Marigold by gardeners and Poor Man's Saffron by cooks. The tangy petals flavour and garnish dishes, colour rice and make Marigold wine. Young leaves can be added to salads. Petals make a rinse for brown hair, a yellow textile dye, an eyewash for tired eyes, and a potpourri additive if dried at low temperatures to preserve their colour. Calendula is antiseptic, antifungal and contains hormone and vitamin A precursors, making it ideal for skin healing. A petal infusion is a rinse for mouth

ulcers, a compress for slow-healing wounds and ulcers, and can be taken internally for gastric and period pains and to stimulate the liver. In creams it treats numerous skin problems, including dry eczema and cracked nipples. An infused oil heals skin, capillaries and hangnails.

ESSENTIAL OIL The dark greenish-brown petal absolute is expensive and rarely extracted. It can help depression and other stress-related problems and is added to a few tangy perfumes. The available orange 'Calendula oil' is normally an infused petal oil.

CAUTION HERB: Do not confuse with *Tagetes* species, also called Marigold.

GROWTH & PROPAGATION Z 6; H & S 70cm (28in). Grow in a sunny position, preferably in fine loam, although it tolerates most soils except those that become waterlogged. Sow seed in spring *in situ* or singly in pots. Plant 30–45cm (12–18in) apart. Deadhead for continuous flowers.

## *Cananga odorata*

### YLANG-YLANG

This tall tropical tree has masses of night-scented greenish-yellow flowers all year round which exude an intense, sweet, jasmine-like fragrance.

USES In parts of Asia the flowers are included in festivals and temple offerings, or may be rolled up overnight in freshly oiled hair to perfume it.

ESSENTIAL OIL The flowers are picked in the early morning and steam-distilled 4 times for their

CARAWAY

pale yellow oil, yielding Extra, First, Second and Third qualities. Ylang-Ylang Extra, the highest quality, is best for aromatherapy; the lower grades are often confusingly sold as Cananga oil. The strong radiating aroma is narcotic, intensely sweet and floral. For many it is too overpowering on its own, but in combination with other floral or woody oils its effect is warm, elegant, languorously relaxing and often aphrodisiac. An important oil for perfumery, soaps and sebum-balancing skin lotions, it is also a commercial food flavouring. Aromatherapists use the oil to reduce high blood pressure, premenstrual syndrome, depression, insomnia and sexual anxiety. It lowers rapid heartbeat and breathing, helping those who dislike crowds or are prone to panic attacks or work frustration. Flowers of the closely related *Artabotrys* species, including Climbing Ylang-Ylang (*A. hexapetalus*), yield an essential oil used in local perfumes.

**CAUTION** OIL: Use only in moderation to avoid headaches and nausea.

GROWTH & PROPAGATION
Z 10; H 25m (80ft); S 10m (30ft).

Tender. In temperate areas, grow in sun or semi-shade in a humid, heated greenhouse or conservatory.

*Carum carvi*

CARAWAY

The slender branches of this feathery-leaved aromatic biennial bear umbels of white midsummer flowerheads, followed by capsules of warm spicy-pungent seed which explode when ripe.

USES The narrow, curved, aromatic seeds combine wonderfully with cooked apples, breads, sauerkraut and rich meats such as goose and sausages. Mixed with cabbage they reduce its cooking smell and with other vegetables they enhance the flavours with a hint of piquancy. As a breath sweetener and digestive aid the seed can be nibbled at the end of a meal, infused as a tea, or sugar coated as 'caraway comfits'. Tender young leaves can be added to salads and the root cooked as a vegetable.

BALM OF GILEAD

ESSENTIAL OIL The seed oil has a similar but more intense strong, spicy aroma which flavours foods, Kummel brandy, schnapps and the cordial *l'huile de Venus*. It is digestive, antiseptic and antimicrobial in toothpaste and mouthwashes, and added to medicines for taste. The fragrance is blended in perfumes, aftershaves and cosmetics.

GROWTH & PROPAGATION
Z 3; H 60cm (24in); S 35cm (14in). Full sun in rich soil. Sow outside in late spring or early autumn. Thin to 20cm (8in). Can be grown indoors in the sun.

*Cedronella canariensis,*
syn. *C. triphylla*

BALM OF GILEAD

This deciduous shrub, also known as Canary Balm, has three-lobed serrated leaves with a musky camphor-lemon-cedar scent reminiscent of camel caravans, and clusters of pale pink flowers borne from late summer to early autumn.

USES This is one of 3 plants known by the name of Balm of Gilead, but it lacks the sweet balsamic fragrance of the other 2: the original Biblical Balm of Gilead (*Commiphora opobalsamum*) and the Balm of Gilead Poplar (*Populus* x *candicans*). Nevertheless, the leaves have an interesting masculine fragrance used in potpourri and herb pillows and added to tea blends. In its native islands, the leaf brew is called *thé des Canares*.

GROWTH & PROPAGATION
Z 2; H 1.5m (5ft); S 1m (3ft). Half hardy. Grow in full sun and well-drained medium loam. Sow

seed in warmth in spring and note that seedlings resemble nettles. Take stem cuttings in early autumn. Plant 45cm (18in) apart. This is also an excellent flowering conservatory plant which requires a 25cm (10in) pot to reach its full size. Prune in autumn or spring to retain a bushy shape.

*Cedrus libani*

CEDARWOOD

This magnificent tree has dark, fissured bark, tiers of horizontal branches bearing dark green to blue needles, and dull green to brown upright cones. The durable timber has a warm, long-lasting, dry spicy-wood aroma.

USES The aromatic timber was used in building the Hanging Gardens of Babylon, Solomon's Temple and Egyptian mummy cases as it repels termites, moths and other insects, making it ideal for linen chests, coat hangers, wall-hanging batons and as fragrant shavings for drawer potpourri. The rich balsamic resin was used for embalming, incense, perfume and cosmetics.

ESSENTIAL OIL Yellow to deep amber Atlas Cedar oil (*C. l.* subsp. *atlantica*) is steam-distilled from the wood and has a warm, tenacious, sweet woody aroma with an aftertone of parsnip-celery. It scents household products, soap, perfumes, men's cosmetics and aftershaves. It is a useful holiday oil as it repels mosquitoes, insects, leeches and rats! Aromatherapists use it to soothe chronic anxiety, stress and skin and bronchial conditions, including tuberculosis. Research indicates that it inhibits tumour cell division.

**CAUTION** OIL: Avoid during pregnancy. Beware of the irritant, abortifacient and potentially fatal 'red cedar oil' from *Juniperus virginiana*, often confusingly called 'cedarwood oil'. It is used in minute amounts in perfumery and fragrancing only, not for therapeutic purposes, although some experts disagree so perhaps sources vary in safety.

GROWTH & PROPAGATION
Z 6; H 45m (150ft); S 10m (30ft). Grow in full sun in well-drained soil. Propagate from seed. Plant small trees in early autumn or mid-spring. Prune in autumn to maintain a single leader and in spring remove old basal branches to avoid a bushy habit.

---

*Chamaemelum nobile* and *Matricaria recutita*

## CHAMOMILE

Both the evergreen perennial Roman or English Chamomile

CHAMOMILE

---

(*Chamaemelum nobile*, syn. *Anthemis nobilis*) and annual German Chamomile (*Matricaria recutita*, syn. *M. chamomilla*) have feathery foliage and yellow-centred white daisy flowers, with a faint earthy green scent, in summer. Only the perennial species have the sweet apple-scented foliage and include the double-flowered 'Flore Pleno' and a non-flowering cultivar 'Treneague'. The short-lived perennial Dyer's Chamomile (*Anthemis tinctoria*) has bright yellow daisy flowers and a green herbaceous scent.

USES For centuries, the apple-scented foliage of Roman Chamomile has been used to cover small lawns and garden seats, and been dried for potpourri. The flowers of both Chamomiles share similar aromatic healing compounds and yield a digestive, relaxing tea, useful after overeating. It is also given to soothe nightmares and insomnia and suppress nausea, including morning sickness. Cooled Chamomile tea bags placed over the eyes reduce inflammation, puffiness and fatigue shadows. Regular applications of a Chamomile infusion lightens fair hair and in baths or compresses softens and soothes sun, wind or eczema-damaged skin. Herbalists prescribe extracts to aid the internal healing of some ulcers and intestinal operations. Cut flowers will last longer if Chamomile tea is added to their water. Spray the tea on seedlings to avoid 'damping off' and on compost to activate decomposition. In the garden, the plant revives nearby ailing specimens, possibly through root secretions.

ESSENTIAL OIL Roman Chamomile oil has a sweet, dry, fruity scent and is pale blue, turning pale yellow on exposure to light and air. Annual German Chamomile has a warm, earthy herbaceous aroma and is dark inky-blue, slowly turning through green to yellow-brown with extended exposure to light. Ormenis oil, also known as Chamomile Maroc/Moroccan Chamomile (*Chamaemelum mixta* syn. *Ormenis mixta*, or *O. multicaulis*) is pale to brownish-yellow with an herbaceous-balsamic scent. All are produced from their flowers and used in perfumery. Although expensive, both Roman and German Chamomile oils are effective and best used very dilute: 0.5 to 1 per cent. Both have a gentle, healing nature, suitable even for children. They share similar compounds but in differing percentages. The most valued, azulene, is most potent in German Chamomile and is only formed during distillation and possibly when flowers are dried. The oils are cell-renewing, anti-inflammatory, analgesic, disinfectant, and inhibiting to viruses and fungi. Aromatherapists prescribe it for anxiety and stress-related illnesses, to stimulate liver regeneration and heal irradiated skin. Inhalations ease hayfever and asthma. A few people experience skin reactions; there are fewer with German Chamomile.

**CAUTION** HERB: Some feel nausea from over-infused tea; if so, remove the flowers/tea bags after 5 minutes. OIL: Avoid in pregnancy. Use the weak dilution for children. Moroccan Chamomile is widely used in perfumery, but has yet to be tested properly for therapeutic safety – avoid for the present.

EDIBLE CHRYSANTHEMUM

GROWTH & PROPAGATION
Z 4; H 15cm (6in); S 45cm (18in). Grow in full sun, in light, well-drained soil. Sow seed in spring. Divide perennials in spring or autumn. Take 8cm (3in) cuttings from side shoots in summer. For a Chamomile lawn or seat, plant 10–15cm (4–6in) apart. Plant annuals 23cm (9in) apart. Plant Dyer's Chamomile 45cm (18in) apart. Pick leaves any time. Pick fully open flowers, dry and store in airtight, lightproof containers.

---

*Chrysanthemum coronarium*

## EDIBLE CHRYSANTHEMUM

This annual has deeply indented, spicy leaves and yellow-orange flowers in late summer.

USES Also known as Chop Suey Greens and Garland Chrysanthemum, the nutritious, tangy young leaves are used as a flavouring and green vegetable – boiled, steamed, blanched, stir-fried or made into soup. They can be rubbed on the fingers to counter fish preparation odours. The bright petals are an eye-catching garnish for salads and fish, and are pickled in vinegar. The sprouted seeds give a winter salad, snack or stir-fry. The flowerheads *C. c. spatiosum* have a unique flavour, and traditionally are boiled for one minute to serve with a savoury sauce. The cooling, antibiotic yellow flower-heads of Wild Chrysanthemum (*Dendranthema indicum*, syn. *C. indicum*) were part of a Taoist elixir of immortality. In traditional Chinese medicine, it is included in medicinal meals for hypertension, blood impurities, flu and infections. In-vitro tests show that both flower and leaf have anti-cancer properties.

ESSENTIAL OIL *C. lavandulae-folium* yields a fresh, green, leafy-scented oil used in some perfumes.

CAUTION HERB: Can cause an allergic skin reaction.

GROWTH & PROPAGATION Z 5; H 80cm (32in); S 35cm (14in). Rich, well-drained soil in a sunny, sheltered position. Sow seed in spring and midsummer for 2 crops. Thin to 12cm (5in). Pick at 15cm (6in) for a tender tall leaf crop. In China, flowers are steamed before being dried to reduce bitterness. A pretty plant for the potager in rows or under sweetcorn.

## *Cinnamomum verum*, syn. *C. zeylanicum*

### CINNAMON

This tropical evergreen tree has aromatic bark, wood and leaves with a sweet, rich, mellow spicy aroma, silky panicles of tiny malodorous cream summer flowers and purple berries.

USES Cinnamon spice is the dried inner bark available rolled

as quills, broken pieces called quillings, or powdered. It flavours savoury dishes in the Middle East, North Africa and Asia, but elsewhere is added to sweet dishes and drinks. It is digestive and quells nausea. Cinnamon is added to potpourri, incense and pomanders, and is a popular male aphrodisiac. Oil from the berries can be made into fragrant candles. Cassia, the stronger-flavoured cinnamon of North America and China, is from *C. aromaticum*. The bark is thicker, more pungent and less sweet. Cassia leaves are used in Eastern Indian cuisine.

ESSENTIAL OIL Yellow Cinnamon Bark oil is too toxic and irritant for domestic or skin use but the powerful sweet, dry, spicy odour is used in pharmaceuticals, the food industry and at very low levels in perfume for a cosy, seductive effect. Yellow-brown Cinnamon Leaf oil has a sweet, green, woody-spicy cinnamon odour with a hint of cloves used commercially by the food, drink and pharmaceutical industries and in perfumes and cosmetics. Although less toxic than bark oil, it is not suitable for home use, except as a fumigant (both are powerful antiseptics), or in very low doses (0.5 per cent) in oil burners. Cassia oil has a strong, spicy odour but less warmth than cinnamon. It is very hazardous and should never be used at home.

CAUTION OILS: Avoid in pregnancy – can cause miscarriage. Irritant to skin and mucous membranes. Can cause sensitization to other compounds, even at low dosages.

GROWTH & PROPAGATION Z 9; H 13m (43ft); S 10m (30ft).

CINNAMON QUILLS

Tender. Can be grown as a glasshouse ornamental in well-drained, moisture-retentive, sandy but fertile soil in sun or part shade, min temp 15°C (60°F). Water sparingly in winter. Propagate by sowing seed or taking semi-ripe cuttings in summer.

## *Cistus ladanifer*

### LABDANUM

This evergreen shrub, also called Cistus or Rock Rose, has large flowers of white petals marked with a crimson spot. Summer heat causes sticky balsamic resin to exude from glandular hairs on the leaves and stems, perfuming the air for a considerable distance. The resin becomes opaque in cold weather to give the plant a ghostly leaden appearance.

USES A traditional medicinal resin with antibiotic and insecticidal properties, it is a pleasantly fragrant fumigant and a commercial food flavouring for meats, sweets, ice cream and soft drinks.

ESSENTIAL OIL The oil distilled from the resin has a warm, dry, woody-spicy musk odour that diffuses well. It is the best natural

substitute for sperm whale ambergris and the scent is widely used as an erogenous fixative in perfumes, aftershaves and cosmetics. Tests show no irritation at 8 per cent dilution, but weak sensitizing above 0.25 per cent.

GROWTH & PROPAGATION Z 7; H & S 2.5m (8ft). Grow in full sun in well-drained, light to poor soil. Sow seed in autumn or spring, and take softwood cuttings in late summer. Remove damaged material and dead flowers in spring, but avoid hard pruning. Dislikes disturbance.

## *Citrus* species

### CITRUS

The *Citrus* genus contains 16 evergreen trees and shrubs with perfumed flowers and segmented, aromatic fruit.

USES Citruses, high in Vitamin C, are enjoyed as refreshing fruits and juice, while grilled Grapefruit with brown sugar suits winter breakfasts. Fruit, peel and juice are used in food and drink production. Bitter Orange flowers (*C. aurantium*) are the source of culinary and cosmetic Orange-flower water. Oranges are the traditional base for pomanders. Citrus peels are dried for

MANDARIN

ORANGE BLOSSOM (*left and below*)
LEMON BLOSSOM (*right*).

potpourri, and that of Mandarin for Traditional Chinese Medicine. Antiseptic and astringent Lemon juice lightens blond hair, cleans and softens skin, removes ink stains and treats colds, sore throats and insect bites. In the Bahamas, Lime juice is used to deter mosquitoes and is applied to bites to stop itching. Grapefruit seed provides an exciting new non-toxic extract with a wide spectrum of anti-microbial, antifungal and antiviral actions. It is a natural antibiotic and has great potential as a natural preservative in skin care products.

ESSENTIAL OILS

**CAUTION** Most expressed Citrus peel oils are phototoxic – avoid direct exposure to sunlight after use, or choose those labelled 'FCF' which have the offending compound removed. Citrus oils have a short shelf life and 'old'

oils can cause skin irritations – use within 6 months to a year.

LEMON *Citrus limon* A pale yellow oil is expressed from fresh Lemon peel. Its lively scent is refreshing and clearing, aiding concentration: Japanese research shows that it can increase productivity among office workers. Lemon is much used in perfumery, particularly in eau-de-Cologne, as a scent most people like and associate with freshness and cleanliness. For this reason, and because it is inexpensive, Lemon is used extensively to scent pharmaceuticals, cleaning products, cosmetics and soaps. It is also added to food and drinks and can help to purify water in emergency situations. Aromatherapists prefer the non-phototoxic FCF oil, to treat skin conditions, improve circulation and for the respiratory and immune system.

ORANGE, SWEET *Citrus sinensis* There are two Sweet Orange peel oils. The yellow-orange oil expressed from fresh peel has a fresh, sweet fruity scent, while the clear to pale yellow distilled oil has a lighter fragrance. Both are valued in refreshing perfumes, commercial foods, drinks and cleaning products. The lively aroma is

LEMON

antiseptic and bactericidal, beneficial in baths and room sprays to banish germs and lift the gloom on a dull winter's day. Its cheerful, regenerating effect helps to boost confidence during anxious periods such as job interviews.

**CAUTION** There are mixed reports of the two oils' photo-toxicity – for the moment, avoid using either on the skin before exposure to sunlight.

GRAPEFRUIT *Citrus x paradisi* Yellow to greenish Grapefruit oil is expressed from the fresh peel. It has a bright, buoyant, sharp scent which kindles enthusiasm without being overpowering. A few drops added to shower lotion or a morning bath, or inhaled from a tissue, help to counter jet-lag or hangovers and give a reviving 'I can do it' scent for busy, stressful events such as job interviews, moving house, maintaining the peace among relatives or just getting on with necessary but unpleasant tasks. Grapefruit oil is useful in massage oils for cellulite and to precede sports activities.

LIME *Citrus aurantifolia* There are two commonly used Lime essential oils. Expressing peel yields a pale yellow to greeny oil with a sweet, lively citrus scent used in perfume and soap. This oil was sometimes used for skin care, flu and circulation, but it is photosensitizing, so aroma-therapists now prefer the clear to pale yellow oil steam-distilled from the whole fruit, as it is not phototoxic and shows no skin irritation. It has a sharper, intense, lively, sweet scent, mainly used in commercial food and drinks and now popular as a refresher in colognes.

TANGERINE/MANDARIN
*Citrus reticulata* Mandarins and Tangerines are from varieties of the same species and although scent differences are sometimes reported, these are more likely due to growing conditions and country of origin. The yellowy-orange expressed peel oil has a lively fresh citrus scent with sweet undertones and an energizing, happy effect. It is an important cologne component and is added to perfumes, cosmetics and commercial foods and drinks. Tested to 8 per cent dilution, there are no reports of phototoxicity, so it is a wonderful oil for the delicate, or those who feel it, and can be used in vaporizers for children, the elderly, pregnant women and the stressed, to spark feelings of cheer. Diluted in a carrier oil and gently rubbed clockwise on to the stomach, it eases many digestive upsets and can even stop hiccups. In massage oils it is useful for fluid retention, problem skin, scars, and stretch marks after pregnancy (avoid during pregnancy just to be cautious – use pure vegetable oils instead).

**CAUTION** Always use in low dilutions for children.

BERGAMOT *Citrus aurantium* var. *bergamia* The pale green to greenish-yellow oil is pressed from the peel of the fruit. It has a fresh, lively, fruity-floral scent which is energizing and inspires confidence. Its wide appeal guarantees its inclusion in numerous eau-de-Colognes and cosmetics, and it provides the perfume of Earl Grey tea. Aromatherapists find it a strong, comforting oil for those suffering from grief, depression and anxiety. Bergamot treats skin infections (a dab is great for spots), and in vaporizers is a refreshing antiseptic for colds and flu.

## NEROLI (BITTER ORANGE) *Citrus aurantium*

This pale yellow oil is distilled from the flowers. It has an intense, fresh, sweet, green floral scent with a hint of bitter spice used in high-class perfumes, and has both a soothing and uplifting effect. Although expensive, only small amounts are needed for a luxurious bath or body oil, hair scent or romantic room fragrance. In skin creams it is gentle enough for dry or sensitive skins and encourages healthy cells, aiding the complexion, mature skins, stretch marks and scars. Neroli is very relaxing and reassuring for depression, anxiety and sexual apprehension.

## PETITGRAIN *Citrus aurantium*

Yellow Petitgrain oil is steam-distilled from the leaves and twigs of the Bitter Orange tree. It has a refreshing, warm, floral-woody scent with an uplifting, supportive effect, and is an important ingredient of many fresh perfumes, colognes, soaps and cosmetics. The aroma is relaxing for insomnia and tension, and regenerating for convalescence and weariness. The popular fragrance is deodorizing, counters greasiness and acne in skin creams, and is ideal for massage, bath oils, hair rinses and perfumes.

GROWTH & PROPAGATION
Z 7–9; H 10m (30ft); S 7m (22ft). Tender trees. Grow in deep, well-drained but moisture-retentive loam. In temperate climates, Oranges, Lemons and Grapefruit can be grown outside during the summer, and brought into a cool, light room before the first frosts. Lemon is easiest to grow, Grapefruit the largest. Pummelo

BITTER ORANGE LEAVES

(*C. maxima*), Meyer Lemon (*C. meyeri*), Lemon (*C. limon*) and Seville Orange (*C. aurantium*) are suitable for large pot cultivation. Pots should be terracotta or have aeration holes drilled in the sides. Under glass, mist daily and keep well ventilated during summer. When watering, soak the plant well, then leave until almost completely dry before watering again. In winter, plants may need watering only once every 10 weeks (too much hinders flowering); increase this from spring onwards, and feed regularly when in full growth. When plants bloom indoors, ensure a good crop-set by touching each flower with a dry camel's-hair brush dipped in pollen. Oranges and Lemons take up to a year to ripen, which can result in fragrant flowers together with colourful fruits. Air- or oven-dry peel and store in an airtight tub.

## *Commiphora myrrha*

## MYRRH

This thorny shrub has 4-petalled yellow-red or white flowers which appear after the rainy season but before the new trifoliate aromatic leaves. The branches and shoots yield a highly valued rich, warm, spicy-balsamic resin. Several of the 180 *Commiphora* species yield this Myrrh resin, with slight variations in quality.

USES Wild-collected Myrrh has been treasured for its long-lasting aroma since the garden of Eden. As the earliest Biblical and Egyptian incense, along with Frankincense, many cultures still include it in holy incense blends. It also has a long medicinal, cosmetic and perfuming history: carried by Greek warriors to heal wounds, fed to Arabian horses to prevent fatigue, used in salves to rejuvenate Egyptian skins and smouldered near clothes and bedding to scent the fabrics. New research shows *C. mukul* to contain guggulipid, which lowers blood cholesterol and is an anti-inflammatory for arthritis.

ESSENTIAL OIL The steam-distilled amber oil has the rich, spicy balsam of the resin with extra sweetness and a hint of camphor. The aroma has an uplifting, positive effect, useful for meditation and healing and in exotic perfumes and cosmetics. A commercial food and drink flavouring, its medicinal qualities are used in toothpastes and as an effective tincture for mouth ulcers. It can be added to creams for mature skin, wrinkles, eczema, and cracked heels and hands. Antiseptic, anti-inflammatory and skin healing, it treats slow-healing wounds including bed sores, and chesty colds.

**CAUTION** Avoid in pregnancy.

GROWTH & PROPAGATION
Z 11; H & S 5m (15ft). Tender. Full sun in well-drained soil. Min temp 10–15°C (50–60°F). Sow seed in spring or take hardwood cuttings at the end of the growing season.

## *Comptonia peregrina*

## SWEET FERN

The fern-like leaves with their rust-coloured hairs and the twigs of this low-growing deciduous shrub sport strongly aromatic resinous glands. Catkin-like male spring flowers and spherical female flowers are followed in autumn by small green burrs containing up to 4 nutlets.

USES The spicy fresh or dried leaves are brewed as a fragrant tea and immature nutlets can be eaten. Worthy of wider cultivation, Sweet Fern is an attractive garden shrub near paths, steps and entrances, where its spicy leaves will be brushed or trodden on, and is most aromatic for early morning and evening garden strolls. Branches are cut to bring their fragrance indoors, used as a strewing herb for aromatic outdoor parties, or tucked under the front door mat to welcome visitors. The astringent leaf is infused to treat diarrhoea and used by Native Americans to stop bleeding or as a cool wash for poison ivy rash.

GROWTH & PROPAGATION
Z 4; H 1.5m (5ft); S 1.2m (4ft). Grow Sweet Fern in sun or partial shade in well-drained acid soil which remains moist in the growing season. It is good for covering banks of poor soil. Sow ripe seed and overwinter in a cold frame. Replant rooted suckers in spring. Sweet Fern dislikes being transplanted. Harvest and dry young leaves in early summer.

LILY-OF-THE-VALLEY

*Convallaria majalis*

LILY-OF-THE-VALLEY

The graceful white, bell-like late-spring flowers of this perennial have a distinctive sweet, elegant fragrance, while the creeping rhizome has a spicy scent.

USES This traditional bridal bouquet flower symbolizes ever-returning happiness. Once called Ladder to Heaven and Virgin's Tears, it represented Mary's tears at the cross, and in the Middle Ages was considered so medicinally powerful that flower infusions were kept in gold vessels. A German country wine is prepared from the flowers mixed with raisins. Distilled flower water, called 'aqua aurea', is an astringent, whitening beauty wash. Legend has Apollo teaching the healer Aesculapius that the flower is a cardiac tonic and extracts are still used to regulate heartbeats. It was given to sol-

diers who had been gassed during World War I. The head-clearing effect of inhaling the root and flower snuff was believed to restore speech and memory. Even a flower tea 'doth strengthen the Memorie and comforteth the harte', wrote the herbalist Dodoens in 1560. With lime water the leaves yield a green dye.

ESSENTIAL OIL The spicy sweet scent of the flowers is highly desired by perfumers but extraction is extremely difficult and very expensive, so most products contain a chemical substitute, hydroxy-citronellal.

**CAUTION** HERB: Poisonous, for use by medical personnel only.

GROWTH & PROPAGATION Z 3; H 23cm (9in); S indefinite. Grow in dappled shade beneath deciduous trees in humus-rich, moist but well-drained soil. Sow seed in spring. Divide clumps in early autumn, then plant shallowly 15cm (6in) apart. Mice may eat the rhizome.

*Coriandrum sativum*

CORIANDER

The delicate, feathery upper leaves and rounder lower leaves of this annual have an unusual strong, pungent, earthy smell

CORIANDER

with an undertone of burnt coffee. The white to pale mauve summer flowers produce small round seeds with a warm sweet spicy scent that increases when they are dried.

USES Fresh young leaves are a popular flavouring in Middle Eastern, Asian, Caribbean and South American cooking and can be frozen for later use. The mildly narcotic seeds, once called dizzycorn and considered aphrodisiac by the Ancient Egyptians, have a spicy-sweet taste with Orange peel overtones, excellent in pickles, curries, fried mushrooms, dessert breads and dishes which mix meat and fruit. Chewed, or brewed, they aid digestion, ease migraine and have a mildly sedative effect. The stems and autumn roots can be used as vegetables.

ESSENTIAL OIL The seed oil has a sweet, spicy, slightly musky scent used in perfumes and incense. Therapists employ it to eliminate toxins and muscular aches, stimulate appetite and treat measles and nervous exhaustion. It is used to flavour liqueurs, meats and medicines and improves the taste of cheap chocolate and tobacco.

**CAUTION** OIL: Use only in moderation.

GROWTH & PROPAGATION Z 7; H 50cm (20 in); S 30cm (12in). Full sun in light, rich soil. Sow in autumn, to overwinter in mild climates, or early spring in the final position, away from Fennel which suffers in its presence. Thin to 20cm (8in) apart. Plants run to seed in hot summer weather. 'Cilantro' gives a good leaf crop, 'Morocco' a bumper seed harvest.

SAFFRON

*Crocus sativus*

SAFFRON

The late-autumn mauve flowers of this crocus, unusually, stay open at night. They have 3 thread-like protruding vermilion stigmas which are picked and dried to become the spice Saffron, with its tenacious rich, aromatic flavour and hint of earthiness. In home-grown British Saffron the underlying slightly bitter tang is tempered with a honey sweetness not found in imported threads.

USES It requires the hand-picked light, wiry stigma from over 1,700 flowers to make 25g (1oz) of dried Saffron; hence it is the world's most expensive spice. The deepest colour yields the best flavour and it should be used within a year. Purchase whole threads, as pieces and powders are easily adulterated, often with harmless and equally coloured but flavourless Safflower or Bastard Saffron (*Carthamus tinctorius*). Saffron's unique taste and warm yellow colour are popular in sweet and savoury foods such as fish and rice dishes including paella and bouillabaisse, in saffron bread, cakes and pastry, ice cream and sauces. For most recipes, the threads are soaked for a few minutes in a little hot water or milk and both are added to the dish. Saffron with henna was part of a paste rubbed on the body of Arab brides to soften their skin and give a warm glow and seductive scent. It is considered an aphrodisiac, but too much may be narcotic. Although water soluble, Saffron, the 'colour of light', is used as an auspicious Tika forehead mark in India and a sacred healing dye for Buddhist robes. For hygiene reasons, Henry VIII forbade people by law to dye Irish linen with Saffron, because they often refused to wash the cloth for fear of losing its healing properties. In Asia and Africa Turmeric powder is often used instead; it gives a more permanent dye but the flavour is very different.

**CAUTION** Do not confuse with the garden crocus *Colchicum autumnale*, called Meadow Saffron or Naked Ladies, which is highly poisonous.

GROWTH & PROPAGATION Z 6; H 23cm (9in); S 10cm (4in). Grow in a sunny, warm position in well-drained, alkaline soil enriched with manure or in pots in a cold greenhouse. Corms increase by producing 'baby' corms, so after 4 years, dig up in late summer, break off new corms and plant them 12cm (5in) deep and apart. They require a long, hot summer to flower. Harvest autumn stigmas in the morning; for a slightly lighter flavour, remove the white base. Wrap loosely in absorbent paper, dry for 2–3 days away from light and damp until brittle, and store in an airtight container.

## Cuminum cyminum

### CUMIN

Annual Cumin has warmly fragrant, delicate thread-like leaves and umbels of white or pink summer flowers, followed by narrow seeds with a strong, warm, dry pungent scent with a hint of turpentine and a tenacious sharp, spicy flavour with a bitter aftertaste.

USES Whole or freshly ground seed is included in many spice mixtures: Northern India's *garam masala*, Thai red curry paste, Cajun seasonings, Mexican chilli

CUMIN

con carne, European pickles and cordials, and Morocco's warming aphrodisiac *ras el hanout* with 20 spices including Ginger, Rosebuds and Spanish Fly, added to couscous and lamb stews. The stems flavour Vietnamese food. Roasted seeds served at the end of a meal aid digestion, relieve flatulence, and provide a general tonic and stimulant. The rare Black or Royal Cumin from Kashmir has smaller, sweeter black seeds used in Moghul cuisine. In Ayurvedic medicine Cumin is a stimulant and digestive.

ESSENTIAL OIL The pale yellow-green oil has a warm, rounded, spicy musk scent used in perfumery, food products and some veterinary medicines. In massage oil it aids the circulation and elimination of toxins and is used for cellulite. It can also ease some types of migraine.

**CAUTION** OIL: Phototoxic – avoid direct sunlight on treated skin; avoid during pregnancy.

GROWTH & PROPAGATION Z 10; H 30cm (12in); S 10cm (4in). Half hardy. Well-drained soil in full sun. Propagate by seed in spring. Seeds may not ripen in cold climates.

## Cupressus sempervirens

### CYPRESS

This tall, narrow conifer has twigs and dark green needles with a pleasant green-resinous odour, yellowish male cones and green female cones, both of which ripen to brown.

USES Used as a purification incense by Tibetans, and dedicated to Egyptian and Roman gods of death and the underworld, the striking vertical shape is a memorable feature of the Italian landscape. Its aromatic timber is woodworm-resistant. It is often made into boxes, and the shavings maintain their fragrance for sweet bags and potpourri.

ESSENTIAL OIL The needles and twigs are steam-distilled for their pale yellow to green oil. It has a refreshing sweet, woody-spicy odour with a hint of lemon camphor which therapists value for its direct, reassuring effect on conditions of stress, overtiredness or weepy irritability. It is included in aftershaves, perfumes, soaps and creams for oily, mature skins. Cypress oil can be inhaled from a tissue to calm coughs, or added to footbaths for sweaty feet. It strengthens capillary walls and is used for varicose veins, broken capillaries, haemorrhoids, sluggish circulation and excess fluid conditions such as occur with cellulite.

GROWTH & PROPAGATION Z 8; H 40m (130ft); S 7m (22ft). Half hardy. Full sun in limestone soil in a sheltered position. Cold winds may scorch the foliage.

## Curcuma longa

### TURMERIC

Perennial Turmeric from the Ginger family has a bright orange-fleshed rhizome with a dry, aromatic, peppery scent when dried, large paddle-shaped leaves and yellow flowers.

TURMERIC

USES The powdered rhizome, high in vitamins and minerals, adds a bright golden-yellow colour and dry musky flavour to curries, vegetarian bean dishes and piccalilli. In the East it is a protection from evil, a dye for Buddhist robes, and a throat-clearing chew for Indian singers. The Amazon Sionas grate the yellow rhizome to dye their hammocks and wear the leaves as perfume armbands. The shoots and inflorescences are Thai vegetables. Antibacterial, anti-oxidant Turmeric is a significant herbal medicine for modern problems; research shows it has a non-steroidal, anti-inflammatory action, increases fat metabolization to assist weight loss, protects the gall bladder, reduces some liver toxins, stimulates circulation to resolve clots and bruises, and it is given for uterine tumours. Zeodary (*C. zedoaria*) rhizomes have a strong aromatic, musky, slightly camphorish fragrance used in Indian perfumes and the Hindu talc 'Abir'. In Chinese trials it has reduced cervical cancer and increased the effec-tiveness of radiotherapy and chemotherapy. A popular South-east Asian garden plant for its fragrant pink flowers, it is now becoming available in the West as an exotic houseplant.

ESSENTIAL OIL The spicy-woody oil is used commercially to flavour foods and condiments and in exotic perfumes.

CAUTION OIL: Use low dosage; possible irritant and sensitizer.

GROWTH & PROPAGATION Z 11; H 1m (3ft); S indefinite. Tender. Well-drained soil in sun, with ample humidity, min temp 15–18°C (60–65°F). Sow seed in autumn; divide in the dormant season.

## *Cymbopogon citratus*

### LEMON GRASS

DESCRIPTION
This aromatic perennial grass has bulbous, leek-like stems topped by blade leaves and panicles of flowers. It has a light, fresh, sweet lemon scent, lacking the acidity of citrus Lemon.

USES The stems and leaves feature extensively in South-east Asian cuisine and are becoming more popular in the West, but should always be used fresh as they lose most of their flavour when dried. The refreshing, antiseptic leaf tea is given in South America and tropical Africa for digestive problems, headaches and fevers. Large areas are planted to control soil erosion as its fibrous roots bind dry soils.

ESSENTIAL OIL Lemon grass falls into two types: the West Indian reddish-amber, boiled-lemon-sweets-scented oil with earthy undertones, and the East Indian with a lighter grassy-lemon scent and colour. Both are relaxing and uplifting and are used in perfumery, antiseptic room sprays and insect repellents, and to treat stress, poor circulation, muscle tone and fungal infections. Palmarosa (*C. martinii*) has a rosy-myrrh odour with lingering liquorice and peppery-ginger hitting the back of the nose. It is added to skin creams for its moisturizing, antiseptic, sebum-regulating and cell-regenerating qualities and prescribed for intestinal infections. Citronella (*C. nardus*), has a light, sweet lemony scent, used to repel insects and cats and as an industrial fragrance.

CAUTION OIL: Use all these oils in the lowest dilutions. Avoid Citronella in pregnancy. There is a very slight possibility of skin irritation or sensitization.

GROWTH & PROPAGATION Z 9; H 1.5m (5ft); S 1m (3ft). Tender. In temperate areas, grow as a houseplant in a moisture-retentive mix in moderate humidity, min temp 10–13°C (50–55°F). Water regularly. Pot on to avoid crowded roots. Propagate by division. Try growing from grocers' fresh bulbous-based stalks – place in water until roots develop, then plant.

## *Dipteryx odorata*

### TONKA BEAN

This tall evergreen tree of tropical South America has large elliptical leaves, fragrant rose-violet flowers and fruit with a large, single dark seed containing coumarin. This seed releases a strong, sweet,

TONKA BEANS

new-mown hay/vanilla scent when dried.

USES The seed is 'cured' to create a white powdery surface of crystallized coumarin. Its odour improves with keeping, which gives fixative qualities to pot-pourri, powdered perfumes and exotic sachet blends. The seed is used as jewellery by the Amazons and can be strung with cedar-wood beads and hung amongst clothes. The fatty oil from inside the seed is used to treat earache and as an insecticide.

ESSENTIAL OIL A seed absolute is solvent-extracted to produce the rich, warm, sweet hay scent with extra herbaceous woody tones. Demand has declined since the advent of synthetic coumarin in 1868, but the absolute is still used in the making of fine perfumes.

CAUTION OIL: The high coumarin content indicates oral and skin toxicity.

GROWTH & PROPAGATION Z 11; H 40m (130ft); S 20m (70ft). Seldom grown outside its native climate zone.

LEMON GRASS

*Elettaria cardamomum*

## CARDAMOM

This large tropical perennial has white orchid-like flowers with violet veins, palm-like fronds and erect or trailing stems of green fruits which have a distinct, mellow, warmly aromatic fragrance when mature.

USES The expensive seed pods are sold green, bleached or sun-dried. To check quality, look for plump pods filled with slightly sticky, dark brown, strongly aromatic seeds. Substitutes are usually brown with a camphor smell. Cardamom features in Eastern spice blends, Indian sweets, Arab coffee, Danish spiced cakes and quality hot cross buns. Seeds chewed after a meal will reduce garlic breath and are digestive, stimulant and antispasmodic. The seeds may counteract the negative effects of caffeine and mucus-forming dairy products.

ESSENTIAL OIL The strong, warm, honey-spice-scented oil with balsamic floral undertones is

CARDAMOM PODS AND SEEDS

steam-distilled from the seeds and used in perfumes, cosmetics, pharmaceuticals and liqueurs. A reputed aphrodisiac, therapists use it for fatigue, nervous strain and anorexia.

CAUTION OIL: No toxicity at 4 per cent dilution but ingestion of spices has caused dermatitis so use in low dilutions.

GROWTH & PROPAGATION Z 11; H & S 3m (10ft). Tender. Rich, moist, well-drained soil in part shade, min temp 18°C (65°F). Sow seed in autumn; divide plants in spring or summer.

*Eucalyptus* species

## EUCALYPTUS

Over 500 species of Eucalyptus trees and shrubs offer a range of refreshing medicinal-balsamic-scented leaves, gums and oils. The flowers are usually white or yellow, but some species produce pink or red.

USES Tasmanian Blue Gum (*E. globulus*) is planted in mosquito areas for its insect-repellent odour, and its white ant-and water-resistant timber to drain swampy land. Cider Gum (*E. gunnii*), the hardiest species, exudes sweet edible gum. Eucalyptus flowers are the most important source of pollen and nectar to Australian honey bees; the small branches are long-lasting and distinctive in floral arrangements, and leaves can be added to potpourri. Aboriginal people bind wounds with the antiseptic leaves and brew them for fevers and coughs.

ESSENTIAL OIL Steam-distilled from the leaves and young twigs,

LEMON EUCALYPTUS

the oils are antiseptic, antiviral and expectorant. Clear, light refreshing camphorous Tasmanian Blue Gum oil is most common medicinally and is also insect repellent, antifungal, an inhalation for respiratory, smoking-related and infectious conditions including pulmonary tuberculosis; it lowers blood sugar levels and treats burns, catarrh and flu. Added to vaporizers, it helps prevent the spread of colds and eases the breathing of sufferers. Blue Gum oil is included in pharmaceuticals and veterinary medicines. Lemon and Peppermint Eucalyptus (*E.citriodora* and *E.dives*) are cosmetic and industrial fragrances, useful in room vaporizers and to treat wounds, asthma, colds and fevers. In addition, Lemon Eucalyptus is antifungal against Athlete's foot and candida, and Peppermint Eucalyptus treats muscular aches and pains.

CAUTION HERB & OIL: Externally, among the safest but internally they are toxic. Slight chance of sensitization with Lemon Eucalyptus.

GROWTH & PROPAGATION Z 10; H 70m (230ft); S 25m (80ft). Tender or half hardy. In temperate climates, grow in a sheltered position in well-drained,

moist soil with a thick mulch, or as a pot plant brought inside when frosts start. Prune Blue Gums annually or biennially to maintain attractive juvenile foliage. Keep conservatory specimens in full sun and well ventilated; water moderately when in growth. Easy from seed.

EUCALYPTUS

*Ferula assafoetida*

## ASAFOETIDA

This tall perennial with feathery foliage produces many umbels of creamy-yellow midsummer flowers. The whole plant has a faint fetid muskiness with fishy notes strongest in the root gum, reflecting its alternative name of Devil's Dung.

USES Gum extracted from the aromatic root loses its unpleasant notes in cooking, and used in minuscule amounts adds an intriguing flavour to exotic

MEADOWSWEET

dishes. It provides the vital musky-to-oniony aroma of many Indian foods, added via the cooking oil, pickles or vegetables. It is also an ingredient of English Worcestershire sauce and aphrodisiac condiments. Graze a little across the grill or meats before barbecuing, or imitate the ancient Romans and store a small piece with pine nuts, using the aromatized nuts to flavour food. Store as powder in the freezer in an airtight container and remove small pinches as needed. The green parts are eaten as a vegetable. The gum aids digestion and research suggests that it is also anticoagulant and can reduce high blood pressure. The milky sap of *F. gumosa* hardens into a rich balsamic gum, burned as incense since Moses' time.

ESSENTIAL OIL Distilled from the gum, it has a strong, tenacious, garlic muskiness with a sweet balsamic side note, used occasionally as a fixative in evening perfumes.

GROWTH & PROPAGATION Z 8; H 2m (6ft); S 1m (3ft). Frost hardy. Grow in a sunny position in deep, moist, well-drained soil. It dislikes being moved. Sow fresh, ripe seed in late summer. The gum is bled from 5-year-old plants and dried.

## *Filipendula ulmaria*

### MEADOWSWEET

This tall, upright perennial has leaves which release a refreshing wintergreen-cucumber scent when crushed, and elegant, frothy cream summer flowerheads with a sweet, romantic almond fragrance.

USES An alternative name, Bridewort, came from the wide use of the flowers for wedding bouquets and the leaves for strewing the aisle – ironically, this was the favourite strewing herb of the Virgin Queen, Elizabeth I. Before the dominance of hops, meadowsweet beer was popular, while the flowers still add a delicate flavour to jams, stewed fruit and herb wines, provide an astringent skin tonic, and are dried to scent handkerchiefs. For dyes, the flowers produce a greenish yellow, leaves and stems blue and the roots black. Flower buds contain salicylic acid from which aspirin was later synthesized, but using the whole herb is gentler on the stomach and less likely to cause gastric bleeding. Herbalists prescribe it for heartburn, headaches, rheumatism and flu, as an antiseptic diuretic for cystitis and for stomach ulcers (tests have shown it to heal aspirin-induced ulcers in rats).

CAUTION Do not take internally if sensitive to aspirin.

GROWTH & PROPAGATION Z 2; H 2m (6ft); S 45cm (18in). Sun or partial shade in moist to wet, fertile, alkaline soil. Sow in spring; divide in spring or autumn. Thin or transplant to 30cm (12in) apart.

## *Foeniculum vulgare*

### FENNEL

All aerial parts of perennial Fennel have a green-anise flavour and scent, from the tall stems, attractive finely cut foliage and umbels of yellow midsummer flowers to the spicy green-anise-flavoured autumn seeds.

USES Fennel leaves and tender stems, and those of its bronze cultivar *F. v.* 'Purpurascens', are increasingly popular as salad ingredients and to enhance oily fish and pork dishes. Spare leaves can be frozen, or infused in oil or vinegar. Bronze Fennel gives vinegar a spectacular claret colour. The seeds are used to flavour bread, sausages and apple pies, or can be sprouted. Chewed, or brewed as a tea, the seeds are breath freshening, digestive and stimulate milk in nursing moth-

FENNEL

ers. The edible autumn 'bulb' of Florence Fennel for crunchy salads and vegetable dishes is the blanched, swollen leaf base of *F. v.* var. *azoricum*.

ESSENTIAL OIL The seed oil is widely used as a commercial food and pharmaceutical flavouring. It is added to chest rubs and muscle-toning oils for athletes, while therapists prescribe it for cellulite, anorexia, rheumatism, the menopause and problems of the respiratory system.

CAUTION OIL: Avoid if pregnant or epileptic and for children under 6. Use a low dilution of 0.5 per cent. Oil from the Bitter Fennel variety is unsuitable for home use.

GROWTH & PROPAGATION Z 5; H 2m (6ft); S 45cm (18in). Full sun in well-drained loam soil; avoid heavy clay. Sow in late spring to early summer. Self-seeds when established. Divide in autumn. Thin or transplant to 50cm (20in). Do not grow near Dill as cross-pollinated seed flavours are muddled, or near Coriander, which reduces Fennel's seed production.

## *Fragaria vesca*

### WILD STRAWBERRY

This perennial has a basal rosette of bright green, toothed leaflets in groups of 3 which turn red and faintly scented in autumn, and small, sweet, aromatic red fruits with an exquisite flavour from summer to autumn.

USES Some market stalls still sell strawberries in pottles, absurdly small for today's large berries but an original measure of this tiny,

WILD STRAWBERRY

wild fruit. Made into fever-cooling drinks, liqueurs, tonic wines and preserves, they are best enjoyed eaten fresh – a tasty reward for the garden weeder who comes across them. Wild strawberries, rich in iron and potassium, are good for anaemia, rheumatic gout, and kidney and liver complaints. Rubbed on the teeth they lessen stains, while a mash can be applied to soothe sunburn or as a face pack to clear dead skin. The leaves are dried for commercial herbal teas, and are prescribed on their own or with autumn roots for diarrhoea and urinary problems.

**CAUTION** For tea, dry early-summer leaves thoroughly to avoid possible toxins.

GROWTH & PROPAGATION
Z 5; H 30cm (1ft); S 20cm (8in). Grow in a cool, sunny or shady position in humus-rich, moist, well-drained alkaline soil. Sow seed in spring. To avoid the erratic germination caused by the seed's hard shell, sow in heat 18°C (65°F) with high humidity. Transplant daughter plants produced on runners to 30cm (12in). apart. Keep well watered. A potash fertilizer is beneficial when fruits begin to set. Pick ripe fruits to encourage more.

*Gardenia augusta*
syn. *G. jasminoides*

GARDENIA

This evergreen shrub or tree has glossy green, leathery leaves and intensely sweet, fragrant, showy ivory flowers from summer into late autumn, followed by orange-red fruit.

USES A prized garden exotic even in its native lands, cut perfumed flowers are floated in bowls of water and used in the East to impart a delicate flavour to tea, while the fruits give a yellow food colouring. In traditional Chinese medicine the fruits and roots treat sores, toothache, dysentery, nosebleeds, flu temperatures, hepatitis and snake bites. In Indonesia the leaves are used for asthma, fevers, hypertension and palpitations.

ESSENTIAL OIL The expensive, rich, warm, heady floral oil produced from the flowers is considered 'osmically balanced' (as are Carnation and Lavender), which

GARDENIA

means that their floral compounds are perfectly balanced, containing a top, middle and base note. For this reason, Gardenia is still enjoyed as a single-flower perfume. It is a component of quality blends, particularly oriental-floral scents, but has largely been replaced with synthetics.

GROWTH & PROPAGATION
Z 11; H 3m (10ft); S 1.2m (4ft). Tender. In temperate climates, grow under glass or indoors in bright indirect light, in lime-free compost. Maintain a temperature of 16–18°C (60–65°F) in summer and 10–16°C (50–60°F) in winter. Keep the soil moist with rainwater, watering more when the plant is in growth, but do not allow it to stand in water, or dry out. Fluctuations in temperature and watering will cause flower buds to drop. Take softwood cuttings in spring, or ripewood in late summer/autumn, with a heel, and root in a sandy mix, in a closed case with bottom heat at 18–21°C (65–70°F). Pinch out young plants in summer to encourage flowering shoots.

*Hesperis matronalis*
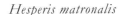
SWEET ROCKET

This pretty upright biennial, sometimes perennial, has lance-shaped leaves and numerous violet-clove-scented, white to purple flowers in the early summer of its second year.

USES Also called Dame's Violet and Vesper-Flower, the flowers attract butterflies and their sweet, soothing fragrance is most intense in the evening. Plant for fragrant pleasure next to windows, doors and garden seats. The flowers have a hint of floral

SWEET ROCKET

taste but are mainly pretty mixed in party salads or sprinkled on puddings, and maintain a faint scent if dried for potpourri. The young bitter leaves can be added sparingly to salads, sandwiches and smoked fish dishes.

GROWTH & PROPAGATION
Z 3; H 1m (3ft); S 25cm (10in). Grow in full sun or light shade in moist, well-drained neutral to alkaline soil. It tolerates poor soils well, but double-flowered forms need more nutrients. Sow *in situ* in autumn or spring; take basal cuttings in spring; divide in autumn or winter. Deadhead to encourage further flowering.

*Hierochloe odorata*

SWEET GRASS

This tuft-forming, creeping meadow grass has fresh green blades each spring which wither soon after the delicate, pyramid-shaped brown grass flowers have finished. When dry, it has a sweet vanilla/new-mown hay scent.

SWEET GRASS

USES Several North American tribes still gather and dry the summer grass to braid and hang in lodges during ceremonies or to burn as sacred incense: the Bow Museum in Calgary, Alberta, has a ceremonial braided piece still fragrant after many years. Sweet Grass is soaked to produce an aromatic hair rinse or placed to fragrance clothes and linen, chopped into relaxing potpourris, added to sweet sachets and woven into baskets and mats. The leaves flavour vodka, and were once made into a tea for coughs and sore throats, and to treat chafed skin.

ESSENTIAL OIL The strong vanilla/hay-scented oil from Sweet Grass leaves is used in perfumery to enhance other scents and act as a fixative, and to flavour confectionery, drinks, tobacco and hand soaps. Its principal scented compound, coumarin, was synthesized in 1868 and both natural and synthetic forms are widely used.

GROWTH & PROPAGATION Z 3–4; H 50cm (20in); S 60cm (24in). Sow seed in spring and grow in a sunny position in moist, well-drained soil. Divide rhizomes in spring or late summer. Harvest and dry whole leaves in summer.

*Humulus lupulus*

HOPS

This herbaceous twining climber with separate male and female plants has large, toothed, 3-lobed leaves with a clean green scent; the catkin-like yellow-green flowers in early autumn have a sharp, green, leathery-valerian-onion scent. The distinctive beery aroma develops in the 'strobiles' (ripe female catkins with papery bracts). *H. l.* 'Aureus' is a gold-leaved form.

USE The aromatic strobiles are used to flavour, clarify and preserve beer. When freshly dried, they are added to sleep pillows for their soporific effect (old strobiles are ineffective). Young leaves can be blanched for soups and the young spring shoots, eaten like asparagus, are a Venetian speciality. Fresh, newly dried or freeze-dried strobiles

HOPS

make a tea which is a nerve tonic, mild sedative and smooth muscle relaxant. It stimulates the appetite, is digestive, increases lactation and, mixed with other herbs, helps relieve irritable bowel syndrome.

ESSENTIAL OIL The amber strobile oil has a rich herbaceous-leathery aroma used in perfumes, lotions, tobacco and condiments. The scent has a direct sedative action on the nervous system and is used for restless tension-headaches, stress and anxiety-related illness, including some sexual problems, but can aggravate depression. Because of its oestrogen content, it is an anaphrodisiac for men.

CAUTION Only fresh strobiles are effective. Hops, and hop products, should be avoided with any history of depression. Pollen may cause contact allergies.

GROWTH & PROPAGATION Z 5; H 7m (22ft); S 6m (20ft). Sunny, open position in fertile, deeply dug soil. Provide climbing support. Reproduce female plants only. Separate rooted stems and suckers in spring; take cuttings in early summer. Pick ripe strobiles in early autumn. Dry or freeze-dry for immediate use.

*Hyssopus officinalis*

HYSSOP

This semi-evergreen subshrub has narrow, fresh peppery-green-scented leaves and spikes of small, bright blue, occasionally white (*H. o. albus*) or pink (*H. o. roseus*) aromatic flowers in late summer that are visited by bees and butterflies. Rock Hyssop (*H. o.* subsp. *aristatus*) is

HYSSOP VARIETIES

a compact form with deep blue/purple flowers.

USES The clean antiseptic scent of Hyssop – from the Hebrew *ezob* meaning 'a good smell' – contributed to its ancient reputation as a herb for purifying sacred places and cleansing lepers. It is one of the Jewish bitter herbs used in the Passover ritual. The sharp, savoury leaves are added sparingly to sweet pies and savoury dishes to give bite and aid the digestion of fatty fish and meat. The flowers provide colour and mild Hyssop flavour to fruit and green salads. The Romans considered it plague protection and also aphrodisiac combined with Ginger, Thyme and Pepper. A weak flowering-top infusion provides a sedative expectorant for flu and coughs. A leaf poultice helps to heal wounds and disperse bruises. It can be used as a strewing herb or dried for potpourri. In the garden, grow it near vines to increase their yield.

ESSENTIAL OIL The clear to pale yellow oil, steam-distilled from flowering tops and leaves, has a sweet herbaceous fragrance with a hint of camphor which is used in perfumes, cosmetics, commercial food products and liqueurs including Chartreuse.

Therapists use it as a tonic for convalescence, to disperse bruises especially after facial surgery, for cold sores and to ease tension.

**CAUTION** HERB & OIL: Use only in moderation. Hyssop should be avoided in pregnancy and with high blood pressure or epilepsy. Not suitable for a spray in public places.

GROWTH & PROPAGATION Z 3; H & S 1m (3ft). Full sun in light, well-drained, alkaline soil. Divide roots in spring. Take stem cuttings from spring to autumn. Sow seed in spring. Grow 60cm (24in) apart, or 30cm (12in) for hedging. Cut back to 20cm (8in) in mild winter areas after flowering; otherwise in spring.

*Illicium verum*

## STAR ANISE

Warm, sweet, cinnamon-liquorice fragrance is carried in all parts of this evergreen tree – in its smooth, pale bark, shiny green

STAR ANISE

leaves, yellow magnolia-like flowers sprouting from the trunk, and strongest of all in the star-shaped seed pods enclosing mildly fragrant seeds.

USES The scent inspired the genus name *Illicium* from the Latin for 'alluring'. Chinese Star Anise gives a distinctive, subtle warm spicy flavour to Asian food, particularly pork and duck. The ground pod and seed are part of Chinese five-spice powder. One Emperor's favourite chicken dish from Hangzhou, China, is flavoured with Star Anise and Cassia, wrapped in Lotus leaves and slow-baked underground. Seed pods can be added whole or ground into packets of tea or coffee to impart subtle fragrance and create a digestive after-dinner drink. The fruit pods have antifungal and antibacterial properties and are an attractive shape, texture and aroma for inclusion in potpourri. Locally, the unripe pods are collected to chew as digestive breath fresheners. Revered but poisonous Japanese Star Anise (*I. anisatum*) has cardamom-scented fruit and is planted near Buddhist temples, where the aromatic bark is burnt as incense.

ESSENTIAL OIL The intensely sweet, warm, spicy, cinnamon-liquorice scent is used in perfumes, soaps, hair oils, liqueurs, soft drinks and to mask unpleasant tastes in pharmaceuticals. Therapists use it to combat rheumatism, colds, respiratory and digestive problems.

**CAUTION** OIL: Avoid during pregnancy. Use in the lowest doses and only in moderation. Unlike other spice oils, it does not appear to be a skin irritant

but it is narcotic in large doses, leading to possible brain disorders.

GROWTH & PROPAGATION Z 8; H 18m (60ft); S 9m (28ft). Frost hardy. Part shade in moisture-retentive, well-drained neutral to acid soil. Take semi-ripe cuttings in summer. Difficult to cultivate outside its native Southern China and Vietnam.

*Iris germanica* var. *florentina*

## ORRIS

The perennial rhizome produces sword-like leaves and large white to pale blue, honey-scented bearded flowers. The dried rhizome slowly develops its valued violet scent over 3 years.

USES The multi-coloured genus takes its name from the Greek messenger Iris, who came to earth on a rainbow. The white form is the heraldic arms of the city of Florence. The dried rhizome has a bitter flavour used in some liqueurs and is added to rosary beads, scented sachets, face packs, tooth powders, dry shampoos, body powders and potpourris as an excellent fixative. It has an ancient history of medicinal uses and recently the seed of *I. lactae* var. *chinensis* were found to inhibit DNA synthesis of cancer cells and to strengthen cell immunity.

ESSENTIAL OIL The essential oil of the rhizomes of Orris and of *I. pallida* (considered the best quality by perfumers) is extremely expensive and has a complex woody, violet, oily scent with sweet, warm-woody, fruity and floral notes. It is used as a fixative in quality perfumes and as a

ORRIS

violet substitute. An even more expensive absolute (three times the price of Jasmine) is produced, with a light, sweet, floral-woody odour, and a less expensive resin with a tenacious dark, sweet-woody, tobacco-like scent used in soaps and perfumes. Synthetic Orris is frequently used.

**CAUTION** HERB: Fresh leaves and roots of all irises are internal toxins. Can be skin irritant. OILS: Frequently adulterated.

GROWTH & PROPAGATION Z 6; H 1m (3ft); S indefinite. Grow in a sunny position in well-drained neutral to alkaline soil. Propagate by removing offsets in late summer. Sow seed in autumn. Lift rhizomes in late summer/ early autumn to dry for 3 years.

JASMINE

## *Jasminum officinale*

### JASMINE

This deciduous shrub with a climbing habit has dark green leaves with 5–9 leaflets and 5-petalled white flowers in late summer which exude an intensely rich, honey-sweet, narcotic perfume with fruity-green undertones. Many attractive aromatic varieties are available.

USES Valued for its beauty and scent, Jasmine is planted around courtyards and verandahs and beneath windows for its romantic night-time fragrance. Flowers flavour desserts and teas, decorate and scent hair, and are given as temple offerings. Chinese Jasmine tea is perfumed with the flowers of *J. sambac*.

ESSENTIAL OIL The dark orange-brown oil is solvent-extracted from the flowers of *J. officinale* and *J. o. grandiflora*. Oil crop plants are kept to 1m (3ft) tall and picked daily in the early morning every day from August to October. It requires 8 million blossoms to make 1 kg (2¼lb) of the exotic oil so it is very expensive, but it is also very powerful so only tiny amounts are needed. It supplies perfumers' most popular floral absolute and flavours a surprising range of drinks and foods, including Maraschino cherries. Aromatherapists find it antidepressant, confidence building and relaxing. It helps dry sensitive skin, tiredness, anxiety-related sexual problems and post-natal depression.

CAUTION OIL: Avoid throughout pregnancy.

GROWTH & PROPAGATION Z 7; H 1–10m (3–30ft); S 2-10m (6–30ft). Sunny position in rich, well-drained soil. Provide climbing support. Sow seed in spring; take semi-ripe cuttings in summer. Thin out shoots or cut back after flowering.

## *Juniperus communis*

### JUNIPER

The fresh, warm, resinous odour of this tree is carried in its needle leaves and gin-scented berries, which ripen to blue-black in their second or third autumn.

USES Among Native Americans, Juniper berries are used to treat colds and small branches are used in atmosphere-cleansing smudge-sticks and burned as protective ceremonial incense. The ripe female berries, which give gin its distinctive flavour, are best used within 6 months. They are added as a flavouring to marinades, pâté, game dishes and savoury preserves.

ESSENTIAL OIL Juniper Berry oil has a stimulating warm, sweet, green-woody gin scent used in masculine perfumes and Chartreuse. Added in the lowest dilutions to massage or bath oils, it is detoxifying and anti-spasmodic for arthritis, muscle pain and cellulite, and treats acne, eczema, cystitis and nervous tension. Juniper oil is calming and considered emotionally cleansing and protective against negativity, so some healers massage a drop on each wrist while working or visiting crowded or hostile environments. Cade, or Juniper Tar oil, distilled from the wood of *J. oxycedrus*, has a smoky, leathery-woody odour used in aftershaves, scaly-skin ointments and veterinary medicines. Juniper Needle oil has a less woody, greener tone used in fragrancing. *J. virginiana* yields Red Cedarwood oil, which has medicinal and insecticide uses.

CAUTION OIL: Avoid during pregnancy or with kidney disease. Do not use internally. Another Juniper oil, Savine, from *J. sabina* is banned in some countries as it is highly toxic, an abortifacient and a nerve poison.

GROWTH & PROPAGATION Z 2–7; H 10m (30ft); S 4m (12ft). Grow in an exposed, sunny site in moist soil. Both male and female plants are necessary for berry production. To ensure plant gender, cultivate from semi-hardwood cuttings taken from known plants in late summer to early autumn.

## *Laurus nobilis*

### BAY

The dark, glossy, evergreen foliage of this tree or shrub has a warm, green, spicy nutmeg-like scent which matures when the leaf has dried for a few days. Small cream spring flowers produce black autumn berries. There is a gold-leaved form, *L. n.* 'Aurea', and a narrow-leaved form, *L. n.* 'Angustifolia'.

USES Sacred to Apollo, a crown of the leaves granted honour to poets, statesmen, athletes and more recently students. Apollo's first temple at Delphi had its roof made of Bay branches for protection. Mildly narcotic in large doses, some suggest the Bay induced his oracle's trance. As further protection, Bay-leaf garlands became an architectural moulding. In Dr Andrew Borde's first book on hygiene in 1542, citizens were advised to burn

BAY

woody stems of Bay during the plague. Bay leaf is a digestive flavouring for bouquet garni, sauces, vinegars and savoury rice and milk dishes. Add twigs to the barbecue for a smoky, aromatic tang. Old leaves can be crumbled into potpourri and 'masculine' sweet bags.

ESSENTIAL OIL The spicy oil from the leaves and twigs is used by the food, drink and perfume industries. In aromatherapy it helps to ease sprains and rheumatism and boost the immune system. The berry oil is used in perfumery.

CAUTION Other laurels are poisonous. OIL: Avoid in pregnancy and with sensitive skin.

GROWTH & PROPAGATION Z 8; H 15m (50ft); S 10m (30ft). Sheltered site in sun; rich, moist, well-drained soil. Mature plants recover from frost if roots are undamaged but young plants and leaves are killed by freezing winds. Difficult to propagate. Take 10cm (4 in) stem cuttings in late summer in a heated, humid propagator. Bring pot-grown plants indoors if temperature drops below -15°C (5°F). Can be clipped into a ball shape.

## *Lavandula* species

### LAVENDER

These silvery-leaved, shrubby evergreen perennials are covered in aromatic oil glands, most concentrated in the summer flowers. With 28 species and numerous varieties, flower colours range from white to deep purple. All carry variations of the unmistakable sweet-balsamic scent. The largest is *L. x intermedia*

LAVENDER VARIETIES

'Grappenhall' at 1.2m (4ft); Old English Lavender (*L. angustifolia*, syn. *L. officinalis*) is 75cm (30in) tall; Sawyer's Selection, crossed with Woolly Lavender (*L. lanata*), is very silver with long purple flowers and reaches 1.1m (3$^{1}$/$_{2}$ft). *L. a.* 'Rosea' and 'Lodden Pink' have pink flowers, 'Alba' has white. *L. a.* 'Vera' is more silver and compact at 65cm (26in); 'Folgate' and 'Twickle' are more compact forms around 45cm (18in); *L. a.* 'Hidcote', with very silver leaves and deepest purple flowers, is 40cm (16in); *L. a.* 'Munstead' is blue and smaller at 35cm (14in) tall. Less hardy are *L. stoechas* with persistent purple bracts above the flowers, and *L. s. pedunculata* with magenta bracts. *L. dentata* is half hardy with bright green toothed leaves

and a rosemary-lavender scent. Also half hardy are the balsamic-scented Woolly Lavender and Green Lavender (*L. viridis*) with pale green flowers.

USES Long valued for its tenacious sweet, clean, relaxing, insect-repellent fragrance, many ideas have evolved to enjoy Lavender's qualities, ranging from potpourri, drawer liners, linen sachets, herb pillows, pet basket lining, hanging bundles and burning incense to simple display bowls of the flowers. These keep rooms sweet-smelling, calm and insect free. Small quantities of flowers make an interesting bitter-sweet fragrant addition to ice-cream, jam, sugars, vinegars, Provençal stews and lamb stuffing, and the bitter leaves are used in southern European cook-

ing. Lavender flowers, once brewed as a health drink, give a pale, delicately flavoured, uplifting tea to ease headaches, nausea and halitosis; add a few drops of Lemon juice and it will turn a deep violet colour. Lavender flower water tones the face, speeds cell renewal and is antiseptic for acne. Ancient Persians and Greeks burned the twigs as defence against epidemics.

ESSENTIAL OIL The most frequently used oil in the home, by aromatherapists and in the perfume industry. There are three significant sources. For perfume and aromatherapy, the best quality is steam-distilled from the flowering tops of True Lavender – *L. angustifolia*, *L. a.* 'Vera' and specially developed hybrids. It has the traditional benevolent, clean, balsamic floral scent with woody undertones and a more intense, penetrating sweetness than the fresh flowers, but evaporates quickly. It is the most versatile of essential oils, with a great many properties including sedative, antidepressant, antiseptic and painkilling to benefit the body, mind and emotions. It is sedative in small doses but stimulating in larger amounts. It blends well with almost all other oils and blending seems to increase its therapeutic qualities.

Its primary importance is in stress reduction. It also enhances the immune system, whose efficiency may be reduced under stress. It has been used to reduce restlessness, the noise sensitivity of tinnitus and panic attacks. Hospitals are beginning to recognize that Lavender can help patients achieve a comfortable, relaxed sleep.

Lavender oil has a rejuvenating effect on all skin types, especially

LOVAGE

delicate and sensitive skins. It speeds cell replacement in dry, inflamed, mature, oily and normal skins. It treats acne, and soothes broken capillaries and eczema. In general, it promotes healing and reduces scarring. In a massage blend it is used to improve circulation, muscle tone and a sluggish lymph system and to reduce cellulite, fluid retention and chilblains.

A must for the home first-aid kit, a single drop of the antiseptic oil used neat soothes and disinfects insect stings and bites, and benefits cooled minor burns. The cleansing, cell-renewing properties are valuable diluted in water to apply on small cuts and slow-healing wounds. Mixed with Geranium oil, it fights the cold sore virus. As a painkiller and circulation booster in a massage blend, it reduces the discomfort of aching muscles and chronic rheumatism.

Spike Lavender oil, at around one-third the cost of True Lavender oil, is distilled from *L. latifolia* (with its dull grey-blue flower, it is not valued as a garden plant) and *L. fragrans*, but is sometimes sold as, or used to adulterate, True Lavender. It has a more herbaceous, soapy, camphorous aroma used in masculine perfumes, cosmetics, soaps, cleaning products and insect repellents. It has sedative, painkilling properties useful for respiratory and catarrhal complaints and dressing burns, and is massaged on for asthma, acute and chronic bronchitis, rheumatic pains, colds, coughs and flu. Lavandin oil is from Lavandin (*L. x intermedia*), a cross between True Lavender and Spike Lavender. This also has the typical lavender scent with a woody, spicy undertone but a distinct sharp, camphorous top

note. It is widely used in cheaper perfumes, toiletries and cleaning products.

GROWTH & PROPAGATION Z 5–9; H 75cm (30in); S 1.2m (4ft). Grow in an open, sunny site in well-drained, open, limey soil. Take 10–20cm (4–8in) stem cuttings in autumn or spring, or divide or layer the plant. Sow species from fresh seed in late summer. Thin or transplant to 45–60cm (18–24in) apart, or 30cm (12in) for hedging. Remove faded flower stems; prune hedges and straggly plants in late autumn or spring. Harvest flowers at maximum opening.

*Lawsonia inerma*

HENNA

The loose, open Henna shrub has pairs of oblong pointed leaves and panicles of intensely scented, small cream summer flowers followed by blue-black fruits.

USES Known as Camphire in the Bible, the flowers made

HENNA LEAF POWDER

Cleopatra's famous seductive perfume Cyprinum and an Arab fragrance called 'Mehndi'. The young leafy shoots are dried and made into a paste to produce the famous red stain for painted patterns on the feet and hands of women, and to colour and condition the hair of both sexes, principally in North Africa and India. Muslim men who have made the pilgrimage to Mecca are entitled to dye their beards with Henna and prized Arab horses have their manes, tails and hooves coloured with it. Introduced to the West in the 1960s, 35 years of experimentation have produced conditioning hair colours which avoid the original strident orange. The cooling astringent and deodorizing leaves are used for fevers, headache, insect bites and painful joints.

ESSENTIAL OIL The sweet, strong oil is distilled from flowers collected in the early morning and is used in Indian and North African perfumes, but is seldom employed in the West.

GROWTH & PROPAGATION Z 10; H 6m (20ft); S 5m (15ft). Tender. In temperate areas, grow in an intermediate to hot glasshouse in a light, loam-based compost. Propagate from seed or by softwood cuttings in spring and hardwood cuttings in winter.

*Levisticum officinale*

LOVAGE

Perennial Lovage has large, beefy-celery-scented leaves and umbels of greenish-yellow flowers ripening to aromatic seeds.

USES All parts have culinary uses: raw shoots are eaten with

French dressing; spring stems are steamed as vegetables, added to stews or crystallized; young leaves are chopped into salads, soups and cheeses or frozen for later use; the root, dug before flowering in the second or third year, is grated into salads, pickled, or powdered as a condiment, and the seeds are sprinkled on rice or mashed potatoes. Seeds steeped in brandy or cordials make a settling digestive, while an infusion of seed, leaf or root reduces water retention. The root is used to treat anorexia, as a mouthwash for ulcers and tonsillitis, and for respiratory infections.

ESSENTIAL OIL The roots yield an amber oil with a warm, celery-spicy, earthy odour, while the leaves and stalks yield a paler, sweeter version; both are used in perfumery and as flavourings.

CAUTION HERB & OIL: Avoid during pregnancy or with kidney problems. Possible phototoxic or sensitizing effects.

GROWTH & PROPAGATION Z 4; H 2m (6ft); S 1.5m (5ft). Full sun or part shade in rich, moist, well-drained soil. Sow fresh ripe seed in late summer; self-seeds readily. Take root cuttings with buds in spring or autumn. Thin or transplant to 60cm (24in). Tie straw around the stems 2–3 weeks before harvesting for use as a blanched, tender vegetable.

*Lilium candidum*

## MADONNA LILY

This bulb produces a rosette of new basal leaves each autumn, and flowering stems in spring carrying 5–20 elegant white summer flowers with pollen-laden golden stamens. Madonna Lilies have perhaps the best fragrance of all Lilies: sweet and exotic, but without the sickly overtones often present in others. *Lilium regale*, popular with florists, yields an essential oil used to make perfume in Bermuda.

USES The bulbs of this and other Lilies are ancient foods, still cultivated and collected by several cultures including Chinese, Japanese and American Indian. The rich, soothing mucilage from late-summer bulbs can be used in cosmetics, burn ointments and creams to reduce inflammation and acne; the distilled flower water is a skin toner, and flower-

infused Almond oil treats eczema and provides an exotically fragranced massage or body oil.

ESSENTIAL OIL The flowers yield a costly, sophisticated, honey-smooth, intensely rich floral scent used in expensive perfumes. It is only available to perfumers.

CAUTION Wild collection has endangered this plant in its native areas – only from reliable sources, ensuring bulbs labelled as commercially grown.

GROWTH & PROPAGATION Z 6; H 2m (6ft); S 45cm (18in). Plant in early autumn in a sunny, sheltered spot in well-drained alkaline soil, with no more than a 5cm (2in) top covering of soil. Do not allow to dry out or disturb the bulbs. Propagate by seed sown in spring or autumn; by 'scales' (outside surface of a large bulb) in summer; or by offsets (mini bulbs) in late summer.

*Lonicera periclymenum*

## HONEYSUCKLE

Climbing, twining perennial Woodbine Honeysuckle bears pink and creamy-yellow summer flowers whose intense perfume drifts across the garden in the evening. Highly fragrant forms include *L. p.* 'Early Dutch' or 'Belgica', with reddish-purple flowers fading to yellow in late spring and again in late autumn; *L. p.* 'Late Dutch' or 'Serotina' with rich reddish-purple flowers from midsummer to mid-autumn; Japanese Honeysuckle (*L. japonica*), China's 'Silver and Gold' flower, a semi-evergreen with white flowers that turn yellow from midsummer onwards; *L. j. repens*, a beautiful garden

climber with purple-flushed evergreen leaves, shoots and flowers from midsummer onwards; and the Cottage Honeysuckle (*L. caprifolium*), with pink-tinged creamy flowers in midsummer.

USES The tenacious twining habit has made this the emblem of fidelity in the language of flowers. Almost evergreen, Honeysuckle is an easy, attractive cover for porches, pillars and pergolas. Under windows and over arbours, its sweet perfume and attendant hypnotizing hum of bees create a soothing, romantic atmosphere. Woodbine flowers can be added to salads, infused in apple jelly or milk puddings at the end of cooking, or picked fresh to decorate a wedding cake. They yield a skin-softening toilet water, and Honeysuckle syrup, made with flowers, sugar and water, provides a cough syrup or can be diluted as a fragrant summer drink. In Chinese medicine, *L. japonica* is used to control blood sugar levels, to detoxify, and to cool high fevers.

ESSENTIAL OIL Although a very popular fragrance, the scent was too elusive to capture until the late 1800s, when extraction with volatile solvents was developed. Then, to the delight of perfumers, Honeysuckle, Carnation, Mimosa and Broom became available. Honeysuckle oil (Chevrefeuille) is distilled from *L. caprifolium* and *L. gigantea*, but the rare and expensive oil is not generally available. It is a favourite scent for cosmetics and room deodorants but usually a synthetic is used.

CAUTION Honeysuckle berries are poisonous.

HONEYSUCKLE

GROWTH & PROPAGATION Z 4; H 4m (40ft); S Climber. Well-drained soil in sun or light shade. Take cuttings from non-flowering shoots in summer and root in sandy compost. Plant out in autumn or winter, preferably in light shade.

*Melaleuca alternifolia*

## TEA TREE/TI-TREE

There are over 150 species of *Melaleuca* trees and shrubs. Tea Tree has papery bark, small white spring flowers and the antiseptic leaves and twigs yield a spicy, camphorous, thyme-scented oil.

USES The leaves of several melaleucas are components of Aboriginal medicine and many species have commercial importance for timber and oils.

LILY (*Regale*)

ESSENTIAL OIL Tea Tree oil is distilled from the leaves and twigs. It is occasionally used in aftershaves, but more often chosen for its clean medicinal scent and antiseptic properties in cleaning products and pharmaceuticals. Issued to Australian servicemen during World War II for dressing wounds, it was pushed aside by the advent of antibiotics. However, since the 1970s much research, particularly in Australia, has confirmed its antiseptic (most powerful known!), antifungal (for athlete's foot and thrush), antiviral and strong immuno-stimulant properties. Fresh oil is dabbed neat on verrucas and warts, but diluted for spots, cold sores and herpes, or used in inhalations for colds and respiratory infections. It is added to lotions for cracked skin on hands and feet and to shampoos for itchy scalp and head lice. Becoming popular in many 'natural' toiletries, it has great potential for use in hospital and restaurant antiseptic soaps. Cajeput oil, from *M. cajuputi* and *M. leucadendron*, shares the camphorous scent of Tea Tree with a sweeter, fruity note; in high concentration it is a skin irritant. It is added to dental preparations, throat pastilles, antiseptic room sprays to combat airborne infections and insect repellents. Niaouli oil, from *M. viridiflora* has a lighter, eucalyptus note and does not appear to irritate skin, although it has not been 'officially' tested. It boosts the immune system, is a tissue stimulant for wounds and acne, and 1–2 drops applied as a thin film before cobalt radiation therapy will reduce burns.

CAUTION Possible sensitization. Avoid Cajeput in pregnancy and on skin. Melaleuca oils, especially Niaouli, are often adulterated – so buy from a reputable supplier.

GROWTH & PROPAGATION Z 11; H 7m (22ft); S 5m (15ft). Tender. Sun in moisture-retentive to wet soil. Min temp 15–18°C (60–65°F). Sow seed in spring; take semi-ripe cuttings in summer. Pinch out young, pot-grown plants to induce bushiness.

## *Melilotus officinalis*

### MELILOT

This graceful biennial has faintly aromatic toothed leaves and late-summer spikes of small, yellow, pea-like, honey-scented flowers. Lining the highways of Alberta, Canadian Sweet Clover (*M. alba*) has white flowers.

USES The dried leaves and seeds were once part of a medieval magic philtre and have a sweet, new-mown-hay scent due to the developing presence of coumarin. The aerial parts are used to flavour Gruyère cheese, Polish vodka and rabbit dishes, or for scented pillows, moth repellents, potpourri and baths. The seeds are mildly antibiotic, while the leaves are used as a tea to ease headaches, indigestion and insomnia, or are prescribed to reduce thrombosis risk and for varicose veins. The herb is also the source of an anticoagulant.

ESSENTIAL OIL The new-mown-hay-scented oil is used in some quality perfumes, but is unavailable for home use.

CAUTION Should not be used with blood-thinning drugs or blood-clotting problems. Use the fresh herb only for home teas – poorly dried or fermented herbs develop a powerful anticoagulant which is toxic in excess.

GROWTH & PROPAGATION Z 3; H 1.2m (4ft); S 1m (3ft). Grow in sun or light shade in well-drained soil. Sow in spring or late summer. Self-seeds in light soils. Thin or transplant to 45cm (18in) apart.

## *Melissa officinalis*

### LEMON BALM

The pretty scalloped leaves of this bushy perennial have a refreshing, soft lemon scent, best when the tiny white flowers begin opening in late summer. There are gold and variegated forms: *M. o.* 'All Gold' and *M. o.* 'Variegata'.

USES The delicately flavoured fresh leaves make a mildly sedative tea which eases headaches, indigestion and nausea and, taken daily, has an ancient reputation for increasing longevity. Leaves are added to fruit and wine cups, vinegars and oils. Fresh leafy stems are ideal for invalid posies, relaxing baths, to soothe insect bites and to attract bees to the garden. They lose scent and possibly their antiseptic and antiviral properties when dried.

ESSENTIAL OIL The pale yellow oil steam-distilled from the leaves and flowering tops is known as Melissa. It has a light, lemony, fresh fragrance which is both cheerful and calming and features in Carmalite water and several perfumes. A gentle, sunny, reassuring oil, therapists find it of great help for the terminally ill and bereaved, as well as in relieving anxiety, shock, depression

LEMON BALM

and nightmares. Antispasmodic, it is given for stress-related digestive, menstrual and respiratory problems, including asthma, and combined with Chamomile it treats eczema and allergies.

CAUTION OIL: Use in low dilutions. Frequently adulterated.

GROWTH & PROPAGATION Z 4; H 1.2m (4ft); S 1m (3ft). Sunny site with midday shade in ordinary, moist soil. Gold leaves scorch in midday sun. Sow in spring; germination is slow. Divide the plant or take stem cuttings in spring or autumn. Thin or transplant to 60cm (24in). Prune to keep tidy shape.

## *Mentha* species

### MINTS

These perennials with invasive creeping rootstocks sport a wide range of refreshing, mint-based leaf scents in a variety of leaf colours, plus purple, pink or white flowers with a milder mint scent. They hybridize freely, producing yet further blended scents. Mat-forming, tiny-leaved Corsican Mint (*M. requienii*) has a powerful peppermint scent and is a groundcover mint for cool, moist soils.

USES The range of Mint flavours includes Spearmint (*M. spicata* – *M. s.* 'Moroccan' and 'Red Raripila' have excellent clean flavours), Peppermint (*M.* x *piperita*), Apple (*M. suaveolens*), Lemon (*M.* x *aquatica* 'Citrata'), Basil (*M.* x *aquatica*), and Eau-de-Cologne (*M.* x *piperita* 'Citrata'), used to flavour sweet and savoury foods such as sauces, salads, vegetables, vinegars, desserts and drinks. Mint is seldom combined with other herbs because of its dominant character. Refreshing Spearmint or Peppermint tea gives a just-brushed-teeth sensation, improves digestion, helps to quell nausea and flatulence, and cools feverish colds. The scent released from sprigs in baths or inhalations is invigorating and eases nasal congestion. The perfume fragrance of Eau-de-Cologne Mint is used in cosmetics and floral waters.

ESSENTIAL OIL Spearmint oil, steam-distilled from the flowering tops of *M. spicata*, has a warm, rounded minty scent. Although

MINTS *(Peppermint, Applemint, and Basil)*

seldom used in perfumery, it flavours toothpastes, mouth-washes and confectionery. This oil is milder than Peppermint and can be used in place of it for children. Spearmint is useful in room sprays against colds and flu both for its antiseptic quality and for its refreshing, stimulating scent, which helps to lift the gloom that can accompany these ailments and to clear the head and aid concentration. Pungent Pennyroyal (*M. pulegium*) and Japanese/Cornmint oils (*M. arvensis*) are unsuitable for home use, but are used industrially. Peppermint oil, steam-distilled from the flowering tops of *M.* x *piperita*, has the sharp, penetrating characteristic peppermint scent, too distinctive for most perfumery but the 'morning freshness' component of many oral hygiene products. It has a head-clearing, enlivening effect, and can be inhaled from a tissue as 'smelling salts' for shock and dizziness, to boost concentration and spirits on a lethargic or oppressive day, or to quell motion sickness. Antiseptic, antiviral and antispasmodic, it makes a good steam inhalation for colds, coughs and asthma. Diluted in oil, a little can be applied to the temples to relieve headaches and fatigue, but, as with Spearmint, should not be used too late in the evening as it will hinder restful sleep.

**CAUTION** OIL: Do not use continuously. Use in low dilution. Avoid in the first trimester of pregnancy. Avoid Mint inhalations, or direct applications of menthol products to the nostrils, for babies. All Mint oils cancel the effect of homoeopathic medicines.

GROWTH & PROPAGATION Z 3; H 1.2m (4ft); S indefinite. Grow in sun or partial shade in

moist, well-drained, nutrient-rich alkaline soil where invasive roots will not be a problem. Divide in spring or autumn. Take cuttings in spring or summer and root in compost or water. Remove flowering stems to avoid cross-pollination between species. If rust appears, dig up and burn.

## *Monarda didyma*

### BERGAMOT

Young purple-veined leaves of this spreading perennial have a sweet eau-de-Cologne scent. Late summer brings faintly scented, shaggy scarlet flowers with red bracts. Pink, mauve and white flower forms are also available.

USES The name 'Bergamot' was given because the leaves smell like the Bergamot Orange (*Citrus bergamia*). Young leaves can be added to pork stuffing, jams and lemonade, and to China tea for an 'Earl Grey' flavour. Leaves and petals are added to salads and potpourri. Brewed leaves (known as Oswego tea) ease sore throats, nausea and insomnia. Bergamot milk is a pleasant nightcap. Leaves contain antiseptic thymol and are added to steam inhalations for colds and bronchitis. Other *Monarda* flavouring leaves include the lemony-oregano-scented *M. pectina* and *M. fistulosa*, and the minty *M. menthifolia* and *M. punctata*, plus the lemon-scented *M. citriodora*, which has important medicinal virtues.

GROWTH & PROPAGATION Z 4; H 1m (3ft); S 60cm (24in). Grow in sun or part shade in rich, light moist soil. Sow seed of species in spring. Plant 45cm (18in) apart. Divide every 3 years,

BERGAMOT

discarding dead centres. Divide or take root cuttings in spring, and stem cuttings in summer.

## *Murraya koenigii*

### CURRY LEAF

This evergreen tree or shrub has aromatic, peppery-curry-scented leaves and bark, and produces large clusters of small white flowers in summer.

USES Throughout Asia, particularly southern India and Sri Lanka, the fresh leaves (they lose flavour when dried) are digestive and essential to vegetarian cooking. The bark, leaves and roots are used in local medicine. Cosmetic Bark or Orange Jasmine (*M. paniculata*), has jasmine-scented flowers several times per year, citrus-scented

CURRY PLANT

medicinal leaves and aromatic bark used in cosmetics.

ESSENTIAL OIL Another curry-scented plant called Curry Plant is the silver-leaved evergreen sub-shrub, *Helichrysum italicum*. A form of this shrub yields an essential oil and absolute known as 'Immortelle'. The pale yellow to red oil has a German Chamomile-Rose Geranium scent, while the yellowy-brown absolute has a stronger floral fragrance. Both are used in perfumery and cosmetics and in aromatherapy for depression, withdrawal from addictive substances and lethargy.

GROWTH & PROPAGATION Z 11; H 6m (20ft); S 3m (10ft). Tender. In temperate regions, grow in a conservatory with min temp 10°C (50°C). Grow in

moist, well-drained, fertile soil in full sun or part shade. Water and liquid feed fortnightly during full growth, moderately at other times. Prune if necessary in early spring. Sow seed in spring; take semi-ripe cuttings in summer.

*Myrica cerifera*

WAX MYRTLE

This shrub has shiny, evergreen leaves with a spicy-resinous aroma shared by its bark and male and female catkins on separate bushes, with berries covered in a pale balsamic wax.

USES Also known as Candleberry Bush, the berries of this and of California Wax Myrtle (*M.californica*) are picked after the first frosts and scalded to melt the wax, which is skimmed off and made into balsamic-scented candles that burn with a clear white flame, shaving soap and cosmetics. Skilled harvesters collect the bark and leaves of Wax Myrtle and Sweet Gale (*M. gale*) for clothes sachets. Sweet Gale leaves repel moths and other insects. The dried berries of all

CURRY LEAF

3 can be used like Juniper berries for flavouring meat. The early-summer leaves are dried as seasoning or steeped (not boiled) as an astringent medicinal tea. Wax Myrtle bark snuff, or its tincture in a massage oil, is used for sinusitis.

CAUTION Wax can be irritant. Use home-grown Sweet Gale only, as the shrub is endangered.

GROWTH & PROPAGATION Z 6; H 10m (30ft); S 3m (10ft). Grow in sun or partial shade in well-drained moist, sandy, acid soil. Remove weak ground-level growth. Sow seed in autumn or spring; layer in spring or take semi-ripe cuttings in summer.

*Myristica fragrans*

NUTMEG

This evergreen tree has aromatic leaves, tiny yellow flowers and apricot-sized fruits which split to reveal the sweet-spicy seed (Nutmeg) and its aromatic aril (Mace), a red lacy coating.

USES The outer part of the fruit is fermented into a brandy-type drink, while the Nutmeg and Mace flavour sweet and savoury dishes and ease digestion, nausea and flatulence. A reputed aphrodisiac, it increases the intoxicating and soporific effects of alcohol. Nutmeg is considered narcotic and large doses are dangerous. Nutmeg powder is added to scented sachets and the nuts yield cosmetic butter.

ESSENTIAL OIL The Nutmeg seeds, from which worms have been allowed to eat away the fat and starch, yield a warm, spicy-sweet essential oil, while Mace

NUTMEG AND MACE

yields a similarly scented oil and an oleoresin with a spicy-balsamic scent. All are used in the food and perfumery industries, with the Mace oleoresin mainly used in male fragrances. In aromatherapy, Nutmeg essential oil is used to help overcome addictions, guilt and depression and to help the sufferer focus on a more positive self-image.

CAUTION HERB: Excessive amounts are toxic. OIL: Use low dilutions and with caution during pregnancy.

GROWTH & PROPAGATION Z 11; H 10m (30ft); S 8m (25ft). Coastal humid tropics.

*Myrrhis odorata*

SWEET CICELY

This perennial has attractive, fern-like leaves with a woodland-anise scent and umbels of small white spring flowers with a light, sweet anise flavour followed by large, narrow, similarly aromatic dark brown seeds.

USES The unripe green seeds

have a sweet, nutty, anise flavour and scent used in an aromatic furniture polish for oak panelling and flooring. Once added to the salads of French kings for perfume and flavour, tender green seeds are now sprinkled in fruit salads, puddings and ice creams or dried. The ripe black seeds flavour liqueurs. Fresh leaves cooked with acid fruits reduce the tartness, and therefore the amount of sugar needed, and are chopped into soups and omelettes. The white autumn root flesh, flavoured like spicy winter-sweets, can be grated into salads, cooked as a vegetable, candied or pickled. A brandy root infusion is an enjoyable tonic and digestive, and leaf and root infusions are given for anaemia in the elderly.

GROWTH & PROPAGATION Z 5; H 1.3m (4½ft) ; S 1m (3ft). Plant in light shade in humus-rich soil. Sow outside in autumn; seed

SWEET CICELY

SWEET MYRTLE

requires several months of winter temperatures to germinate. Self-seeds. Allow 75cm (30in) spacing. Divide the plant in autumn after it dies down.

## Myrtus communis

### SWEET MYRTLE

This shrub has small, thick evergreen leaves with deeply embedded oil glands, 5-petalled ivory summer flowers with pronounced stamens and small blue-black berries. All parts have a fresh, spicy-sweet, orange-blossom scent.

USES Popular in bridal wreaths as a symbol of beauty and chastity, the leaves and branchlets are also dried for sweet pillows, strewn as an insect repellent, or dipped in water then laid under grilling barbecue meats for the final 10 minutes to add a sweet-smoky flavour. Flower buds with the green parts removed are added to salads or infused with ripe berries to give creamy dishes a subtle orange blossom scent with a faint resin taste. Berries can be dried as a spice. Flowers are infused for Angel Flower Water, a skin tonic; flowers and antiseptic leaves are

infused for acne creams and to scent furniture polish.

ESSENTIAL OIL The essential oil, steam-distilled from the twigs, leaves and sometimes the flowers, has the plant's fresh green, orange-blossom scent with a hint of eucalyptus. It features in toilet waters for its fresh, sweet aroma and therapeutic action on oily, problem skin. It is a mild oil, used by aromatherapists for children's chest complaints and for colds and flu. Therapists find Myrtle oil fragrance helps people to feel good about themselves.

GROWTH & PROPAGATION Z 8; H 5m (15ft); S 3m (10ft). Almost frost hardy. In warm areas, grow in full sun in a sheltered position in well-drained neutral to alkaline soil. Protected during the winter, it may survive temperatures down to -10°C (14°F), but prefers an average min temp of 5°C (40°F). Take stem cuttings in mid- or late-summer. Transplant to large pots. An ideal tidy conservatory or topiary plant.

## Narcissus poeticus

### POET'S NARCISSUS

This perennial bulb sends up blade-like green leaves and a late-spring flower of glistening white petals around a red-trimmed shallow yellow cup, with an intense narcotic floral perfume.

USES Roman perfumers captured the fragrance in an unguent, the Arabs consider it an aphrodisiac and the French used the flowers for their antispasmodic effect to treat epilepsy. Narcissus refers not to vanity, but to numbness due to its powerful paralyzing

effect on the nervous system, as though the youth Narcissus was benumbed by his own beauty. It was carried in Roman soldiers' kit bags and applied to gladiators' wounds to numb pain, but always with caution as it can also paralyze the heart. Later, the bulbs were used to draw splinters and treat raw heels. The flower scent in a closed room is too powerful for some and can cause headaches.

ESSENTIAL OIL The flowers yield both a concrete and an absolute with a sweet, heavy floral scent used in expensive exotic floral perfumes. The fragrance is considered empowering, aiding creativity and spiritual concentration, and helpful in the treatment of addiction.

NARCISSUS 'CHEERFULNESS'

**CAUTION** Internally, all Narcissus and Daffodil bulbs are poisonous, potentially fatal.

GROWTH & PROPAGATION
Z 4; H 50cm (20in); S 15cm (6in). Plant bulbs 1½ times deeper than their size in moist but well-drained soil in dappled shade, in late summer or early autumn. Do not cut the leaves until at least 4–6 weeks after flowering. Alternatively, plant in deep pots in a 'double layer' for mass flowering. Divide bulbs at the base or remove offsets in early summer or autumn.

## *Nepeta cataria*

### CATNIP

The leaves of this herbaceous plant have a camphorous minty scent, and its whorls of small bee-attracting, tubular summer flowers are white-spotted lavender. Catmint, the smaller *N. racemosa*, syn. *N. mussinii*, has less scent

CATMINT

CATNIP

but is a prettier plant with its silver-grey leaves and blue flowers.

USES Cats recognize pheromone overtones in the scent of this herb, and they love it! While rolling in it in complete bliss, they can flatten or even pull up a young plant. Leaves are dried to stuff cat toys or to soothe cats when moving house or visiting vets. Tender young leaves add flavour to salads and meat, or can be brewed, especially the lemon-scented *N. c.* 'Citriodora'. The leaves and flowering tops contain vitamin C, are mildly sedative, lower fevers and yield a useful tea for colds, flu, headaches and to help sick children relax and sleep. Dried as herbal tobacco, the leaves produce feelings of general well-being and mild euphoria, with no known harmful effects. Planted near vegetables it will repel some beetles and aphids, and near duck and hen houses will deter rats.

GROWTH & PROPAGATION
Z 3; H 1m (3ft); S 60cm (24in). Sun or light shade in well-drained soil. Sow seed or divide the plant

in spring. Take softwood cuttings in late spring. Thin or transplant to 30cm (12in). Cut back in autumn. Plants sown *in situ* are less likely to be damaged by cats than transplanted plants, which may need protection.

## *Ocimum basilicum*

### BASIL

The delicious sweet-spicy clove-like scent of Sweet Basil leaves is popular worldwide. Varieties vary from annual to short-lived perennial, from tiny-leaved Greek Basil to large Lettuce Leaf, and from green to purple *O. b.* 'Dark Opal'. There are the lemon-scented leaves and seeds of *O. b.* var. *citriodorum*, various spice-scented leaves with names like Anise, Cinnamon, Thai and Morpha Basil, and the balsamic Sacred Basil *O. sanctum*. They bear small, white, lipped flowers in late summer with clove-flavoured nectar, and release their leaf scent in hot sun or when crushed. Holy Basils *O. sanctum* and *O. album* are widely grown in India, but never used in cooking as they are sacred plants. The only culinary Basil in Indian cooking is Camphor Basil, *O. kilimandscharicum*, known as Kapoor Basil.

USES Tear, rather than cut, fresh leaves to release the warm, spicy flavour into salads, tomatoes, peppers, fish, egg and chicken dishes. They flavour oils, vinegars and pesto sauce. Use flowers in salads and as garnish. Leaves steeped in wine are tonic and stimulant-aphrodisiac. Paint the leaves with olive oil if freezing them for later use. Leaves can be added to potpourri and sweet bags, and grown in window pots to deter flies.

ESSENTIAL OIL Steam distillation of the flowering tops and leaves supplies this top-note oil. The oil of French Basil is less harsh and less toxic than Exotic or Comoran Basil, although classified botanically as identical. French Basil Oil has a penetrating, refreshing, energizing, sunny, light-green fragrance with a hint of cloves, and like old-fashioned smelling salts, a whiff can revive a fainting spell. The oil is antiseptic, a general tonic and selectively antiviral.

**CAUTION** OIL: Basil oil should not be used directly on the skin and requires caution as many species contain oestragol, a compound which can have adverse reactions on sensitive skins and in high doses may be carcinogenic. It should not be used for babies or children, nor during pregnancy. The industry is looking for Basil species with little or no oestragol and these presently include *O. canum*,

PURPLE AND SACRED BASIL

EVENING PRIMROSE (White)

syn. *O. americanum*, and *O. gratissimum*. Although these are much safer, it is still wise to avoid contact with undiluted oil.

GROWTH & PROPAGATION
Z 10; H 60cm (24in); S 38cm (15in). Tender. Warm sun, well-drained moist soil. Water at midday, not in the evening. Sow seed thinly with heat. Avoid over-watering: seedlings are prone to 'damping off'. Protect from wind, scorching sun and frost.

*Oenothera biennis*

## EVENING PRIMROSE

This biennial, sometimes annual, has a rosette of narrow leaves in the first year, and in the second year stems of large butter-yellow flowers from summer to autumn, which unfurl at twilight and last for one day. The flowers have a sweet, clean honey scent, strongest in early evening, and a slight luminescence. *O. speciosa* is a fragrant white form.

USES First-year roots were dug and dried in autumn by the Blackfoot tribe as winter food. 'Twice boiled', they taste like sweet parsnip, and can be stewed, pickled, candied or fried. Young leaves can be picked in late winter and used sparingly in mountain salads or 'twice boiled' as a vegetable and eaten with butter or vinegar. Roots or tops, slow boiled in twice their volume of honey, make a soothing cough syrup. The seed oil contains gamma-linolenic acid (GLA), the fatty acid needed for healthy skin, and anticoagulant compounds. GLA reduces eczema, premenstrual and menopausal tension, helps hyperactive children and rheumatoid arthritis, lowers blood pressure and aids red blood cell mobility in multiple sclerosis and other degenerative conditions. It can ease withdrawal from alcohol, reduce alcohol liver damage, and a large dose (2–3g), can cure a hangover.

GROWTH & PROPAGATION
Z 4; H 1.5m (5ft); S 30cm (12in). Sunny, open position in dry soil. Sow seed in spring to early summer. Self-seeds in light soil. Transplant to 30cm (12in) apart by autumn. May need staking.

*Origanum majorana*

## SWEET MARJORAM

This perennial, biennial or annual has small leaves with a sweet, spicy scent more refined than that of Marjoram or Oregano. It has narrow, rooting stems, tiny white to mauve summer flowers and knot-like seed clusters.

USES Grow it in window boxes or hanging baskets as a spicy green fragrance and convenient seasoning. It adds fresh sweet spiciness to salads, sauces and cheese, meat and vegetable dishes when added near the end of cooking. Dried leaves retain their flavour well and the seeds are a commercial food flavouring. Leaf tea eases colds, tension headaches and painful menstruation, and is added to baths to ease anxiety and rheumatic pains. The spicy leaves and flowering tops can be enjoyed in clothes sachets, pot-pourri and relaxing pillows. A popular Victorian fragrancing idea was to use mashed leaves to perfume furniture polish.

ESSENTIAL OIL The oil, steam-distilled from the flowering herb, has a warm, nutty, spicy scent with a hint of camphor and a comforting, confidence-building effect. Aromatherapists find these qualities useful when treating alcohol withdrawal, phobias, overwork, stress headaches and irritability, while a few drops near the pillow at night promote restful sleep. This calming quality is considered to reduce sexual impulses, although Marjoram is used in perfumes, masculine fragrances and cosmetics. Its antioxidant property reduces skin-aging free radicals, with future skin cream potential. Marjoram oil is antiviral, stimulates local circulation, and eases spasms, and also treats colds, the chest tightness of asthma and muscular and rheumatic pain.

CAUTION HERB: Avoid medicinal doses in pregnancy. Cooking quantities are safe. OIL: Non-toxic but avoid in pregnancy.

GROWTH & PROPAGATION
Z 7; H 60cm (24in); S 45cm (18in). Half hardy. Grow in a sunny position in well-drained, dryish, nutrient-rich alkaline soil. Sow seed in spring and avoid overwatering. Thin out or transplant to 30–45cm (12–18in).

*Origanum onites* and *O.vulgare*

## POT MARJORAM & OREGANO

Both these perennials have small pungent-spicy leaves and dense clusters of tiny white to dark pink late-summer flowers attractive to bees and butterflies. There are gold and gold-variegated forms of each, plus Curled Leaf and Compact Oregano and Greek Oregano/Winter Marjoram (*O. v.* subsp. *hirtum*) which has sweeter, spicier leaves and a small compact habit useful as edging.

USES Pot Marjoram, the milder of the two, is included in bouquet garni, rubbed on roasting meat, and flavours cheese, egg and fish dishes. Oregano is the classic accompaniment to pizza, tomato and chilli dishes. Oregano tea is a tonic and mild sedative, helping to prevent sea-sickness, headaches, irritability, coughs and menstrual pain. Externally, it is

OREGANO

PEONY

used as a poultice for easing rheumatic pains and stiff necks.

ESSENTIAL OIL Oregano oil has a savory-camphor scent used in men's fragrances and commercial food products. Most oil labelled Oregano or Spanish Oregano is distilled from *Thymus capitatus*. Both sources are toxic and unsuitable for home use.

**CAUTION** HERB: Avoid medicinal doses in pregnancy. OIL: Irritant to the skin and mucous membranes. Avoid during pregnancy and on skin. Not suitable for home use.

GROWTH & PROPAGATION Z 5; H 1m (3ft); S 75cm (30in). Frost-hardy/ hardy. Grow in full sun, except for ornamental golden forms which appreciate midday shade, in well-drained, dryish, nutrient-rich alkaline soil. Sow seed in spring; germination can be slow. Divide in spring or autumn. Take root or stem cut-

tings from late spring to midsummer. Thin or transplant to 45cm (18in). Cut back plants by two-thirds before winter or leave seed heads as bird food.

*Paeonia officinalis*

PEONY

This perennial has indented foliage and sumptuous, often sweetly fragrant, showy single or double summer blooms in red, pink or white.

USES Peony, from the Greek Pæon, physician to the Olympic gods, has been variously regarded as the 'food of dragons', a good luck charm, averter of storms and witchcraft, and a symbol of the sun and moon. In the past the roots were made into babies' teething beads – despite their poisonous potential. The tonic, anti-spasmodic roots were once considered a cure for 'lunacy', and do aid some types of epilepsy. Chinese Peony (*P. lactiflora*) and Moutan or Tree Peony (*P. suffruticosa*) are important in traditional Chinese medicine. The former is immunostimulant and reduces blood pressure, pain and inflammation, and the latter is antibiotic and stimulates circulation. Together, they are part of a successful treatment for children's eczema.

**CAUTION** Can be poisonous; for use by qualified personnel only.

GROWTH & PROPAGATION Z 6; H & S 60cm (24in). Grow in sun or part shade in rich, well-drained soil in a sheltered position. Dislikes disturbance. Sow seed, which may take 3 years to germinate, in autumn. Divide in autumn or early spring; take root

cuttings in winter. Tree peony can be layered or semi-ripe cuttings taken in spring.

*Pandanus odoratissimus*

SCREWPINE

This evergreen tree, often with visible stilt roots, has long, blade-like aromatic leaves which grow in spiral clumps at the ends of branches, hence the common name. Mature trees have rose-jasmine-scented white bracts around the male flowers, and pineapple-like fruits.

USES In India the fragrant flowers are floated in silver dishes, thrown into wells to scent the water and decorate trellises at lavish weddings. In some areas the leaves are a sacred offering to Shiva. The flower water, Kewra, a by-product of essential oil production, is used to flavour syrup desserts and savoury rice dishes. Fresh or dried leaves flavour South-east Asian and Pacific Island food. The seeds and sweet fruits are edible after careful preparation. Cleaned bundles of ripe flower stamens are used as brushes; leaves and roots are used in local medicine. The leaves, known as Rampe or Curry Leaf (*P. latifolius*), have a savoury flavour used in curries, especially in Sri Lanka.

ESSENTIAL OIL The rose-jasmine-scented oil is popular in Indian perfumes, skin-care products and sweetmeats. Stimulant and antiseptic, in Nepal it is given for headaches and rheumatism. No safety data is available.

GROWTH & PROPAGATION Z 11; H 6m (20ft); S 3m (10ft). Tender. Marshy land. The tree is

seldom grown outside its native South-east Asia, but a compact form would be worthy of garden consideration in hot, moist climates.

*Pelargonium* species

PELARGONIUMS

The shrubby perennial Scented Geraniums have highly aromatic leaves and small five-petalled flowers. The Rose Geraniums, with a rosey-green scent, have pink spring to summer flowers.

USES From the African Cape of Good Hope, pot-grown scented Geraniums were a favourite of Victorian interiors, where long skirts would brush the leaves to release their fragrance. Today's scented varieties include the peppery-lavender scented *P. dichondrifolium*, the sweet-scented *P.* 'Sweet Mimosa', orangey *P. crispum* 'Prince of

PELARGONIUM

Orange', rosey *P.* 'Attar of Roses', cedar-rosey *P.* 'Clorinda', balsamic *P.* 'Royal Oak', peppermint *P. tomentosum*, and piney-spicy *P. x fragrans*. The Rose, Apple (*P. odoratissimum*) and Lemon (*P. citronellum*) Geraniums flavour syrups, preserves and drinks – try adding a leaf to a cup of delicate tea. *P. crispum* varieties (usually lemon-scented) can irritate stomachs – avoid internal use. Leaves are a popular addition to potpourri.

ESSENTIAL OIL Rose Geranium is a complex oil steam-distilled from the flowering aerial parts of *P. graveolens* and *P. capitatum*. Its sweet, rosey-spice odour with fruity-green tones, widely used in perfumery, varies significantly with variety and source. Bourbon oil from the island of Réunion is considered the best quality. It is tonic, antiseptic, antifungal and antidepressant, treating stress, sluggish circulation, cellulite, broken capillaries, unbalanced skin sebum and eczema. It is popular in massage for its uplifting, relaxing, cherishing fragrance and is probably the most pleasantly scented insect repellent. Other varieties produce differently scented oils, but are far less in demand.

GROWTH & PROPAGATION Z 10; H & S 1m (3ft). Tender. Grow in pots in well-drained potting compost. Keep in a sunny, warm, well-ventilated indoor position during the winter months, and a sheltered outdoor position in summer. Sow seed in early spring or take 7.5cm (3in) tip cuttings in late summer or spring from overwintered plants. Pinch out the growing tips when the plant reaches 15cm (6in). Feed every 10 days in summer.

FLAT LEAF PARSLEY

*Petroselinum crispum*

## PARSLEY

This biennial has fresh, pungent, green-scented curled leaves, umbels of tiny cream summer flowers and pungent seed.

USES Rich in vitamins, minerals and chlorophyll, the antibiotic, anti-allergen, anti-oxidant and breath-sweetening leaves are a nutritious garnish described as 'the summation of all things green'. Leaves and stems are added to bouquet garni and savoury dishes towards the end of cooking. Hamburg Parsley root (*P. crispum* var. *tuberosum*), boiled as a vegetable, has a nutty taste. The larger, hardier, Flat Leaf (Italian or French) Parsley (*P. c.* 'Italian') has a stronger flavour; the stems are eaten in the same way as celery.

ESSENTIAL OIL The seed essential oil, with a spicy-woody scent, is used in industrial and men's fragrances. It, and the spicy-sweet herb oil, are used as flavourings in the food and drink industry.

CAUTION HERB & SEED: Avoid excessive consumption and during pregnancy or with kidney disease. Toxic to some birds. OILS: moderately toxic; restrictions as for the herb.

GROWTH & PROPAGATION Z 8 (grow as an annual in colder regions); H 80cm (32in); S 30cm (12in). Frost hardy. Grow in sun or part shade in rich, moist, well-drained and deeply dug neutral to alkaline soil. Sow seed in succession from spring to late summer. To speed germination (which takes 3–7 weeks), soak seed overnight in warm water and pour boiling water in the drill before sowing. Self-seeds freely. Thin to 22cm (9in) apart and keep watered and weed-free. Give cloche protection from winter weather and wildlife.

*Pimenta dioica*

## ALLSPICE

This small, tropical evergreen tree has grey aromatic bark, leathery green leaves and dark purple berries, all with a cinnamon-nutmeg-clove scent when touched. The summer panicles of green-white flowers also waft a spicy perfume.

USES Allspice plantations in Jamaica are popular for romantic strolls when the flowers perfume the landscape. Berries are picked green for maximum flavour and grated to release the exotic fragrance of the shell. It flavours sweet and savoury foods including curries, drinks and pickles, and is added to medicines to disguise the taste. Allspice provides a warming medicine for chills, indigestion and flatulence, and is a tonic for the nervous system.

ESSENTIAL OIL Leaves and berries yield spicy, clove-like oils. Berry oil is added to commercial digestive medicines and stimulating liniments. Industry uses both oils to flavour drinks, foods, cosmetics, aftershaves and exotic perfumes. Leaf oil from *P. racemosa*, syn. *P.acris*, gives Bay Rum its distinctive scent. The crushed leaves of *P. r.* var. *citrifolia* emit a delightful lemon scent but the oil is not in demand.

CAUTION OIL: Can irritate skin and mucous membranes. Use at very low dilution.

GROWTH & PROPAGATION Z 11; H & S 9m (28ft). Tender. Grow in a heated dry glasshouse in well-drained, friable soil. Plant fresh ripe seed or take semi-ripe cuttings in summer.

ALLSPICE (DRIED BERRIES)

*Pimpinella anisum*

## ANISE

The summer umbels of white flowers of this tender annual with sweetly aromatic leaves are followed by aromatic, strongly-flavoured seeds.

USES

The sweet, spicy seeds, gathered when they turn grey-green at the tips, are popular in Eastern cookery and are used to enhance bread, apple pies, curries, cream cheese and figs. Who recalls the old-fashioned aniseed balls that feature an anise seed in the centre? The seeds are lightly roasted as a breath sweetener or crushed for use in potpourri and freckle-bleaching face packs. Add young leaves and flowers to fruit and savoury salads; add autumn stems and roots to soups and stews to provide a liquorice hint. Comforting infused seed-tea aids digestion, coughs, colds and nausea, and stimulates lactation and the libido. Tests show that it increases liver regeneration in rats.

ESSENTIAL OIL The extremely toxic seed oil is used by industry in minute amounts to flavour food and drinks such as Pernod, and in medicines to mask any bitterness.

CAUTION OIL: Not suitable for home use.

GROWTH & PROPAGATION
Z 10; H 50cm (20in); S 30cm (12in). Grow in a sunny, sheltered position in well-drained alkaline soil. Avoid similar, poisonous plants by using well-sourced seed. Sow *in situ* in late spring. Thin to 20cm (8in) apart.

*Pinus sylvestris*

PINE

The aromatic, evergreen Scots Pine has attractive peeling, red-brown bark and blue green needle-like leaves with the characteristic pine scent.

PINE

USES Pine needles from any species release their resinous scent when sprinkled on winter fires or pressed in pillows. Fresh spring needles are brewed by woodsmen for tea; root tar is used to stimulate hair growth, the resin flavours Greek retsina wine, and Pine branches decaying in large ponds help to inhibit pond algae. Edible Pine kernels from Stone Pine (*P. pinea*) provide a real culinary treat and can be used raw, toasted or salted.

ESSENTIAL OIL Scots Pine oil is dry distilled from the needles to yield a balsam-turpentine pine scent with a clearing, energizing effect. Powerfully antiseptic, expectorant and antiviral, Pine is excellent for vaporizers to treat and prevent coughs, colds and chest infections. It is added to masculine fragrances, bath products, detergents and floor cleaning products for its 'clean' antiseptic scent. Turpentine, distilled from the oleoresin of *P. palustris* and other Pines, has pharmaceutical and industrial uses but is not suitable for use in the home.

CAUTION OIL: Use in low dilutions. Avoid if you suffer from skin allergies.

GROWTH & PROPAGATION
Z 4; H 35m (120ft); S 10m (30ft). Grow in full sun in well-drained soil. Propagate by seed sown in autumn or spring, or by grafting. Remove dead branches in winter.

*Piper nigrum*

PEPPER

This stout-stemmed vine has drooping, white flowering spikes that yield long clusters of pungent, peppery green fruit which ripen to dark red.

USES An essential luxury of foreign trade which helped to drain the coffers of the Roman Empire, black, green and white peppercorns all come from one and the same plant. Green, unripe fruits are picked and used fresh or pickled; black peppercorns are picked green, fermented and sun-dried; white corns are the ripe, red fruits soaked, de-skinned and dried.

A spice best used freshly ground, Pepper stimulates saliva and gastric juices, aids digestion and kills bacteria, and also eases colic, headaches, diarrhoea and flatulence. Long Pepper (*P. longum*) is sweeter and is used in Asian cooking; Cubeb (*P. cubeba*) has an allspice flavour which is also used in Asian dishes and is powdered to treat amoebic dysentery. Those sold as pink peppercorns are from different plants, *Schinus terebinthifolius* or *S. molle*, and have a very different sweetish, resinous flavour.

ESSENTIAL OIL Black Pepper oil has a warm, spicy, woody aroma that is used in perfume and commercial foods to provide a peppery note without pungency. In low dilutions it is added to sports massage oils and is used to improved circulation and muscle tone. In oil vaporizers it helps to improve concentration.

PEPPERCORNS

**CAUTION** OIL: Use in the lowest dilutions to avoid causing skin irritation.

GROWTH & PROPAGATION
Z 11; H 4m (12ft); S Climber. Tender. Rich soil in shade. Seldom grown outside its zone.

*Pogostemon cablin*

PATCHOULI

This square-stemmed bushy perennial has spikes of violet-marked white flowers and toothed oval leaves with a light, fresh, green version of the distinctive and familiar, penetrating earthy scent from the dried leaves.

USES The fragrance of carefully dried leaves improves with age and in Asia they are popularly placed among clothes to act as an insect repellent. This is how imported nineteenth-century Indian shawls acquired their characteristic earthy odour. The whole plant is also considered to be antiseptic, antidepressant, insect repellent and aphrodisiac.

ESSENTIAL OIL The steam-distilled, dried fermented leaves yield a penetrating sweet, cedar-earthy scent. As an intensifier of woody notes and a fixative, it is widely used in perfumes and incense and to mask unpleasant scents. Patchouli oil imparts the distinctive odour to Chinese red paste ink and original Indian ink. Aromatherapists use it to help deal with stress-related problems, including reduced libido, and to promote new skin cells in the treatment of wrinkles, open pores, acne, eczema, cracked skin and fungal infections such as athlete's foot.

GROWTH & PROPAGATION
Z 11; H & S 1m (3ft). Tender. In temperate areas grow in a humid glasshouse min temp 17°C (63°F) and peaty compost. Sow seed in spring; take softwood cuttings in late spring; divide in spring or autumn.

*Polianthes tuberosa*

TUBEROSE

This tuberous perennial has long blade leaves and spikes of waxy, lily-like white summer flowers with an intense, honey-sweet, narcotic fragrance.

USES Originally from pre-Columbian Mexico, where it flavoured chocolate, Tuberose was later used to fragrance the cool interiors of Italian churches. In temperate climates it can be grown as an exotic summer garden plant or in conservatories in small numbers to perfume the air. The scent can be overpowering in an enclosed space.

ESSENTIAL OIL Tuberose is a dark orange to brown absolute which is solvent-extracted from the flowers. It has a heavy, sweet-floral, sensuous scent with narcotic undertones and is one of the world's most expensive floral perfume ingredients. It is rarely available to the general public. No safety data is available.

GROWTH & PROPAGATION
Z 9; H 50cm (20in); S 20cm (8in). Tender. Grow in a warm, sunny position during the summer, but lift in autumn and store in sand away from frost. Under glass, grow singly in pots in manure-enriched, fibrous loam. In full growth, water well and feed fortnightly; dry off as leaves fade in

winter. Propagate by sowing seed or removing offsets in spring.

*Populus balsamifera*

BALSAM POPLAR

This smooth-trunked, fast-growing deciduous tree has balsamic-incense-scented sticky buds which unfold into large, heart-shaped serrated leaves.

USES The fresh resinous fragrance of the buds is released by touch. Collect them in spring and add to potpourri or infuse in alcohol to use the perfumed spirit in room sprays or aftershaves. It was used by native North Americans as an inhalant for colds and a treatment for skin sores. Called Medicinal Balm of Gilead, the antiseptic painkilling resin from the unopened buds of this tree and its hybrid *P.* x *candicans*, the Balm of Gilead Poplar, contains aspirin-like compounds used in cough mixtures, ointments for cuts, skin diseases and rheumatism, and in potpourri, soaps and perfume as a fixative. In the 1970s Soviet doctors recorded success using it to heal resistant bed sores and infections. The bark is also medicinal.

**CAUTION** HERB: Avoid if allergic to aspirin. Balsams may irritate some skins.

GROWTH & PROPAGATION
Z 2; H 30m (100ft); S 11m (35ft). Tolerant, but prefers deep, moist, well-drained soil in sun. Propagate from suckers or 30cm (12in) cuttings in autumn. Prune *P.* x *candicans* 'Aurora' hard in late winter for new pink-and-cream-flushed leaves. Root damage from mowers will cause suckers to spread widely.

BALSAM POPLAR

*Pseudovernia prunastri,*
syn. *Evernia prunastri*

OAKMOSS

This blue-green to ghostly white lichen grows on deciduous trees, mainly on the shady side of oaks. When dried and processed, it has an extremely tenacious, rich earthy-mossy scent with just a hint of leather.

USES North American tribes used Oakmoss as an antibiotic, absorbent binding for wounds and for coughs. Europeans used it for asthma, bronchitis and children's coughs. Research shows that it inhibits tuberculosis. Today it is dried to add texture and fixative properties to potpourri. All lichens are extremely sensitive to air pollution, making them a good indicator of air quality – hence, their decreasing numbers in the West are a cause for great concern.

ESSENTIAL OIL The solvent extracted, dark green absolute has a fragrance which pulls together all the green, mossy and dry bark scents of a forest. It combines well with all fragrance groups and is used in classy perfumes. It makes a pleasing room spray and adds an interesting note to home-made perfumes. The rich earth-scented concrete and resin have low solubility and so are restricted to soaps, hair products and industrial perfumes.

**CAUTION** OIL: Use in lowest dilutions. May irritate sensitive skin. Frequently adulterated.

GROWTH & PROPAGATION Z 5–6; Wild plant of deciduous northern temperate forests. Difficult to cultivate.

MIGNONETTE

---

*Reseda odorata*

MIGNONETTE

This oval-leaved, upright, branching annual has spherical heads of small white flowers with yellow-brown stamens and a strong sweet-spicy scent, from summer to early autumn.

USES Used by the Romans to treat bruises, the plant impressed Napoleon during his Egyptian campaign, although more for its perfume, and he sent seeds to Empress Josephine. It makes an excellent town balcony plant because its strong, fresh-spicy scent counters urban smells and attracts bees and butterflies. Cut, it can last several weeks in a cool room, but its scent is much fainter out of the warm sunshine.

ESSENTIAL OIL The vibrant green-floral-scented absolute is expensive to extract and only small amounts are available to perfumers to give a distinctive mark to high-class perfumes; in others, synthetics are employed.

GROWTH & PROPAGATION Z 8 or colder zones as an annual; H 60cm (24in); S 30cm (12in). Grow in sun or light shade in well-drained neutral to slightly alkaline soil. Sow seed in spring *in situ* or in plug trays. Thin and pinch to encourage bushy plants. Deadhead to prolong flowering. In warm areas, sow in pots on a sunny windowsill in early autumn for spring houseplants. To grow in a conservatory during winter as a standard or 'tree', sow seeds or take cuttings in mid- to late summer, water moderately and pot on. Train along a cane, remove lower side shoots and pinch leading shoot to form a bushy head.

---

*Ribes nigrum*

BLACKCURRANT

This musky-scented deciduous shrub has lobed leaves, greenish-white spring flowers and soft, edible black berries in summer.

USES The fruit's rich claret flesh and sweet-tart flavour make it ideal for jam, summer puddings, cordials, country wines and Cassis liqueur. The berries are Vitamin C-rich and their seeds yield gamma-linolenic acid, as do those of Evening Primrose. The tannin-rich, astringent, dried summer leaves were once used to extend black tea and are often found in blended herb teas. The leaf brew is cooling, lowers blood pressure and is taken for colds, sore or hoarse throats and urino-genital infections. A berry infusion helps mouth and throat infections, hypertension and weak capillaries.

ESSENTIAL OIL A powerful, pungent, expensive absolute and an essential oil called Cassis are extracted from the buds of plants grown in the clear air of Norway for use in deluxe perfumes. Analysis shows 247 compounds and an intricate fragrance which results from the interaction of minty-green, fruity-spicy, woody-mossy notes with foxy overtones, to give a special cachet to fragrances. Recently, synthetic Cassis compounds with spicy-pungent odours have been developed, but none can reproduce the complexity of the original.

GROWTH & PROPAGATION Z 5; H & S 2m (6ft). Sheltered spot in sun or part shade in well-drained clay soil. Take hardwood cuttings in winter. Prune in autumn. Replace every 10 years.

---

*Rosa* species

ROSE

These mainly deciduous shrubs and climbers have prickly stems, flowers with a range of scents around the traditional sweet, fresh, rosey, floral fragrance, and vermilion autumn hips. The cerise double flowers of 'Mme Isaac Pereire' have the strongest scent; the pure soft pink semi-double flowers of 'Celestial' have the 'purest' rose scent; *R. eglanteria*, Shakespeare's Sweet Briar, has apple-scented leaves and *R. primula* has leaves with an incense-like perfume.

USES One of the most 'herbal' of all plants, the Rose has culinary, medicinal, cosmetic, craft, symbolic and perfume uses and is a beautiful, versatile garden plant. The flowers, leaves and hips are used, and it yields rosewater, Rose absolute and Rose oil. Petals with the bitter white heel removed are added to salads, desserts, jams, exotic chicken and rice dishes, sherbets and punches, used to flavour China tea and sugars, and crystallized. Rosebuds are pickled and the Vitamin C-rich hips are made into syrup, conserve and tea, but must be strained to remove irritant hairs. For wine, pick rosehips after the first frost and use a pressure-cooker recipe to avoid the hair-straining. The fragrance of the deep pink flowers of the Apothecary's Rose (*R. gallica* var. *officinalis*) deepen when dried and had many medieval medicinal applications. Rosewater has never been surpassed as a soothing wash for tired, sensitive skin, and can also be used to fragrance the hair. The dark-coloured, deeply scented old-fashioned Roses retain the best colour and scent for use in potpourri. An extract from 'Mosqueta', the Amazon *R. rubirinova*, is used in various skin products and after surgery to speed healing.

ESSENTIAL OIL The main species for the intensely fragrant oil are the Damask or Bulgarian Rose (*R.* x *damascena*), the Cabbage Rose or Rose Maroc (*R.* x *centifolia*) with a spicier scent, and *R. gallica*. Flowers are collected at sunrise before they lose fragrance and processed within 24 hours. Clear Rose oil (called 'otto') is steam-distilled from the petals and is the preferred extract for aromatherapy; the yellow-orange Rose absolute is solvent-extracted, closer to the original scent and preferred by the perfume industry. English Rose Phytol oil, from a new low-temperature solvent method, uses 'Roseraie de L'Hay', 'Louise Odier', 'Mme Isaac Pereire' and 'Belle de Crécy' Roses to create a Rose oil nearest to the fresh flower scent. With luck, it will result in landscapes of luscious Roses to fill the extractors. All Rose oils are extremely expensive, but for their exquisite fragrance and the way they combine with others they are used in most quality perfumes and a few soaps and cosmetics. Rose oil is a major ingredient of England's Holy Coronation Anointing Oil. In creams, it benefits dry, mature and sensitive skins and can be added to home-made cosmetics, perfumes and massage oils. Its benefits can be inhaled from a handkerchief, but it does not work well in burners. It is an excellent oil for meditating, treating stress and anxiety about femininity, offering comfort to the terminally ill, and helping the bereaved to express grief. Rose leaf oil is used in perfumery.

GROWTH & PROPAGATION Z 2–9; H 25cm-10m (10in–30ft); S 25cm–7m (10in–22ft). Grow in an open, sunny or light position in medium-rich, well-drained loamy soil. Provide protection from strong winds, but also good air circulation. Sow ripe seed of species in autumn or take hardwood cuttings of all types in autumn. Plant from autumn to spring; lightly prune in spring; deadhead in summer. Banana skins are a good Rose fertilizer: bury them among the roots.

## 20 OLD SHRUB ROSES WITH EXCEPTIONALLY REFINED PERFUME

'BELLE DE CRÉCY' Petals pink, grey and mauve, quartered, green eye.
'CELESTIAL' Purest soft pink, semi-double, 'purest' rose scent.
'CHARLES DE MILLS' Large purple and deep red, quartered, vigorous.
'CONRAD F. MEYER' Robust, large thorns, large silver-pink blooms.
'EMPRESS JOSEPHINE' Thick, loose, double, deep-pink veined petals.
'FANTIN LATOUR' Soft pink double flowers, relatively thornless.
'GÉNÉRAL KLÉBER' Globular moss Rose with bright, shiny pink petals.
'GLOIRE DES MOUSSEUX' Moss Rose, large clear pink double flowers.
'HUGH DICKSON' Tall, lanky rose, rich dark red, long arching stems.
'KAZANLIK' Soft warm pink, used in Bulgaria to make Attar of Roses.
'KÖNIGIN VON DÄNEMARK' Healthy plant, rich pink, quartered petals.
'LOUISE ODIER' Vigorous bush with clusters of bright double pink blooms.
'MME HARDY' Elegant plant, pure white, fully double, green eye.
'MME ISAAC PEREIRE' Cerise, double, said to have strongest scent.

APOTHECARY'S ROSE

'MAIDEN'S BLUSH' Blush pink, many petalled, refined scent.
'PARFUM DE L'HAY' Large globe buds become flat, bright red flowers.
'REINE DES VIOLETTES' Velvet mauve, flat and quartered, thornless.
*R.* x *centifolia* Deep pink, deep cup/cabbage shape, lax and thorny.
'ROSERAIE DE L'HAY' Rugosa semi-double crimson-purple, continuous flowering.
'SOUVENIR DE LA MALMAISON' Powder pink globe opens flat and quartered.

## 10 OLDER CLIMBERS WITH EXCEPTIONAL FRAGRANCE

'ÉTOILE DE HOLLANDE' Velvety-red petals age purple, plum shoots.
'GLOIRE DE DIJON' Soft cream-apricot, tolerates shade.
'GUINÉE' Rich, dark velvet-crimson with perfect buds for drying.
'LONG JOHN SILVER' Vigorous, large silky white, double cupped bloom.
'MME CAROLINE TESTOUT' Vigorous, thorny, silver-pink cabbage-like flowers.
'MRS HERBERT STEVENS' Tolerant, shapely white flowers, repeats.

ROSEMARY

'SOUVENIR DE LA MALMAISON' As above, sometimes repeats, hates rain.
'SOUVENIR DU DOCTEUR JAMAIN' Rich ruby-red, semi-double cup, shade.
'SURPASSING BEAUTY' Laxish, early, deep red-crimson, opens blowsy.
'ZÉPHIRINE DROUHIN' Cerise, semi-double blooms, long flowering, thornless.

## *Rosmarinus officinalis*

### ROSEMARY

The branches of this clean, resinous aromatic shrub are densely packed with narrow, leathery leaves and small blue late-spring flowers (sometimes repeated in autumn). White- and pink-flowered, prostrate and upright forms are available.

USES Rosemary, an ancient protective herb once used in European temples, is grown as a bush, hedge or topiary specimen. The antiseptic, anti-oxidant leaves help preserve food and digest fat, and are added to roast potatoes, lamb, pork and fatty fish, oils, vinegars and butters. They are a spicy ingredient in biscuits, ice-cream and sweet oranges in wine. The delicately flavoured flowers are added to salads or crystallized. Bundles of

freshly cut stems are used by Arabs to cool and refresh a sickroom. Smouldered, or added to clothes sachets, the leaves are moth and insect repellent. Added to baths, Rosemary stimulates circulation, helping to ease aching muscles and joints, as well as to clear tired, sluggish mental states.

ESSENTIAL OIL Steam-distilled from the flowering tops, the oil's strong, refreshing, woody-balsamic scent is used in perfumes, including eau-de-Cologne and Hungary Water, soaps and household products, as well as by the food and drink industry. The antibacterial, antifungal oil provides a head-clearing steam inhalation for colds. It stimulates the circulation (grounds for its aphrodisiac reputation), opens surface capillaries and is used in several hair care products, dandruff shampoos and skin creams, particularly for excessive oil, eczema and varicose veins. Rosemary helps to reduce blood cholesterol levels and in massage oil eases tense, tired and overworked muscles.

CAUTION HERB & OIL: Do not use in baths during pregnancy, or with high blood pressure or epilepsy. OIL: Avoid in pregnancy. Use in low to moderate dilution. May irritate skin.

GROWTH & PROPAGATION Z 6; H & S 2m (6ft). Frost hardy. Grow in a sunny position in well-drained soil. Chalky soil gives a smaller but more fragrant plant. Provide protection from cold winters and biting spring winds. Rosemary can be grown in a pot, sunk into the ground in summer and removed to a greenhouse or windowsill for the winter. Germination of seed is erratic, cuttings of all types are easy.

## *Salvia officinalis*

### SAGE

This shrub has textured evergreen leaves with a distinctive warm, clean, spicy pungent scent and small mauve-blue (sometimes white or pink) summer flowers. Various varieties of Sage offer gold, purple and variegated leaves and different fragrances, like the half-hardy *S. elegans*, with both pineapple- and tangerine-scented forms, the silver-leaved *S. prostrata* with a balsamic aroma, and *S. dorisiana* with fruit-scented leaves.

USES The strong, distinctive taste increases when dried, so use sparingly with pork, goose, sausage, liver and stuffings to aid digestion. On a hungover morning, pick a Sage leaf and rub it over teeth and gums for a fresh, clean sensation. The flowers make a light summer tea, while antiseptic leaf tea is a good gargle for mouth and throat infections.

CLARY SAGE

Smouldering dried leaves dispel unpleasant cooking smells.

ESSENTIAL OIL Sage oil is steam-distilled from the leaves and has a spicy, herbaceous scent with camphorous tones. Although used commercially in minute amounts in perfumes, vermouth, mouthwashes and by the food industry, this oil is toxic and unsuitable for home use. Clary Sage (*S. sclarea* – see separate entry) is preferable and some therapists use Spanish Sage (*S. lavandulifolia*) in moderation for massage of deep muscular aches and pains, and treating rheumatism and poor circulation.

CAUTION HERB: Avoid medicinal doses during pregnancy. OIL: Avoid all Sage oils during pregnancy and *S. officinalis* oil at all times. Use Spanish and Clary Sage oils in low dilutions and in moderation only.

GROWTH & PROPAGATION Z 5; H 80cm (32in); S 1m (3ft). Grow in full sun in light, dry, well-drained alkaline soil. Grow species from seed. All forms take easily from cuttings. Plant 45–60cm (18–24in) apart. Cut back after flowering; replace woody plants every 4–5 years. Prune frequently to keep bushy. Yellowing leaves can mean roots need more space. A small green caterpillar eats the leaves; remove it by hand, or prune off and burn the leaves.

## *Salvia sclarea*

### CLARY SAGE

This biennial has a rosette of large, woolly grey leaves in the first year and spikes of dusty-lilac to rose flowers with a white lip

SAGE (PINK FLOWERED)

and persistent coloured bracts in the second summer. The whole plant has a clean, pungent, muscatel, 'love it or loathe it' scent. *S. s.* var. *turkestanica* has pale blue and white flowers with pink bracts.

USES The tall, aromatic flowering spikes which last through to autumn offer a dramatic garden plant in appearance as well as aroma. Tender Clary leaves and Elderflowers are infused in Rhine wines to impart a muscatel flavour. The flowering spikes can be cut for a room-freshening bouquet and the leaves dried for potpourri. Clary Sage has been called Clear Eye, as the seeds soaked in water produce mucilage which painlessly dislodges foreign bodies from the eye, while distilled flower and leaf waters are applied as a compress to soothe and brighten tired eyes.

ESSENTIAL OIL Clary Sage oil is steam-distilled from the flowering aerial parts to produce a warm, herbaceous, slightly nutty-scented oil, used in several perfumes. It confers a remarkable feel-good factor which can range from relaxing, mildly inebriating or uplifting to an almost spiritual experience, and can result in vivid dreams. So relaxing is this oil that aromatherapists advise clients to avoid driving directly after a massage with it. It is considered aphrodisiac and counters stress and tension from physical and emotional sources including asthmatic spasms, muscle pain, swollen legs from standing all day, migraines, sexual problems and depression during convalescence. The re-emergence of tuberculosis means it may once again be used to combat intense night sweats.

CAUTION OIL: Avoid during pregnancy. Avoid alcohol during use, as the combination can cause nightmares and nausea.

GROWTH & PROPAGATION Z 5; H 1m (3ft); S 60cm (24in). Sow seed in spring or summer. Self-seeds in light soils. Dislikes wet winters.

*Sambucus nigra*
....................................................

ELDER

The wood and leaves of this deciduous, shrubby tree have a green, catty-animal scent, while the flat heads of creamy-white early-summer flowers are musky-sweet. Deep purple-black fruit is borne in pendulous clusters.

ELDERBERRIES

USES The flowers give their muscatel flavour to Elderflower 'champagne', Rhine wines, milk dishes, fruit fools, fritters and jams. Flower tea or tincture helps to strengthen the respiratory system before the worst pollen onslaught for hay fever sufferers; the tea mixed with Peppermint and Yarrow helps to break cold and flu fevers. Cool tea is an eye-wash for tired or sore eyes, a facewash and an anti-inflammatory aftershave and gargle. Birds love the raw berries, but they should be cooked for human consumption in jams or pies or made into wine. In colder areas, the seeds should be strained out as they contain a slightly nauseating alkaloid. Rich in vitamin C, as a syrup or cordial they help to prevent winter colds. A leaf brew deters insects from skin and plants. Bark and roots yield black dye, leaves green, berries violet.

CAUTION HERB: Leaves and raw berries should not be eaten.

GROWTH & PROPAGATION Z 5; H 10m (30ft); S 4.5m (13ft). Sun or partial shade in rich, moist neutral to alkaline soil. Take softwood cuttings in summer and hardwood in winter. Can be invasive from suckers. Freeze whole flowerheads as a flavouring.

*Santalum album*
....................................................

SANDALWOOD

The high demand for this slow-growing, semi-parasitic, semi-wild evergreen with aromatic wood, roots of a dry, warm, seductive woody aroma and small pale yellow to purple flowers puts its future in jeopardy. Indian government restrictions and planting

ELDERFLOWERS

schemes are bypassed by many suppliers and today's higher prices seldom reflect improved industry ethics.

USES The fragrant, insect-repellent wood is important for Buddhist and Hindu rituals, and is used for carved boxes and clothes sachets. It is finely powdered and mixed with rosewater to treat skin problems, and used as powder or oil to flavour Indian sherbets and sweet dishes, especially in summer for its 'cooling' properties.

ESSENTIAL OIL Nearly all parts of the tree contain essential oil, but the highest percentage is in the roots and heartwood, from which the oil is steam or water distilled. The viscous oil has a deep, persistent, sweet-woody scent with a warm, relaxing, balancing effect and a long history as an aphrodisiac. An ancient unguent, it is still used extensively in perfumes and in incense as an aid to meditation. In aftershaves it calms shaving rash and in cosmetic creams it benefits eczema, dry or chapped skin and cracked heels. In massage it is valued both as a sensuous fragrance and as a treatment for conditions related to stress and tension.

CAUTION West Indian Sandalwood is from a different species, *Amyris balsamifera*, and should at present be avoided for safety reasons.

GROWTH & PROPAGATION
Z 11; H 18m (60ft); S 3m (10ft).
Tender. Grow in a sunny to semi-shaded position in fertile, well-drained, moist soil. The plant is difficult to cultivate in glass-houses due to its semi-parasitic nature.

## *Santolina* species

### SANTOLINA

The smoky silver-grey, finely divided foliage of these evergreen subshrubs is pungently aromatic with a lemony undertone; the button-like small yellow flowers in late summer faintly echo the

SANTOLINAS

aroma. *S. viridis* has green thread-like leaves; *S.* 'Lemon Queen' has willowy grey-green leaves with cream flowers.

USES Also known as Cotton Lavender, the subtle variations of leaf colour between the species and their compact, 'clippable' growth make them ideal for knot gardens and as edging plants. Sprigs can be placed under rugs, among books and linen, and hung near windows and doors to make full use of their insect-repellent properties. Leaves are occasionally dried with Chamomile and Coltsfoot for herbal tobacco. A flower and leaf wash is is still used in some local medicines to reduce inflammation and heal ringworm and scab.

ESSENTIAL OIL An oil steam-distilled from the seeds has a strong, acrid, green odour. It is a powerful insecticide and vermifuge (expels intestinal worms) but is far too toxic for any domestic use.

CAUTION OIL: Very toxic.

GROWTH & PROPAGATION
Z 7; H 60cm (24in); S 1m (3ft).
Grow in full sun in well-drained, preferably sandy soil. If soil is too rich, the growth will be soft and less silvery. Take 5–8cm (2–3in) stem cuttings in spring or from midsummer to autumn (give protection in frosty weather). Grow plants 50cm (20in) apart, or 30cm (12in) apart for edging. Clip to shape in spring or summer, never in frosty autumn weather. Deadhead in autumn. If temperatures drop below –15°C (5°F), give protection with a sleeve of 2 layers of chicken wire filled with straw, spruce or bracken, 13cm (5in) thick. Santolina can be grown indoors.

## *Saponaria officinalis*

### SOAPWORT

The 'cottagey' soft pink flowers of this spreading, upright perennial have a sweet, raspberry-clove scent which wafts through the air in late summer.

USES The rhizomes, leaves and stems contain water-softening saponins, producing a mild soapy liquid when boiled in lime-free (soft or rain-) water. Cut plant parts into small pieces in autumn, dry in the sun, then soak them well before boiling in minimum water for 30 minutes, to produce a liquid which is the finest delicate fabric cleaner and used by museums to clean and restore vibrancy to old tapestries, furnishings and lace. The gentle soapy liquid is tolerated by many acne, eczema and psoriasis sufferers and is used to soothe poison ivy rashes, but should be kept away from the eyes. Scatter the pretty flowers through green and fruit salads, or dry them for bedroom potpourris.

CAUTION HERB: Keep soap away from the eyes. Do not plant next to fish ponds as rhizomes and leaves are poisonous to fish.

GROWTH & PROPAGATION
Z 4; H & S 60cm (24in). Grow in a sunny or partially shaded position in fertile, moist soil. Sown plants are variable, so obtain propagating material from a well-scented mother plant. Divide the plant or take pieces of underground runners and replant from late autumn to early spring. Grow 60cm (24in) apart. Use twiggy sticks to support the stems; cut back after flowering to induce a second blooming. Large clumps are needed for soap wash.

SOAPWORT

## *Satureja hortensis*

### SAVORY

The narrow, gland-dotted leaves of this annual are strongly aromatic and it has lilac to white flowers in late summer.

USES Summer Savory leaves, like those of the more bitter evergreen subshrubs Winter Savory (*S. montana*) and Creeping Savory (*S. spicigera*), have a spicy, peppery taste, enhancing the flavour of all bean and pulse dishes – even tinned and frozen ones, with the added benefit of aiding digestion and reducing flatulence. They are also added to salami, fish, stews, soft cheese and tonic wines, and to 'perk up' salt-reduced diets. Leaves and flowering tops make an antiseptic gargle for sore throats.

ESSENTIAL OIL Both Summer and Winter Savory oils, with their sharp, herbaceous-peppery medicinal odour, are used commercially to flavour meats and canned products, but are not suitable for home use. Oil extracted from *S. thymbra* is used by the pharmaceutical industry.

CAUTION HERB: Avoid medicinal doses during pregnancy.

GROWTH & PROPAGATION
Z 8; H 50cm (20in); S 75cm
(30in). Grow in full sun in well-
drained, chalky, rich soil (moderately fertile for Winter Savory).
Sow seed in spring. Sow seed of
Winter Savory preferably in early
autumn when ripe, or in late
spring press lightly into soil; and
do not cover with soil. Take side
cuttings in summer; divide in
spring or autumn. Allow 45cm
(18in) between perennials, 23cm
(9in) between annuals. Straggly
perennials benefit from hard late-
spring pruning. May need some
winter protection. Cut back
annuals in early summer to prevent plants becoming woody.

*Spartium junceum*

## SPANISH BROOM

This upright, bright green, deciduous shrub has masses of pea-like
golden-yellow flowers with a
strong, sweet, Orange blossom
fragrance from summer to early

SUMMER SAVORY

autumn. Other ornamental and
fragrant Brooms in the closely
related *Genista* genus include
*G. aetnensis*, *G. cinerea*, *G. spartium* and *G. x spachiana*.

USES The abundant flowers can
be gathered and dried for their
colour in potpourri and yellow
dyes, but with caution, for they
were once a potent heart medicine and should be kept away
from small children. The local
name Weaver's Broom refers
both to the flexible stems, which
can be woven into baskets, and to
the strong bark fibre, once a
source of coarse cloth and ropes.

ESSENTIAL OIL The flowers
yield a seductive dusty-sweet fragrance once extracted by
enfleurage or alcohol, but now by
volatile solvents. It is known to
perfumers as Gênet and is used
in floral fragrances, combining
well with Ylang-Ylang. It also
flavours some alcoholic drinks.

**CAUTION** HERB & OIL:
Potentially fatal, for external use
only.

GROWTH & PROPAGATION
Z 8; H & S 3m (10ft). Frost
hardy. Full sun in not-too-fertile,
well-drained soil. Tolerates urban
pollution and salty winds.
Remove weak shoots; prune
strong growth. Soak ripe seed;
sow under glass in spring. Protect
young plants from rabbits.

*Styrax benzoin*

## BENZOIN

This shrubby, grey-barked deciduous tree has simple pointed
leaves, short racemes of small,
nodding, bell-like fragrant white
flowers in spring and summer,

SPANISH BROOM

and aromatic resin called Gum
Benzoin. *S. officinale* produces the
fragrant resin Storax used in
incense, medicine and perfumes.
The aromatic fixative resins from
the Sweet Gums (*Liquidambar*
species) are also called Storax.

USES Benzoin resin is tapped
from deep cuts in the trunks of
wild trees which are more than 7
years old and dried to yield its
orange-brown, powerful vanilla-
like scent. It provides an important fixative and a rich warm
fragrance for incense and potpourri.

ESSENTIAL OIL The oil is available in small amounts as a true
absolute for perfumers, but more
usually as a viscous resinoid (this
means more solid particles and
less 'purity') dissolved in ethyl
glycol or wood alcohol. In
aromatherapy, it has been found
to ease anxiety and produce feelings of well-being. It is used by
the food and drink industry and
as a fixative and fragrance in perfumery. In cosmetics it prevents

fats turning rancid, in French
pastilles it treats colds, and it is
added to anti-asthmatic tablets
and Friar's Balsam for coughs
and sore throats. Traditionally
used in soothing antiseptic
creams for chapped or irritated
skin, it can cause allergies in some
people, and until further research
has been done should be avoided
on fissured or broken skin.

**CAUTION** OIL: Some essential
oil companies have withdrawn
the oil following fears of allergic
dermatitis. The recommended
maximum amounts for the
resinoid are 0.03 per cent in
creams and 0.08 per cent in perfumes. It can increase sensitization to other compounds.

GROWTH & PROPAGATION
Z 11; H 9m (28ft); S 6m (20ft).
Tender. In temperate zones,
grow in moist soil in medium to
hot glasshouse, min temp 15°C
(60°F) in bright filtered light.
Water well in growing season,
sparingly in winter. Sow seed in
autumn or take semi-ripe cuttings
in summer.

LILAC

acetanisole. The new English phytonic low temperature solvent system will probably bring the goal closer.

GROWTH & PROPAGATION
Z 5; H 7m (22ft); S 5m (15ft). Grow in a sunny, open position, but sheltered from wind, in fertile neutral to alkaline loam enriched with manure. Remove faded flowerheads and suckers from young plants. Prune old and dead wood from older plants after flowering. Mulch and feed well. Take summer softwood cuttings or autumn semi-ripe cuttings in a cold frame. Propagate species from seed or suckers. Plant 3.5–5m (11–15ft) apart in spring or autumn.

*Syzygium aromaticum*

CLOVE

All parts of this glossy, green-leaved evergreen tree smell of cloves when bruised. Its fragrant cream summer flowers turn a deep red-pink when the stamens drop, and are worn by the local women in their hair.

USES Clove spice is the sun-dried, nail-shaped flower bud, and those of good quality should exude a little oil when pressed with a fingernail. Their strong, warm aroma and taste are valued for Indian garam masala and Chinese 5-spice mix, pickles, hams and desserts. Cloves are studded over oranges for traditional pomanders, distinguish Indonesian cigarettes, and can be chewed in small pieces to quell dry, ticklish night-time coughs. In water room-fragrancers cloves give off a warm, comforting spicy aroma. The flowers are used locally as an eye treatment.

*S. jambos*, the Rose Apple widely cultivated in the tropics, has edible, rose-scented and flavoured fruit, used to make perfume.

ESSENTIAL OIL The spicy-sweet oil is water distilled from the buds, although lower-grade oils can be extracted from the leaves, stalks and stems. Used commercially in perfumery, cosmetics, food, drink and dental preparations such as toothpaste and pain-numbing Oil of Cloves, it is very irritant and for home use is only suitable for room fragrancing or to repel ants. Clove-based anaesthetics are now being produced.

**CAUTION** OIL: Irritant to the skin and mucus membranes.

GROWTH & PROPAGATION
Z 11; H 20m (70ft); S 10m (30ft). Restricted to low-altitude maritime tropics. Tender; temp min 15°C (60°F). Sun in well-drained, fertile soil. Sow seed in spring or take semi-ripe cuttings in summer.

CLOVES (*Dried flower buds*)

*Syringa vulgaris*

LILAC

This deciduous shrub or small tree with heart-shaped leaves is an old garden favourite for the intense rich, sweet, warm floral fragrance of its waxy spring flower clusters, which are available as purple, blue, pink or white cultivars.

USES On warm days, one shrub can perfume an entire garden and attract large numbers of butterflies, particularly the blue varieties. Use a vase of fresh flowers to scent rooms and the dark-coloured florets as a dessert garnish or to scatter on potpourri.

ESSENTIAL OIL Lilac is difficult to capture and though there may be a potential absolute, at present there is no known commercially produced flower oil. It was historically popular as a single flower perfume, part of floral colognes, a garments and glove scent, and is present in modern 'fantasy florals', but the scent is created by blending other floral essences (as is done for Sweet Peas) or created chemically as

*Tagetes patula*

## TAGETES

This annual, the French Marigold, has purple-green upright stems, pungently scented foliage and golden-orange flower-heads. *T. tenuifolia pumila* 'Tangerine Gem' has orange-scented leaves and *T. signata* has lemon-verbena-scented leaves; both add zest to potpourri.

USES The petals yield a yellow dye for wool, silk and dairy products, are added to hand-made paper and dried for colour in potpourris. The root secretions of French and African Marigolds (*T. erecta*) and, most strongly, the Inca Marigold (*T. minuta*) deaden the detector mechanisms of potato, rose and tulip eelworms, and the leaf scent of all three deters white fly from tomato plants. Plant Inca Marigolds 15cm (6in) apart to clear earth of ground elder, reduce bindweed and deter couch-grass and ground ivy, or plant double or triple rows to contain them, as the root secretions inhibit their growth. Try the Andean use of leaves in doorways and bedding to deter insects. In South America the leaves of Sweet Marigold (*T. lucida*) provide a seasoning and tea (once given to dull the senses of sacrificial victims), while Mexican tribes smoke them to induce visions.

ESSENTIAL OIL The aerial parts of all 3 types are steam-distilled to produce a distinctive, strongly aromatic bitter-green oil or are solvent-extracted for an absolute with an intensely aromatic, sweet-herbaceous odour with a hint of fruit. Both have antifungal uses and are found in perfumes, food, drink and tobacco.

CAUTION OIL: Use in low dilution. Its main constituent, tagetone, may be harmful, and cause dermatitis. Max recommendation for creams is 0.03 per cent; for perfumes 0.2 per cent. Occasionally wrongly labelled as Calendula (*C. officinalis*) which is a safe oil.

HARVEST & PROPAGATION Z 9; H 50cm (20in); S 30cm (12in). Grow in an open, sunny position in well-cultivated, preferably rich, soil. Sow seed under glass in early spring. Plant out in late spring 30cm (12in) apart. Deadheading improves growth and size.

*Tanacetum balsamita*

## ALECOST

The silvery-green scalloped leaves of this perennial have a clean, spearmint chewing-gum aroma. In late summer it has small yellow flowers with white daisy petals, if grown in the sun.

USES The name Alecost refers to its use in clarifying and flavouring ale before the introduction of hops. Another name, Bible Leaf, comes from long Puritan sermons when the scent of its leaf, used as a bookmark, helped to allay hunger and maintain alertness. The young leaves now add their refreshing, minty scent and sharp tang to carrot soup, salads, game stuffing and fruit cakes. A leaf rinse perfumes hair and laundry, and offers an astringent, antiseptic skin and blemish wash. Crush fresh leaves to treat bee stings or dry them to repel insects and scent linen and potpourri. Alecost leaf tea relieves colds, catarrh and stomach upsets. The almost identical Camphor Plant

ALECOST

(*T. balsamita* var. *camphoratum*) has camphor-scented leaves which repel moths and animal fleas, but these are not edible.

CAUTION HERB: Use Alecost with discretion.

GROWTH & PROPAGATION Z 6; H 80cm (32in); S 45cm (18in). Grow in full sun in rich, dryish, well-drained soil. Divide roots in spring or autumn. Seed is not viable in cool climates.

*Tanacetum vulgare*

## TANSY

The feathery leaves of this perennial have a pungent rosemary scent, echoed in the clusters of mustard-yellow, button flower-heads in late summer. For the garden, *T. v.* var. *crispum* is less rampant, with compact fern-like foliage and a milder scent. *T. v.* 'Silver Lace' has subtle light markings; *T. v.* 'Isla Gold' is a recent sport with gold leaves.

USES Spicy and bitter, the leaves are added sparingly to omelettes, or are used to make 'tansy', a traditional custard pudding. The strongly insect-repellent leaves were used to wrap meat for flavour and protection before refrigeration, and can be placed under door mats and carpets to ward off ants and mice, or secured beneath pet baskets to repel fleas. Add the whole plant to compost heaps for its potassium, or use the flowers to make golden fabric dye, and the leaves yellow-green. A gypsy healing herb once used in local medicines, Tansy is today restricted to homeopathic treatment for worms.

ESSENTIAL OIL The sharp, spicy, herbaceous-scented oil was once used in perfumery and by the food and drink industry, but was found to contain toxic thujone, an abortifacient, and was therefore discontinued.

TANSY

**CAUTION** HERB: Avoid in pregnancy. Large internal doses can cause brain and kidney damage. Externally, can irritate skin.

GROWTH & PROPAGATION
Z 4; H 1.2m (4ft); S indefinite. Grow in full sun or light shade in any soil that is not too wet. Sow seed in spring or divide the creeping rootstock in spring or autumn. Thin or transplant to 60cm (24in) apart; it is a vigorous spreader.

## *Thymus* species

### THYME

Thymes grow either as subshrubs (*T. vulgaris* species) with woody stems, or creeping (*T. serpyllum* species) with rooting stems. All have numerous tiny leaves and offer a range of fragrances, from tradition spicy-peppery common Thyme, to several

THYME (*T. Serpyllum*)

shades of lemon (*T.* x *citriodorus*), caraway (*T. herba-barona*), piney-resinous (*T. azoricus*), fruity (*T. odoratissimus*) and sweet (*T.* x *c.* 'Fragrantissimus'), all with the medicinal undertone which gives the herb its antiseptic qualities. Discover gold- and-silver variegated forms; woolly, blue and all shades of green leaves; plus flowers from white, pink and purple to cochineal.

USES Thyme herb lore ranges from fairy charms to a scent that pervades haunted sites. Common Thyme (*T. vulgaris*) is a constituent of bouquet garni, co-operates with prolonged cooking, aids digestion and reduces flatulence. Add it to stew, stuffings and slow-cook wine dishes. Lemon Thyme accompanies chicken, fish and vegetables, Caraway Thyme enhances beef and Pine Thyme is a novelty in Greek dishes. The many varieties provide scope for 'patchwork carpets', scented garden seats and pathways, and all attract butterflies and honeybees to the garden.

ESSENTIAL OIL *T. vulgaris* oil is water or steam-distilled from the leaves and flowering tops. The sweet, herbaceous, peppery oil with a medicinal edge is sometimes sold as Sweet Thyme. It has a stimulating, energizing effect and is an important aspect of many perfumes. It is a powerful antiseptic and in a weak steam inhalation or room sprays, it treats colds, sore throats and respiratory infections – in all treatments it stimulates the white corpuscles which fight infection. Aromatherapists add tiny amounts to creams for acne and to massage oils for cellulite, arthritis, rheumatic and muscular pains, and low blood pressure. It can be mixed with alcohol and

THYME (*T. Vulgaris*)

sprayed on papers and herbarium specimens to protect them from mould, while commercially the oil and its extracts are added to mouthwashes, toothpastes, surgical dressings, cleaning products and food and drinks.

**CAUTION** OIL: Avoid in pregnancy or with high blood pressure. Use in lowest dilutions. Often adulterated, so buy from a reputable supplier. Use only *T. vulgaris* oil. (See *Origanum onites O. vulgare* Oregano entry)

GROWTH & PROPAGATION
Z 5–7; H 38cm (15in); S 50cm (20in). Grow in full sun in light, well-drained, preferably alkaline soil. Take 5–8cm (2–3in) 'heeled' stem cuttings any time except in winter. Divide roots or layer stems in spring or autumn. Sow species seed in spring. Thin or transplant to 25cm (10in) apart. In summer, prune frequently. In very cold areas, protect in winter.

## *Tilia species*

### LINDEN TREE

Linden, or Lime, trees have heart-shaped serrated leaves and numerous small cream summer flowers with a fragrance capable

of scenting an entire street. These trees hybridize freely, making identification difficult.

USES The flowers of Common Lime (*T.* x *vulgaris*, syn. *T.* x *europaea*), Large-leaved Lime (*T. platyphyllos*) and Small-leaved Lime (*T. cordata*) are all used to make Linden tea, a relaxing digestive popular in France after an extended meal when 'a crisis of the liver' is felt to be looming. It helps ease headaches and insomnia, soothe fractious children, is expectorant and induces sweating (thereby lowering temperatures) in feverish colds and flu. It also lowers blood pressure and helps to heal blood-vessel walls. Lime blossoms flavour honey, make a skin tonic for rashes and can be added to relaxing and rheumatic-soothing baths. The twigs are made into charcoal for medicinal, artistic and food-smoking purposes. To avoid the dripping 'honeydew', from the suckers and

LINDEN BLOSSOM

dense twiggyness of many Common Limes, plant the Large- or Small-leaved Limes – these do not encourage the greenfly which cause the honeydew.

ESSENTIAL OIL Solvent extraction of dried flowers yields a concrete with a herbaceous hay-like odour, and an absolute with a dry, green herbaceous scent nearer to the fresh flowers. It treats indigestion, stress-related nervous tension, headaches and insomnia and is found in a few perfumes.

CAUTION HERB: Stale flowers may cause mild 'intoxicated' symptoms. Flower tea from some species, if drunk in quantity, causes nausea and heart damage – be certain of species before use. OIL: no safety data available. Difficult to obtain unadulterated.

GROWTH & PROPAGATION Z 5–7 (Z 3 for *T. cordata*); H 40m (130ft); S 20m (70ft). Grow in full sun or semi-shade in well-drained soil. Sow seed in a cold frame in early spring, plant suckers in spring, or layer. Plant out in nursery beds in mid-autumn. Grow on for 4 years, then transplant to permanent positions. Remove suckers as they appear.

*Tropaeolum majus*

## NASTURTIUM

This happy climbing or dwarf annual has round wavy-margined leaves, large seeds, and spurred red, orange and yellow faintly peppery-scented summer flowers, which at dusk on hot days sometimes emit sparks.

USES The peppery-cress-flavoured leaves add bite to summer salads and sandwiches, while the milder, vitamin-rich flowers cheer salads, seafood and cucumber soup and can be frittered. The unripe seeds, picked as soon as the petals drop, are pickled as capers and chopped into mayonnaise or tartare sauce. Believed rejuvenating, it is included in commercial scalp tonics. The seeds contain a natural antibiotic and, together with the leaves and flowers, are prescribed for respiratory and genito-urinary infections to fight bacteria without destroying intestinal flora (unlike conventional antibiotics). It is planted around fruit trees and in vegetable patches to attract aphid-feeding hoverflies. Andean wives feed testosterone-reducing 'Mashua' (*T. tuberosum*) to husbands who are going away, to suppress libido and temptation.

ESSENTIAL OIL Known to the perfumery trade as Capucine, the pungent oil, both spicy and floral, is added to modern 'fantasy' and sultry floral perfumes.

GROWTH & PROPAGATION Z 8; H 60cm (24in); S 30cm–2m (12in–6ft). Full sun or partial shade in free-draining, moist, average to poor soil. Sow seeds singly 20cm (8in) apart in late spring. Poor soil encourages more flowers.

NASTURTIUM

*Valeriana officinalis*

## VALERIAN

This perennial has compound leaves with a green pea-pod scent and clusters of tiny lilac-pink summer flowers with a honey scent, and both hint at the foxy undertones for which its rhizomes are famous.

USES As the root dries, its scent matures from old leather to an animal musky sweat and is a bait for trapping rodents or wild cats (reported to be the real decoy of the Pied Piper). The growing plant benefits its neighbours and the soil by stimulating phosphorous production and attracting earthworms – infuse leaves in water and sprinkle on the soil – and the mineral-rich leaves add value to compost heaps. The unskinned roots of two-year-old autumn plants, given as a shell-shock treatment during World War I, are prescribed by herbalists for anxiety, insomnia and irritable bowel syndrome; a decoction is added to baths for nervous exhaustion and research indicates that Valerian has an anti-tumour action. The root of

**VALERIAN**

Spikenard (*V. jatamansi*) from the Himalayas yields a long-lasting musky leathery scent used as devotional incense in India, and by Mary Magdalen to anoint the feet of Jesus, representing the most costly aromatic then available.

ESSENTIAL OIL The steam-distilled rhizome oil has a warm, woody-leathery, musky odour with a fresh green top note; the solvent-extracted absolute has a strong bitter-sweet, woody-leathery odour. Both are used in moss- and forest-type perfumes and some herbal teas. The oil is a relaxant and flavouring for foods, root beer and liqueurs and is used by therapists to treat restless nervous tension and insomnia.

**CAUTION** HERB: Internal use must be by professional prescrip-

tion only. Avoid large or continuous doses and with liver problems. OIL: For external use only, in moderation; may cause sensitization.

GROWTH & PROPAGATION Z 7; H 1.2m (4ft); S indefinite. Grow in full sun or light shade – prefers cool roots and warm foliage – in rich, moist loam. Sow seed in spring, pressing it into the soil, but do not cover with soil. Divide roots in spring or autumn. Plant 60cm (24in) apart. Harvest the complete root in the second season in late autumn. Discard pale fibrous roots, slice and dry.

*Vanilla planifolia*

## VANILLA

This perennial climbing fleshy orchid has fragrant, waxy, pale greenish-yellow trumpet flowers in spring followed by long, narrow seed pods. It grows on support trees or shrubs but is not a parasite.

**VANILLA PODS**

USES Exotic even in cultivation – the flowers are pollinated by hummingbirds or by hand in its native Mexico. Vanilla has been a luxury ingredient since the time of the Aztecs, who used it to flavour chocolate. Unripe pods are 'cured' to develop their intensely sweet, creamy, vanilla aroma. The pods flavour sugar, sauces, drinks and potpourri, and can be washed, dried and reused. Vanilla extract flavours puddings, ice-cream, confectionery and liqueurs and is popular in aphrodisiac foods. The widely used synthetic vanilla is inferior in flavour. Added to the hot water of a vaporizer, a pod imparts a warm, relaxing, sensuous aroma. Infuse vanilla pods in a carrier oil or pure alcohol as a base ingredient for recipes, but do not use on sensitive skin.

ESSENTIAL OIL A warm, sweet, richly scented resinoid from the pods is used in perfumes, foods and some medicines. It is usually adulterated and seldom available outside the industry. As it is a skin sensitizer, use only in low dilutions and never internally.

GROWTH & PROPAGATION Z 11; H 15m (50ft); S Climber. Tender. Take tip cuttings at a node, dry, then insert in damp perlite with bottom heat 27°C (80°F). When thick roots have developed, move into coarse orchid compost in well-drained pots. Support by tying to a moss pole. Water well and maintain high temperature.

*Vetiveria zizanoides*

## VETIVER

This perennial, densely clumped, sturdy tropical Khus Khus grass

has a fibrous, rhizomatous root system with a fresh, woody, myrrh-violet scent.

USES In tropical Asia, Vetiver roots are woven into aromatic shade screens and fans. When dampened with water, the scent is reactivated and the air cooled to carry the calm, woody violet fragrance along verandahs and courtyards. Sachets of the finely chopped root are placed with clothes and in cupboards to scent them and repel insects, including cockroaches. The densely rooted grass is planted in Nepal and India to reduce soil erosion. The sweet balsamic scent of Sudanese grass (*V. nigritana*) is used as a body and clothes perfume.

ESSENTIAL OIL Clean, dried, chopped roots are steam-distilled for their dark brown oil which develops a rich, earthy-woody, sweet-molasses odour. Bourbon Vetiver from the Réunion Islands is considered the best quality but the supply is diminishing. Known in Sri Lanka as the 'oil of tranquillity', it is relaxing and uplifting. Many find the fragrance sensuous, and it is used for aftershaves, soaps and as a perfume fixative. In Asia it flavours sherbets and sweets, while in the West it makes an unexpected appearance as a preservative for asparagus. Added to massage and bath oils, Vetiver eases muscular pain and is relaxing for those with insomnia, depression and other stress-related ailments.

GROWTH & PROPAGATION Z 9; H 1.8m (6ft); S indefinite. Tender. Grow in moisture-retentive compost in sun. Maintain a min temp 10°C (50°F) and moderate humidity with good air circulation. Propagate by seed or division.

SWEET VIOLET

## *Viola odorata*

### SWEET VIOLET

Delicate and beautiful, the strongly sweet-scented violet or white flowers of this perennial appear amid the heart-shaped leaves from winter to spring.

USES The scent and appearance of Violets evoke both sweet innocence and exotic mystery, and therein lies their appeal. Goethe loved Violets so much that he carried seed to sprinkle on his country walks, while Napoleon's affection for the flower earned him the nickname Corporal Violette. Smelling the flower directly is only possible for several seconds, after which the olfactory receptors shut down and begin to work again after a short break. The flowers flavour alcohols, are crystallized, added with young leaves to salads and provide a colouring agent. Once made into throat pastilles praised by Charles II, the flower syrup is antiseptic, a mild laxative and, with the leaves (which contain pain-killing salicylic acid), treat coughs, headaches and insomnia. The dried aerial parts reduce eczema and skin eruptions and are a folk treatment for breast and lung cancer. *V. striata* shows test-tube anti-tumour activity.

ESSENTIAL OIL Violet was the favourite imported perfume of the last Empress Dowager of China. The flowers are solvent-extracted for an absolute with the sweet-soothing floral fragrance of the fresh flower, and the leaves yield an absolute with a clean, deep earthy-green leaf odour; both are used in high-quality perfumes. Violet leaf oil is used by therapists for skin refining of large pores, thread veins and acne, for the bronchial system and for insomnia and nervous exhaustion.

GROWTH & PROPAGATION Z 8; H 15cm (6in); S 30cm (12in). Grow 10cm (4in) apart in semi-shade, with early or late sun, in rich, moist soil. Easy to propagate from runners. Seed germination is erratic as many early flowers miss pollination. Divide established plants immediately after flowering.

## *Zingiber officinale*

### GINGER

This tropical perennial has erect stems of compound leaves, spikes of fragrant white flowers and a large knobbly, yellowish rhizome with the characteristic warm, pungent, spicy ginger aroma.

USES
The shoots, leaves and flowering stems are all edible, but the rhizome is most valued. Fresh or 'green' ginger has a milder, sweeter taste than mature rhizomes; it is used for relishes and chutney and is a fundamental ingredient in Chinese and Indian cuisine. Ginger's digestive qualities make spicy foods more palatable – it suppresses the nausea of travel, of morning sickness (used in small amounts) and of eating garlic foods. It is pickled, preserved in syrup as stem Ginger, crystallized (after a brine and vinegar soak), or dried and ground for the spice used widely in European baking. Ginger tea is taken for colds and, together with Ginger wine, is a popular warming winter drink. The flowers are used locally as hair decorations and included in flower garlands. In India, cooks can buy green varieties of ginger with mango or camphor overtones.

ESSENTIAL OIL Ginger oil is steam-distilled from unpeeled dried rhizomes. Warm, fresh and spicy, it is traditionally added to masculine and Oriental fragrances, but is becoming increasingly popular as the taste for more adventurously scented cosmetics and bath products grows. Widely used by the commercial food and drink industry, it is also added to several over-the-counter medicines and digestives. A single drop in massage blends helps to relieve muscular pain, rheumatism and fatigue.

CAUTION OIL: Only tiny amounts are needed; excess can cause skin irritation.

GROWTH & PROPAGATION Z 10; H 1.5m (5ft); S indefinite. Tender; min temp –1°C (34°F). Buy a fresh plump culinary rhizome in spring and plant in well-drained, neutral to alkaline, humus-rich compost. Maintain high humidity but do not overwater. A striking houseplant, it requires 10 months to produce new Ginger, which can be dug up when further new shoots appear. Clean and dry the rhizome, which will keep fresh for up to 3 months in a cool, dry place; then dry in small pieces and grind as required.

GINGER RHIZOME

# Safe Use of Essential Oils

Essential oils are potent and precious substances which we are privileged to use. Because they are so potent they can also be dangerous if misused, and we must therefore each take responsibility for understanding the safety aspects of their use and encourage others to do the same. Certain industries would prefer that we did not have access to essential oils and any accidents would give ammunition to those who wish to restrict our access. Oils are constantly being researched and it is prudent to try to keep as up-to-date as possible with new information. Then you can enjoy these wonderful plant gifts with confidence.

## Buying and Storing Essential Oils

Always buy essential oils from a reputable supplier who tests the oils for purity. Choose organically grown if available. Contact the appropriate organization (in the UK, the Aromatherapy Trades Council) for a list of registered members. Bottles and packaging should be labelled with both the common and botanic Latin plant name; plant part used; country of origin; purity (which should be 100 per cent, although sometimes very expensive oils like Rose are diluted to 5 per cent); and volume.

Be aware that true essential oils vary enormously in price, from the least expensive Eucalyptus to Rose at 40 times the price and Narcissus (only from specialists) at 150 times. Crop vagaries can cause price fluctuations. Store oils away from children and pets in dark glass, tightly lidded bottles and protect from extremes of temperature. Most will keep for several years. Citrus oils, once opened, are best used within six months.

## Using Essential Oils

When using essential oils, always follow the safety procedures listed below.

• As essential oils are very concentrated, use only a few drops at a time and always dilute them. Only rarely will a single drop of neat oil, such as gentle Lavender, be recommended. Buy bottles with individual droppers or use a pipette for accuracy.
• Never take essential oils internally.
• Keep essential oils away from your eyes.
• Label all your dilutions and mixtures with the contents and date.
• Avoid continuous use of the same oil over long periods.
• Some oils, such as Peppermint and Camphor, are considered incompatible with homoeopathic medicine, so consult your homoeopath.
• If you are pregnant, have a medical condition, or wish to use oils for children, it is advisable to consult a registered medical aromatherapist. Those working in the beauty and leisure industries are not qualified to give health advice.

## Patch Test

Always patch test essential oils you have not used before. Dilute the essential oil in carrier oil (begin with 1 per cent: 1 drop in 5ml), apply to your inner elbow and leave for 12 hours. If you experience an adverse reaction, apply almond oil, then rinse off with cold water. A reaction can mean that you are allergic to that particular essential oil, but contact the supplier as it may be due to an impure or poor-quality batch.

## Dangerous Oils

The following oils should not be available to the general public and are unsafe for home use. Do not attempt to home distil or infuse them in oil:
Aniseed, Bitter Almond (*Prunus dulcis* var. *amara*), Boldo (*Peumus boldus*), Box, Buchu (*Agathosma betulina*), Broom, Sweet Flag (*Acorus calamus*), Camphor (Brown and Yellow), Cassia, Cinnamon Bark, Costus (*Saussurea lappa*), Elecampane (*Inula*

*helenium*), Exotic Basils, Bitter Fennel, Ho leaf (*Cinnamomum camphora*), Horseradish, Jaborandi (*Pilocarpus jaborandi*), Mugwort, Mustard, Oregano, Parsley Seed, Pennyroyal, Rue, Sassafras (*Sassafras albidum*), Santolina, Savin (*Juniperus sabina*), Savory (*Winter and Summer*), Tansy (*Tanacetum vulgare*), Thuja, 'Red' Thymes, Tonka, Wintergreen (*Gaultheria procumbens*), Wormseed (*Chenopodium ambrosioides*) and Wormwood.

## Photosensitizing Oils
Essential oils can sensitize the skin, so avoid using them before exposure to sunlight or a sunbed. Common photosensitizing oils are Angelica root, Citrus oils (especially Bergamot) and Tagetes. (Rue oil, the most dangerous, is not available, but wear gloves when picking the plant.)

## Irritant Oils
The following oils are unsuitable for the skin, inhalations or therapeutic use. Use them for room fragrancing and in potpourri only:
Basil, Benzoin, Texas and Virginian Cedarwoods (*Juniperus ashei* and *J. virginiana*), Citronella, Clove bud (avoid leaf and stem oils altogether), Cinnamon leaf, Lemon Verbena, Dwarf Pine (*Pinus mugo* var. *pumilio*), Sage, Tagetes, Tarragon, Turmeric, West Indian Sandalwood (*Amyris balsamifera*), 'Wild' Thyme (*Thymus serpyllum*) and Yarrow.

## Medical Guidelines
Medical conditions have a variety of causes and individuals differ in their responses. The following advice should therefore be regarded as a general guide only. For more detailed information, consult a qualified aromatherapist.

EPILEPSY Avoid Fennel (Sweet), Hyssop, Rosemary, Sage.

PREGNANCY Avoid those on the irritant oils list above, plus Angelica, Bay, Cajeput, Cedarwood, Cinnamon, Clary Sage, Fennel, Hyssop, Jasmine, Juniper, Lovage, Marjoram, Myrrh, Nutmeg, Parsley, Sage, Star Anise, Spanish Sage, Sweet Marjoram, Tarragon, Thyme and Virginian Cedarwood.
During the first trimester avoid Chamomile, Fennel (Sweet), Frankincense, all Mints, Rose and Rosemary, and use with caution for the remainder of the pregnancy.

HIGH BLOOD PRESSURE
Avoid Hyssop, Rosemary, Sage and Thyme, plus Peppermint if you have cardiac fibrillation.

## Final Note
Think carefully about what you want from a product. If you want a fun, scented bath foam, for example, then artificial fragrances are perfectly acceptable, but for therapeutic use real herbs and essential oils are required. Be aware that words such as 'pure' and 'natural' have very broad legal definitions – 'natural flavours' for example, are 'nature identical' flavours, and the new expression in perfumery, 'Headspace', for the capturing of the 'natural' scent of a flower, is an analysis of the fragrant compounds released into the air around a living plant, which are then copied in the laboratory.

# Index

# *Acknowledgments*

Publishing Director:
Anne Furniss

Art Director:
Peter Windett

Design:
Paul Welti

Photographic Art
Direction & Styling:
Margaret Caselton

Researcher:
Catriona MacFarlane

Illustrations:
David Atkinson

Herbal Arrangements:
Sandy James

Stylist:
Maya Babic

Food Stylist:
Marie-Ange Lapierre

Copy Editors:
Sarah Widdicombe,
Lewis Esson

Editorial Assistant:
Katherine Seely

Typesetting:
Pete Howard

Production:
Vincent Smith,
Candida Lane

## AUTHOR'S ACKNOWLEDGMENTS

I would like to dedicate this book to my husband, J. Roger Lowe, for his inspiration and integrity and to our four wonderful lads: Toby, Rory, JJ and Cameron 'Jedi Master' Lowe. Here's to a fragrant future.

A big bouquet to Quadrille and the talented team who produced this beautiful book, especially the design work of Paul Welti and the sympathetic editing of Sarah Widdicombe. A flower-strewn path to my assistant Catriona MacFarlane for her sparkling contributions and witty equilibrium. Horticultural points to Inka Hilgner and Clare Higson for keeping our herb nursery thriving, and therapeutic thanks to Jane MacFarlane for magical fragrant massage, Charlotte Prud'homme for yoga amongst the trees, and my sister Adrienne Bremness for the final relaxation treats.

## CLAY PERRY'S ACKNOWLEDGMENTS

I would like to thank my wife Maggie for help in styling, arranging and propping the herb and garden photographs. I also owe an immeasurable debt to Christine and Trevor Forecast, of Congham Hall, and their gardener David Roberts. They gave me carte blanche to plunder their wonderful herb garden.

## PUBLISHER'S ACKNOWLEDGMENTS

Grateful thanks to the following for providing herbs or for allowing us to photograph in their gardens: David Austin's Roses, Albrighton, Shropshire; Kate Cambell, Eye Abbey, Suffolk; Anthony Lynam Dixon, Arne Herbs, Bristol; Annie Huntington, Old Rectory, Sudborough, Northants; John & Leslie Jenkins, Wollerton Old Hall, Shropshire; Phillip Norman, the Tradescant Museum of Garden History, London; Lyn Raynor, The Herb Garden, Hall View Cottage, Hardstoft, Chesterfield; Hexham Herbs, Northumberland; Geffrye Museum, Shoreditch, London; Mrs Charles Kitchener, Croylands, Nr Romsey, Hants; Marylynn Abbot, West Green House, Hartley Wintney, Hants; Amanda & Chris Dennis, The Citrus Centre, Pulborough, Sussex; Chelsea Physic Garden; Hestercombe Gardens, Somerset; Caroline Pakenham; Monsieur Robert Carvallo, Chateau de Villandry, France; Mme Cargère, Bois des Montiers, Varengeville, Normandy; The Romantic Nursery, Swannington, Norfolk; The Abbot of Das Münster, Insel Reichnau, Bodensee; Cressing Barns Museum Garden, Essex; Barry Ambrose, RHS Garden, Wisley, Surrey; The Church of St Michael & St Martin, Eastleach Martin, Glos; Lady Paget, Haygraff House, Taunton, Somerset; Sue Windett, Maggs Farm Nursery, Mountain Bower, Wilts; Wells Reclamation, Coxley, Nr Wells, Somerset.

Thanks to the following for supplying props for photography: Avant Garden, 77 Ledbury Road, London W11 2AG; Blake's Baskets, Holt, Norfolk; Damask, Unit 7, Sulivan Enterprise Centre, Sulivan Road, London SW6 3DJ; Descamps, 197 Sloane Street, London SW1X 9QX; Designers Guild, 267-271 Kings Road, London SW3 5EN; The General Trading Company, 144 Sloane Street, London SW1X 9BL; Thomas Goode, 19 South Audley Street, London W1Y 6BN; Lunn Antiques, 86 New Kings Road, London SW6 4LU; David Mellor, 4 Sloane Square, London SW1W 8EE.

## *John Evelyn's Dream for a Fragrant London*

The quote on page 1 is taken from John Evelyn's *Fumifugiu, or the Smoake of London Dissipated* (1661), in which he outlines his grand vision for fragrancing the city of London. He suggested to Charles II that large areas, 30-40 acres in extent, should be filled with all manner of scented plants. The beds and borders should be filled 'with pinks, carnations, stocks, gillyflowers, primroses, avunculas, violets, etc'. Evelyn suggested that when the shrubs were pruned, the waste 'be burnt to visit the City with a more benign Smoake'.